aFFIRMING FAITH

United Church Press
Cleveland, Ohio

aFFIRMING FAITH

a congregation's guide to confirmation

United Church Press, Cleveland, Ohio 44115

© 1996 by United Church Press

Biblical quotations are from the New Revised Standard Version of the Bible, © 1989 by the Division of Christian Education of the National Council of the Churches of Christ in the U.S.A., and are used by permission

All rights reserved. Published 1996

Printed in the United States of America on acid-free paper

01 00 99 98 97 96   5 4 3 2 1

Library of Congress Cataloging-in-Publication Data

Affirming Faith : a congregation's guide to confirmation / [Gordon J. Svoboda II, Grant F. Sontag, and R. Kenneth Ostermiller, project developers ; Kathleen C. Ackley, project editor ; writers : Kealahou Alika . . . [et al.]].
             p.   cm.
    Includes bibliographical references.
    ISBN 0-8298-1065-X (alk. paper)
    1. Confirmation—United Church of Christ—Study and teaching.
I. Ackley, Kathleen C.   II. Alika, Kealahou.
BX9886.A35   1996
264'.05834082—dc20   96-41421
                                                                 CIP

Affirming Faith: A Congregation's Guide to Confirmation, ISBN 0-8298-1065-X
Affirming Faith: A Confirmand's Journal, ISBN 0-8298-1066-8

CONTENTS

Sessions

COMMUNITY LIFE

OUR HISTORY AND HERITAGE

GOD

JESUS CHRIST

Affirming Faith is the result of input gathered during the last decade from United Church of Christ congregations across the country. We would like to express our thanks to those who have repeatedly asked for a new confirmation resource, to the local churches that participated in the 1980s survey on confirmation practices, to all those who have contributed their thoughts and ideas during the formative stages, and to the writers, readers, and editors who gave final shape to *Affirming Faith*.

Most of all, thanks go to you who will use this resource to help youth in your congregation affirm their faith. It will take your openness to the Holy Spirit and your skill as pastors and teachers to make *Affirming Faith* come alive. As you become familiar with the curriculum, you may have comments or suggestions. We welcome your response on the form provided on page 303.

God bless you in your teaching—and learning.

Project Developers:	Grant F. Sontag and Gordon J. Svoboda II
Project Consultant:	R. Kenneth Ostermiller
Project Editor:	Kathleen C. Ackley
Writers:	Kealahou Alika, Elizabeth Ann Bassham, Dale E. Carmen, Cynthia J. Carr, Gary L. Davis, Barbara J. Essex, Stephen R. Hanning, Ted E. Huffman, William Noel Koch, Rosemary McCombs Maxey, Fé R. Nebres, Margarita Sánchez De León, Kent J. Siladi, Michael O. Simmons, Hamilton Coe Throckmorton, Rodney C. Yee

The words of the Preamble to the Constitution of the United Church of Christ speak boldly to affirm "the responsibility of the Church in each generation to make this faith its own in reality of worship, in honesty of thought and expression, and in purity of heart before God."[1]

Affirming Faith: A Congregation's Guide to Confirmation is an attempt to do just that—to keep company with the understandings of the Christian faith and the movements of the Holy Spirit in order to aid persons in affirming and renewing faith. It seeks to communicate the gospel message while striving to be contemporary in its outlook.

This resource is designed for those planning, leading, and participating in a local church's program of faith formation for youth ages twelve to sixteen. The term "faith formation" is used throughout *Affirming Faith* in place of "confirmation." *Confirmation*, strictly speaking, is a rite of the Christian church, celebrated during a service of worship. *Faith formation* is what happens over time through the intentional teaching efforts of the church, the worship of the congregation, the Christian witness of persons, and the work of the Holy Spirit. *Affirming Faith* is a resource for a local church to use in a process of intentional faith formation for youth. At its completion, participants—including leaders and mentors—may wish to affirm their faith through the rite of confirmation.

Affirming Faith has two components:

@ *Affirming Faith: A Congregation's Guide to Confirmation*
@ *Affirming Faith: A Confirmand's Journal*

The congregation's guide includes session and retreat designs to help leaders plan and lead a comprehensive faith formation experience for youth ages twelve to sixteen. Each session design has detailed instructions for leading a ninety-minute experience, as well as suggestions for additional activities. A unique feature, "Connecting with the Congregation," offers ways the confirmands can be involved more fully in the life of the congregation as they go through the faith forming process. It also includes planning guides for establishing a mentoring program, engaging in witness and service projects, conducting field trips and retreats, and working with youth, as well as liturgical resources, a bibliography, and a list of additional resources.

The confirmand's journal includes session-related material for confirmands' reflection and "Questions to Consider" that can be used to initiate discussions with a mentor—an adult who will be a companion in faith throughout the confirmation process. It also contains music related to the sessions, a glossary of terms, and space for drawing or journaling.

Each leader, who will be instrumental in planning the faith formation program, will need a copy of *Affirming Faith: A Congregation's Guide to Confirmation*. Each leader, youth, and mentor will need a copy of *Affirming Faith: A Confirmand's Journal*.

The sessions of *Affirming Faith* are based on the United Church of Christ Statement of Faith. The statement is the focal point for this faith formation program because of its unique role in the life of the church. The statement is a powerful expression of God's saving acts and our invited response. Challenging Christians to "accept the cost and joy of discipleship, to be God's servants in the service of others, to proclaim the gospel to all the world and resist the powers of evil" are important steps in discovering what it means to be a follower of Christ and a member of Christ's church. These units are introduced by two foundational units about the church: "Community Life" and "History and Heritage." Sessions include the following segments:

@ Themes

@ Scriptures

@ Objectives for This Session

@ Session at a Glance

@ Biblical and Theological Background

@ Materials Needed

@ Preparing for This Session

@ Gathering

@ Exploring

@ Connecting

@ Going

@ Connecting with the Congregation

@ Thinking About This Session

@ Planning Ahead

Affirming Faith uses a teaching-learning model that assumes that all persons involved in the teaching will also be learners—actively exploring faith and its meaning in the lives of each participant. It also assumes that the whole of a congregation's life will contribute to the teaching and learning process. Consequently, leaders may include ministers, teachers, past and present confirmands, family members, church elders and deacons, and other members of the local church.

Congregations are encouraged to choose leaders who will provide opportunities for mutual learning and openness to the Holy Spirit. It is important that leaders be thoroughly familiar with each session and meet together regularly to plan and experience the session before meeting with the confirmands.

The Bible is used throughout this resource. In keeping with more traditional confirmation programs, particular passages of scripture have been selected for each session, but the emphasis is on encounter *with* scripture rather than knowledge *about* scripture. The goal is life transformed through continuing exposure to the Word of God.

Confirmation, theologian Urban Holmes said, is "a rite by which the mature Christian gives assent to Faith." And yet, he continues, it is also a "rite in search of a reason."[1] In churches across the country these words ring true. Many congregations are embracing the need to reexamine the reasons for the rite of confirmation and to look for new ways to interpret this important rite in the life of the community of faith. They are asking the questions: Why do we have confirmation? To whom should it be available? What does it signify? How can it, as a rite of the church, support the faith journeys of its members? How can the practice of this rite help to strengthen the church, the body of Christ, for ministry in the world? What reasons would you give for your congregation's interest in confirmation? Research conducted throughout the United Church of Christ in preparation for *Affirming Faith* revealed a variety of practices regarding confirmation, such as: Confirmation is:

@ a process of preparing young people for church membership.

@ a prerequisite for Holy Communion.

@ a program preparing youth for Christian living.

@ a rite acknowledging the strengthening and maturing of faith.

In many local churches of the United Church of Christ, confirmation is an educational program. It is usually conducted by the ordained minister, taught in a classroom format, attempting to cover what may have been missed in earlier years of Christian education or to introduce unchurched youth to the language and practice of faith.

In addition, a growing number of local churches incorporate a mentoring program and retreats to help prepare young people for confirmation. Some programs continue to emphasize the historic creeds and catechisms of the church, while others see confirmation more as an adolescent rite of passage. With greater frequency, children and young persons are invited to Holy Communion without the prerequisite of confirmation. The *United Church of Christ Book of Worship* states:

Until recently the principal objection to [children's] participation in the sacrament was their inability to "discern the body of Christ" in the meal (1 Corinthians 11:29). Recent biblical scholarship challenges this interpretation of scripture. It recognizes in Paul's words not a concern for a cognitive understanding of sacramental presence but a concern for an experience of the body of Christ present in the community of faith that Christ gathers as the church.

With this communal understanding, in which discernment is primarily a recognition of belonging and not merely a matter of intellectual comprehension, adult Christians are urged to ask "whether, by excluding children from the Lord's Supper, we are not equally guilty [with the offending Corinthians] of failing to 'discern the body' and, therefore, of endangering the reality of the supper."[2]

This resource is intended for those planning a faith formation program. We use the term "faith formation" here instead of "confirmation" to describe a process of engaging young people on a faith journey that encompasses more than a cognitive approach to the language and doctrines of the Christian faith.

PLANNING AND LEADERSHIP

Affirming Faith is designed to help those responsible in a local church plan an intentional program of faith formation for youth. One or more persons will need to assume responsibility for reviewing the material in the congregation's guide and confirmand's journal in order to plan the process that will follow. The following steps may be helpful:

1. **Recruit members to serve on a Faith Formation Committee, convene the group, and pray for the church's process.** Consider who might plan and lead your local church's faith formation program. Think of these people as the Faith Formation Committee. Try to include people from the following groups:

   @ Youth, both confirmed and yet-to-be confirmed
   @ Parents and guardians
   @ Mentors, if there are to be any, new and experienced
   @ Lay spiritual leaders (elders, deacons, and so forth)
   @ Clergy and other church staff
   @ Church educators and teachers
   @ Board and committee members
   @ Other persons interested in faith formation

   If your faith formation program will include other age groups or persons with special needs, they also should be represented.

   In forming the Faith Formation Committee, explain that it will be responsible for a program of worship, fellowship, learning, and service that will lead confirmands toward the rite of confirmation.

Depending on the size, structure, and style of your local church, some or all of the committee members may be the leaders of your congregation's program of faith formation.

When the Faith Formation Committee is convened, begin with prayer that asks God for guidance in shaping a program that will enable all to grow in faith. Or use the following prayer:

> *Loving God, you made us and invite us into a faithful relationship with you and one another. At times our faith seems smaller than a seed, at other times large enough to move mountains. Open us now to your presence and your power. Let your Holy Spirit lead us. May we and all members of this congregation be strengthened in faith in this time of planning. Be with the youth of this church and encourage them in faith. In the name of Jesus Christ, amen.*

Review the role of the Faith Formation Committee in planning a program of faith formation for youth using the *Affirming Faith* resources. Attend to the following details:

- Choose a convener or chairperson or some process for sharing leadership.
- Establish a process for beginning meetings with devotion and prayer and concluding with a review of the process and progress.
- Determine how records of your work will be kept for future reference.
- Decide in what ways your work will be communicated to the congregation and its leaders.
- Set a regular meeting time, place, and length for meetings.

2. **Invite the planning group to share faith formation and confirmation experiences with one another.** Take time to have the committee members to discuss and reflect upon two questions:

- What has helped you to grow in faith?
- How, if at all, have you experienced confirmation?

3. **Review the biblical, historical, and theological rationale for the rite of confirmation and your congregation's history and practice of confirmation.** Read (or review) the section "Confirmation: Then and Now" on page xix of *Affirming Faith*. Discuss as a committee how your congregation's practice of confirmation relates to this history. What has been gained? What has been lost or misplaced? What, if anything, would you like to change?

Remember that your local church's history is an important part of the foundation upon which to build any program of faith formation. Find out which past programs worked, which did not, and why.

You may need to interview those who were involved in earlier confirmation programs in your church, both youth and adult leaders. The earliest practice of confirmation was as a rite of the church framed by baptism and Holy Communion. Discuss how the rite of confirmation is connected to the sacraments in your congregation. What constitutes membership—is it baptism? confirmation? attending a membership or inquirer's class? Who receives Holy Communion—is it the baptized? those confirmed? others? In what ways does your congregation provide faith formation for all its members? In what ways does the congregation celebrate affirmation of faith for persons of all ages? Would you consider celebrating the rite of confirmation and including those leaders and mentors who also wished to affirm their faith?

4. **Address the concerns of youth in your congregation.** Confirmation of faith during early adolescence takes place during a time of rapid and radical change in the lives of young people. A program of faith formation for that age group needs to take that change into account. In general, youth (as well as adults) often are in the realm of searching faith. That is, they are in a time of seeking and testing more than they are of arriving at ironclad affirmations. Any faith formation program for youth must provide room for questions and doubts. Youth must be given explicit permission both to affirm what they believe and to ask questions of God and the church. They must be allowed and encouraged to speak their minds regarding what gives them hope and what disturbs them.

If youth are members of the Faith Formation Committee, invite them to express their needs and concerns. You might ask: How is it to be a part of our church these days? What would *you* change?

As you listen, pay attention to the language youth use. What are the key symbols in their worldview? Are they more visually, aurally, or physically oriented? What words are most likely to reach them? What experiences will most likely motivate them? Imagine what might lead them to say yes to their growing Christian faith in a rite of confirmation.

Whatever the age group in your faith formation program, the committee needs to consider individually the persons whose faith formation is being addressed. The educational component of faith formation should be a response to the learning needs of each group and to the needs of particular individuals. It should also take into account the learning styles of members of the group. What approaches to teaching will most fully communicate the essentials of the congregation's shared faith?

5. **Explore the *Affirming Faith* resources.** Read the introductory materials in *Affirming Faith* for general information about sessions, retreats, and mentoring. Make sure the Faith Formation Committee understands that these components may be used in any combination. That is, your congregation may offer a faith formation program using only sessions, only retreats, or only mentors. Or you may have sessions and retreats, sessions and a mentoring program, or retreats and mentors. Or you may combine all three.

One of the best ways to begin a faith formation program is in a retreat setting. A retreat takes participants away from their routines, allowing for new experiences to occur. It provides a time for community building and an opportunity for intimacy and sharing in a relaxed atmosphere. Worship, spirituality, and recreation are also enhanced in a retreat setting. The units can be conducted in a retreat setting by leading each session within a retreat format (see "A Guide for Retreats," page 275).

Mentor programs have grown in popularity in many congregations because they are an effective way of sharing faith and integrating young people into the life, faith, and work of the church. They are also a way to revitalize the faith and dedication of the lay people who serve as mentors, helping *them* to learn and grow also.

In addition, *Affirming Faith* offers suggestions for field trips, witness, and service projects that will undergird the session plans. Detailed help may be found in the appropriate planning guides ("A Guide for Field Trips," pages 289–91, and "A Guide for Witness and Service," pages 271–74).

Field trips are opportunities to move beyond the familiar setting of your congregation or community. Faith may be expanded when we experience how other people worship God, see how they live out their faith, and learn how they have been informed and shaped by their heritage. The insight gained from field trips often surprises even the leaders. We encourage you to include field trips as an integral part of your faith formation program, rather than as an optional component.

Experiences of witness and service can expand the faith of Christians of all ages. It is important for youth who are preparing for the rite of confirmation to participate in these ministries. The "A Guide for Witness and Service," pages 271–74, gives direction for incorporating these experiences into your congregation's faith formation program.

6. **Determine a time line for the faith formation process.** The resources in *Affirming Faith* allow for a program of a few months to a year or more. Six to nine months is a reasonable amount of time to allow for a program of weekly sessions, monthly retreats, or some combination of the two formats. In many congregations, new programming begins in the fall of the year and parallels academic schedules with the celebration of the rite of confirmation occurring on Pentecost. However, some congregations choose to begin in Advent or Lent. Allow six months to a year for advance planning.

7. **Train leaders.** Once your committee has decided how *Affirming Faith* will be used, and what the time line will be, you will need to train leaders. It is possible that those who will lead will be on the Faith Formation Committee already. If this is the case, the work you have done to this point will be valuable leader preparation. For further help, consult the clergy and other teachers in the congregation.

Affirming Faith is intended to be team-led. That is, two or more leaders should work together in guiding the faith formation program. The leadership team should read through the material (session designs and confirmand's journal) before meeting with the confirmands. One possibility, especially if your leadership team includes mentors, is to experience the material together before going through it with confirmands.

Another way to train leaders is to conduct a faith formation program for interested adults and older youth in the congregation. When the program is completed (perhaps six to nine months), enthusiastic leaders can be recruited from this group.

8. **Have an organizing meeting.** Invite prospective confirmands and their parents or guardians to an organizing meeting. Introduce the leaders, explain the *Affirming Faith* process, distribute a schedule, and invite the youth to participate. Give them a way to indicate their interest and commitment by verbally agreeing to participate, signing a commitment sheet, or making individual commitment cards.

9. **Involve the entire congregation.** At the very least, the Faith Formation Committee should report its work to the congregation and appropriate subgroups (youth, education committee, deacons, elders, clergy, parents/guardians). Beyond this, note the ways the members of the congregation can be involved in the program of faith formation

    @   as planners, leaders, or mentors
    @   as examples whose life, faith, and work provide a Christian witness
    @   as resource persons for faith formation as deacons, elders, teachers, missionaries, and board and committee members
    @   through an adult faith formation program
    @   through involving the youth in worship as readers, greeters, servers, preachers, and musicians
    @   through involving the adults in youth gatherings, field trips, witness and service projects
    @   through retreats
    @   in worship services celebrating the faith formation process in the congregation
    @   through periodic reports and testimonies as to how the program is progressing and affecting members of the congregation
    @   through the rite of confirmation

Traditionally, the rite of confirmation has been associated with the laying on of hands and invocation of the Holy Spirit in conjunction with baptism. The scripture reference that connects the act of confirming with baptism is Acts 8:17, where Peter and John pray for and lay hands upon the recently baptized converts of Samaria. Later in the early church, this laying on of hands was done by the bishop during the rite of confirmation; but because the number of converts was growing and the church was expanding geographically, the bishops could not keep up with the demand. Consequently, by the fourth century, confirmation of the newly baptized was delayed until the presence of a bishop could be counted upon. In some respects, the need for a practical solution to this problem gave rise to a new understanding of confirmation.

Early on the church saw a need for catechesis—the education and faith formation of Christian persons. Originally this was focused on adults, who learned and grew as part of a worshiping community. The Council of Trent, beginning in 1545, determined that the appropriate age for catechumens was six through twelve, and baptized children began to be instructed in the faith. In the past century, for most Christian churches, the normative age for confirmation has been adolescence.

Confirmation has ties to Holy Communion as well as to baptism. In the early church, households of baptized Christians broke bread together as a regular part of their worship. By the fourth century, adult catechumens were dismissed from corporate worship before the celebration of Holy Communion, receiving it for the first time following their baptism. Protestants traditionally have delayed first communion until after confirmation while Roman Catholics offered first communion prior to confirmation. Interestingly, Orthodox Christians continue the practice of unifying the rite and sacraments. Newly baptized infants are immediately confirmed and receive their first communion on a spoon.

The evolution of church practice over the centuries has left the church far from where it started. Catechesis, initially associated with adult baptism, has become connected to adolescent confirmation. Holy Communion is now received with increasing frequency before confirmation. Confirmation, originally practiced as a charismatic and apostolic act, has become a graduation exercise upon completion of a prescribed educational program.

The centuries-old tension between the invocation by the faithful of the Holy Spirit in a person's life on the one hand and the need for effective education and formation on the other hand informs the United Church of Christ today. The *Book of Worship* contains a confirming prayer, invoking the Holy Spirit after baptism: "The Holy Spirit be upon you, (name), child of God, disciple of Christ, member of the church."[1] But it also affirms the need for effective education: "Before a service of confirmation is scheduled, the appropriate leaders of the local church shall be satisfied that the participants have been instructed properly in the Christian faith and personally desire to affirm their baptism."[2]

It is also popular to look at confirmation in light of its root meaning of "to make firm" or "to strengthen." To this end, some contemporary confirmation programs emphasize the educational model of reflection upon experience, remembering that "for most people rational learning is not transformative and does not bring about a radical reorientation of the personality towards a new way of being."[3]

Several points are clear from this history:

- Confirmation means affirmation of faith. It is an acknowledgment by both the individual and the faith community of the presence and power of the Holy Spirit.

- Confirmation is inextricably linked to baptism and, as such, it is also an affirmation of baptism. While the rite of confirmation may include acceptance into the membership of a particular local church, when one is baptized, he or she becomes a member of the Christian church.

- Confirmation is tied to Holy Communion along with baptism. While practices may vary among congregations, Holy Communion is first and foremost a privilege of the baptized, not only of those confirmed. Increasingly, any of these rites may serve as a point of entry into the Christian community.

- Confirmation, strictly speaking, is an act of the church gathered in worship. It is not solely the accomplishment of an individual. While the rite may be rooted in a meaningful program of education and formation, confirmation itself is not that program.

- The rite of confirmation is celebrated both in response to and in anticipation of the work of God in the life of a believer. Thus, it is appropriate for persons of all ages, and it can be repeated throughout a person's life. While the concept of repeatability may seem novel, it is consistent with the traditional understanding of confirmation as a rite that recognizes God's presence and transforming power in the lives of Christ's followers. Practicing confirmation in this way can be an enriching ministry that acknowledges those moments throughout life when faith is strengthened.[4]

Our story as the
people of God
is contained
in Scripture,
in Christian
communities,
and in the lives
of individual
Christians.

Community Life

COMMUNITY LIFE

ON A FAITH JOURNEY

This opening retreat, "On a Faith Journey," invites the youth to a process to form faith and helps them build relationships with one another, leaders, and mentors along the way. During the retreat they will explore some basic Christian spiritual disciplines, such as prayer and scripture reading, consider the meaning of confirmation, and plan witness and service projects.

The retreat is designed for a twenty-four-hour time period but can be adapted to fit your group's needs. For example, you could start the retreat at twelve midnight as a "lock-in" at your church building or at a retreat center. You could spread the retreat over two or three days and incorporate more leisure activities into the schedule. Leaders will need to review all the materials in *Affirming Faith* and be familiar with the confirmation schedule your congregation is using. Helpful information about organizing the program is in the "Planning Guides for Congregations" section, pages 255–91.

Retreat Schedule

Activities in this retreat are for a group of four to six confirmands. If your group is smaller, you may wish to have the retreat with another congregation in your area. If your group is larger, the retreat design indicates when to divide into smaller groups.

DAY ONE

Arrive and check in

Serve dinner (optional)

Worship together (45 minutes)

Get acquainted (45 minutes)

Introduce the purpose of the retreat (15 minutes)

Explore prayer (1 hour)

Have leisure activities (as appropriate)

DAY TWO

Serve breakfast (30 minutes)

Explore Scripture (2 hours, including breaks)

Serve lunch (45 minutes)

Build community (45 minutes)

Plan for witness and service projects (1 hour)

Review the United Church of Christ Statement of Faith
    (15 minutes)

Make a "time capsule" (45 minutes)

Reflect about the retreat (15 minutes)

Take a break (15 minutes)

Worship together (30 minutes)

Pack up, clean up, and depart (30 minutes)

Objectives for the Retreat

- Begin to build relationships with one another, their leaders, and their mentors.
- Experience some spiritual disciplines that will be practiced throughout the journey.
- Explore the definition of *confirmation*.

Materials Needed

- Bible for each participant (New Revised Standard Version, if possible)
- A copy of *Affirming Faith: A Confirmand's Journal* for each participant
- Pens or pencils
- Low table, cloth, candles
- Paper, name tag supplies
- Songbooks (optional)
- Musical instruments (optional)
- Cassette tapes or CDs
- Cassette or CD player
- Games for leisure time
- Markers, newsprint
- "Time Capsule: My Hopes for the Journey" handout for each participant (page 15)
- "Reflections about the Retreat" handout for each participant (page 16)
- Envelopes
- Bowl of water
- Supplies for opening worship (see "Prepare for the Retreat")

Prepare for the Retreat

Gather a basket of items for the opening worship and prepare the worship center for the service. *Or ask the youth to bring an item from home to show during the opening worship that reminds them of someone who has been influential in helping their faith grow.* If you gather objects for the confirmands, make sure you have a wide variety of items. Some suggestions are:

common household medicines like aspirin or ointments, hot water bottle, hairbrush, brooch or other jewelry, hats, windup toys, dolls, bubbles, sports equipment (such as baseball, tennis ball), playing cards, children's books, literary works (small copies), yarn or other craft material, handheld fan, jars or cans of spices, salt, cooking and eating implements (such as wooden spoons, chopsticks), small flower pot, small gardening implements, small carpentry tools, small stone, seashells

This list is just a suggestion; use your imagination and let the Spirit guide you as you gather the objects. You will need at least twice as many objects as the number of people participating.

The activities during the retreat are varied. Consider which leaders will be most effective in leading each one. Singing is suggested as an optional activity. A song leader should prepare music the group will like to sing. There are times for community building and recreation. Leaders need to prepare a variety of group games for these times.

There are two sessions, one on exploring prayer and another on exploring scripture. Make "Prayer Is . . ." signs to display in the room for the session on prayer by copying the quotes from the confirmand's journal, page 3. You will also need to recruit volunteers in advance to help with the reading of the Gospel of Mark. Assign them a portion according to the outline on page 12. Read that section and decide if you will decorate the room(s) with scenery and/or props. The other session on planning for witness and service will be most effective if the leader follows the suggestions in "A Guide for Witness and Service," pages 271–74.

The activity "Time Capsule: My Hopes for the Journey" gives confirmands an opportunity to express their hopes, expectations, and concerns about the faith-forming journey. Make a copy of this handout for each participant. Make copies of the "Reflections about the Retreat" handout as well.

Upon arriving at the retreat, set up a worship center on a low table or bench in the middle of the room. Use your creativity and imagination. Some suggestions for the worship center are:

- Cloth the color of the current liturgical season
- Candle(s)
- Basket for the objects
- Cross
- Open Bible
- Baptismal font or bowl and pitcher of water

Arrange for volunteers to light the candles and read scripture during opening worship.

Day One

ARRIVE AND CHECK IN

Have the participants make name tags as they arrive. When all are present, welcome the group.

SERVE DINNER (OPTIONAL)

You may plan to arrive at the retreat site or the church building around dinner time. For some groups, gathering for a meal is a good way to begin. For others, asking the group to eat before they arrive will make planning easier. Assign sleeping rooms.

WORSHIP TOGETHER (45 MINUTES)

OR – write a word or draw a picture of something that speaks to them

As people gather for worship, ask them to bring the item from home that reminds them of someone who has influenced their faith, or invite them to look at the objects and take something that reminds them of this person. This could be someone who has taught them about God, showed them the love of God, or been especially active in the life of the church community.

Light the candle(s). Sing together the chant "Gathered Here" on page 211 in the *Confirmand's Journal* and page 221 in this guide.

Have a volunteer read Proverbs 2:1–6. Invite each person to name the person(s) who has influenced his or her faith as he or she shows the object, to tell why the object reminds him or her of the person, and to describe how the person was influential. Then they may place it on the worship table saying, "Thank you God for [name of person]."

After everyone who wishes has shared, a leader may say:

Go, remembering that there are many who have gone before us encouraging our faith. As we grow in faith, may we become aware of the ways we will care for and nurture the faith of the next generation. Amen.

GET ACQUAINTED (45 MINUTES)

Lead one or more of the activities below, which will help people get to know one another.

Sing together (optional). Singing together can unify a group. Recruit youth before the retreat to help with the music. Work with them to select a list of songs the youth will enjoy. Be sure these songs are simple and easy to learn. Also, be open to the variety of music available to the church. The musical taste of youth may be different from that of adult leaders. The only criteria should be the appropriate use of language. Print the lyrics on newsprint for everyone to see. If you can get an overhead projector, print the lyrics on transparencies. This frees hands for clapping and other movements. Also, be sure to secure permission if you are copying music. If this is not possible, locate songbooks that include many familiar and singable songs.

Play games. Play an introduction game to "break the ice." It is important to have everyone participating, including mentors. "Bob! Bob! Bob!"[1] is an enjoyable game that helps the group learn names. Have everyone sit in a circle with a leader in the center. The leader moves around and randomly points to a different person. The person shouts his or her name and everyone else echoes shouting "Bob! Bob! Bob!" or "Jane! Jane! Jane!" or whatever the person's name is. Repeat the pointing activity until everyone's name is known.

"Identity"[2] is another fun game. Each person fills out two name tags (the adhesive-backed type) as they enter the room. One is to wear and the other is placed in a basket. After everyone has arrived, gather in a circle. Pass the basket around and have each person take a name tag other than his or her own without letting anyone else see.

Then have everyone turn to the left and stick the name tags they are holding on the back of the person in front of them. The object of the game is for each person to discover the name printed on the name tag stuck on his or her back. They find out by asking questions which can only be answered by yes or no. Each person may ask only two questions of any one person.

When people discover whose name they have, they go to that person, place their hands on his or her shoulders, and proceed to follow him or her around the room. As more people discover their identity, the lines of people will lengthen until the last person finds his or her identity.

Introduce a partner. During this time, participants will spend time getting to know another person. Ask each participant to find a partner or you may make assignments. Partners should find a quiet place to share with each other. Encourage partners to listen carefully so that they will be able to introduce their partner to the rest of the group.

Some of the things they may talk about include:

- Birth date and birthplace
- School life, family life, work
- Favorite hobbies and pastimes
- Favorite foods and places to go
- Favorite movies or books

Give pairs fifteen minutes to exchange information. Call the group together and ask each person to introduce his or her partner.

INTRODUCE THE PURPOSE OF THE RETREAT (15 MINUTES)

Share the purpose of the retreat: to build community within the group, to explore the definition of confirmation, and to practice some basic Christian spiritual disciplines. Review the rest of the retreat schedule. Post the times and activities on a sheet of newsprint and describe each activity. Talk about the ground rules for the group and discuss any covenant you will establish for behavior (see "A Guide for Retreats" on page 275). Take a break and get ready for the next activity.

EXPLORE PRAYER (1 HOUR)

Background. This activity introduces participants to prayer. Prayer is an important spiritual discipline and is foundational in our lives as Christians. Henri Nouwen, in his book *Reaching Out*, says, "Prayer is the language of the Christian community. In prayer the nature of the community becomes visible because in prayer we direct ourselves to the one who forms the community. . . . Praying is not one of the many things the community does. Rather, it is its very being. Without it the community quickly degenerates into a club with a common cause but no common vocation."[3] It is important therefore that confirmands learn about prayer as a Christian spiritual discipline and about how to pray.

The desire to learn how to pray was something Jesus' disciples experienced. They saw him praying and after he had finished, one of his disciples said to him, "Teach us to pray, as John taught his disciples" (Luke 11:1). So Jesus taught his disciples what was to become the most known and often recited prayer in the church today—the Prayer of Our Savior. Here are two versions, a traditional version and an inclusive-language version. There are other variations, as well.

Our Father in heaven,
hallowed be your name,
your kingdom come,
your will be done,
on earth as in heaven.
Give us today our daily bread.
Forgive us our sins
as we forgive those who sin against us.
Save us from the time of trial
and deliver us from evil.
For the kingdom, the power,
and the glory are yours
now and forever. Amen.

Our Father-Mother, who is in the heavens,
may your name be made holy,
may your dominion come,
may your will be done,
on the earth as it is in heaven.
Give us today the bread we need,
and forgive us our debts,
as we have forgiven our debtors;
and do not put us to the test,
but rescue us from evil.
For yours is the dominion, and the power,
and the glory forever. Amen.[4]

The prayers we offer to God come in many different forms and styles. Some are very simple and focus on only one thing. Others are lengthy and involve a variety of topics. Prayer often includes the following actions or attitudes, which are grounded in our relationship with God. These are praising, giving thanks, asking, and listening. These elements may interact or overlap one another. During the retreat, the confirmands will have the opportunity to look at the Prayer of Our Savior and identify which elements of prayer outlined above are found in it (see the *Confirmand's Journal*, pages 5–6).

Prayer may be offered in many ways. Many people pray with heads bowed, hands folded, and eyes closed. Others pray on their knees. Prayer may be offered standing with arms and heads raised. Prayers may be given with eyes open or closed. What is most important is the acknowledgment that God is present and hears our prayers.

On the retreat. Begin by offering a prayer of petition seeking God's guidance for the group. Offer your own prayer or use one of the preparatory prayers from the *Book of Worship:*

Eternal God we come to you with hungry hearts, waiting to be filled: waiting to be filled with a sense of your presence; waiting to be filled with the touch of your spirit; waiting to be filled with new energy for service. Come to us, we pray. Be with us. Touch us. Empower us as your people that we may act in the world for Jesus' sake. Amen.[5]

Consider What Prayer Is

Using the background material on prayer, introduce the idea of prayer as an essential part of the faith community. Call attention to the signs "Prayer Is . . ." that are displayed around the room. Ask the confirmands to move to the sign that most closely describes what they think prayer is. Once everyone is in place, talk about why they chose that particular definition. Gather the group together again. Then introduce the four elements of prayer—praising, giving thanks, asking, and listening. Ask them to look at the questions in their journal and write or draw their responses. The questions are also listed here. Then discuss the questions with the whole group. Ask leaders to share what prayer means to them. Take care to respect all the responses given. Also respect persons who do not wish to share.

- If you were asked to explain prayer to someone, what would you say?
- What does prayer mean to you?
- Can you recall a time when you or someone else you know prayed? What was that like?
- Some people think praying is only for asking God for something. What other purposes are there for prayer?

Look at the Prayer of Our Savior

Use the background information to talk about the Prayer of Our Savior. Ask the confirmands to find the versions of the prayer in their journal, page 6. Have them work in pairs to define the words in the prayer and decide which elements of prayer are found in it. Then have each one write the prayer in his or her own words in the space provided in the journal. An optional activity would be to interpret the prayer using creative movement or art, such as paint or clay.

Close the session by leading the group in a process to develop a breath prayer that they can use as a spiritual discipline throughout their faith journeys.[6]

Distribute pencils and paper. Explain that a breath prayer is a simple, six- to eight-syllable sentence prayer that can help us be aware of God's presence. It can be a prayer that comes out of our heart and is unique to each of us. It can be prayed in silence to the in-and-out rhythm of our breathing.

Have the confirmands sit in a comfortable position. Invite them to close their eyes and remind them how much God loves them and is present with them now. Recall words from scripture that convey this, such as, "Do not be afraid, for I am with you" (Isaiah 41:10).

Ask them to imagine God calling them by name saying, "[Jackie], what do you want?" Invite them to listen from their heart for the answer to the question God is asking. The answer might come as one word, such as "love," or "guidance," or "strength." It also could come as a short phrase, such as, "I want to feel your forgiveness." Have them write the word or phrase on the paper.

Ask the group to think of their favorite name or image for God. It may be names such as "God," "Jesus," "Spirit," "Holy One," "Creator," "Shepherd." Invite them to write this on the paper.

These two elements combine to make the breath prayer. Have the group work with the words or phrases to come up with a six- to eight-syllable sentence that flows easily when spoken aloud or expressed internally. For example, if the answer to God's question is "love," and the name for God is "Holy One," a possible prayer might be, "Holy One [breathe in], let me feel your love [breathe out]." When everyone has formed a prayer, explain that words used in our breath prayers may change and evolve throughout our lives as we grow and change.

Close by leading the group through a guided prayer. Start by inviting them to find a comfortable sitting position again and asking them to notice the rhythm of their breathing. Then begin the prayer, pausing between sentences.

Welcome God into your thoughts; hear God say, "Be still and know that I am God . . ."
Consider what you can see, hear, touch, feel, or think that helps you be aware of God . . .
Pray your breath prayer several times, confident that God is listening . . .
Consider the things for which you are thankful, and give thanks to God . . .

Make a request of God for yourself, asking God for something you may want or need,
> *something you may need help in doing . . .*
Make a request of God on behalf of another person, asking God to be present in the
> *life of someone or some situation you care about . . .*
Again, pray your breath prayer . . .
Give thanks to God . . .
Amen.

HAVE LEISURE TIME (AS APPROPRIATE)

This is a time where youth and others can get to know each other informally. Bring some board games such as Pictionary, Taboo, or Password in which there is team interaction. Others may want to play Hearts or other card games.

To end the evening, play some favorite soft and reflective taped music or sing songs that are reflective in nature. Thank the group for their participation and share briefly what will occur tomorrow. Invite persons to share any reflections they have about the evening and close with prayer.

Day Two

A leader will need to wake the group. If you wish, play some music or serenade the group to start the day in a lighthearted and playful way.

SERVE BREAKFAST (30 MINUTES)

Announce at breakfast that for the morning session confirmands will need their journals, a pen or pencil, and their creativity. Take a brief break to prepare for the morning session.

EXPLORE SCRIPTURE (2 HOURS, INCLUDING BREAKS)

Background. Exploring scripture is the second Christian spiritual discipline being introduced during this retreat. Christians understand that God is known in Scripture and that the Scripture helps us to know better how to live a faithful life. By reading, hearing, and seeking to understand Scripture, we gain a better understanding of what God wants us to be and to do.

This activity will be a telling of the Gospel of Mark from beginning to end, with a few breaks. Recruit others from the congregation to help with this activity. Divide the Gospel into the following segments:

- The Prologue—Mark 1:1–15
- Part One—Mark 1:16–3:12
- Part Two—Mark 3:13–6:6
- Part Three—Mark 6:7–8:21
- Part Four—Mark 8:22–10:52
- Part Five—Mark 11:1–13:37
- Part Six—Mark 14:1–16:8

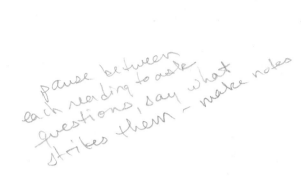

pause between each reading to ask questions, say what strikes them – make notes

Ask the volunteers to practice reading the portion of the story they are given, so that they are familiar with the words, can be expressive, and can use eye contact. If you wish, the group could move from one part of the retreat setting to another, with simple scenery or props used to provide the background for the telling.

Very rarely do we hear the whole gospel story told in one sitting. This activity will give the confirmands the opportunity to hear the scope of Jesus' ministry as it is told in Mark. End the reading at Mark 16:8. That is in agreement with most ancient authorities and makes for a dramatic finish to the Gospel, leaving the challenge to spread the good news to the hearers. There are many good commentaries that provide background information about this gospel and can help readers as they prepare to tell the story. One such is *Mark* by Lamar Williamson Jr. It is part of *Interpretation: A Bible Commentary for Teaching and Preaching*, published by John Knox Press.

Following the reading of the Gospel, allow a time of silence. Then have a brief time for questions and discussion with the presenters. Close with a prayer, if desired.

SERVE LUNCH (45 MINUTES)

BUILD COMMUNITY (45 MINUTES)

This is a good time to move around and play—outdoors, if possible! Two good games that youth enjoy are Blob Tag and Blob Hide and Seek. Modify these games if any of the confirmands are physically challenged.

In Blob Tag, the group has to run from one side to the other in an area marked off by boundaries (a volleyball or basketball court is good) and avoid being tagged by a person who is "it." "It" calls out when the group is to run. As "it" tags people, this group becomes a "blob" by holding hands with "it." The "blob" tries to catch more people by encircling individuals as they run from one side to the other. The game ends when all are caught.

In Blob Hide and Seek one person is designated "it" and everyone else must find that person. As people find "it," they remain with "it" forming a "blob." The "blob" gets bigger until everyone has found the "blob."

This game should be played within agreed upon boundaries. It would be helpful if the person designated "it" hides in a place that is not too difficult to find.

For more games, consult *The New Games Book* (San Francisco: Headlands Press, 1976) and *More New Games* (Tiburon, Calif.: Headlands Press, 1981). These books are filled with games for groups of all sizes and physical abilities.

PLAN FOR WITNESS AND SERVICE PROJECTS (1 HOUR)

Introduce the idea of witness and service as a part of the faith formation program. There is an outline for presenting this session in "A Guide for Witness and Service," pages 271–74.

REVIEW THE UNITED CHURCH OF CHRIST STATEMENT OF FAITH (15 MINUTES)

Read together the United Church of Christ Statement of Faith from the journal, page 234. Point out the references to God, Jesus Christ, the Holy Spirit, the church, and God's gifts and our response.

Ask the group to discuss the following questions. List their responses on newsprint:

@　As you read the Statement of Faith, what statements do you believe or find especially meaningful?

@　What words or phrases do you question, doubt, or just don't understand?

Indicate that you will save these questions and comments for times when you will be looking at portions of the Statement of Faith in more detail.

MAKE A TIME CAPSULE (45 MINUTES)

Youth on this retreat have come from a variety of places and backgrounds. Some are ready to begin a program that will lead them to the rite of confirmation. Others may appear to need more time to explore before they decide. Still others may have come to be with friends or to see what is going on. Affirm where each person is and express your hope that the whole group will continue to journey in the process toward the rite of confirmation.

Distribute paper, pens or pencils, and envelopes to all the participants. Have them open their journals to page 7. Read the letter to the group. Distribute the handout "Time Capsule: My Hopes for the Journey," which you have copied from page 15 of this guide. Give the group time to complete their "time capsules" and have them place the paper in the envelope and seal it. Say that you will collect them, put them in a safe place, unopened, and give them back at the closing retreat.

Let the group know when the next session or retreat will occur. Make sure everyone has the written schedule that was distributed at the organizing meeting.

REFLECT ABOUT THE RETREAT (15 MINUTES)

Distribute the handout "Reflections about the Retreat," which you have copied from page 16. Ask each person to find a quiet place to think about the questions and complete the handout. Let them know that their reflections will be collected and used to evaluate the retreat and to plan further events.

TAKE A BREAK (15 MINUTES)

WORSHIP TOGETHER (30 MINUTES)

Leader preparation. Fill a bowl with warm water. In the closing worship, you will celebrate your relationship to God and invite youth to grow in this relationship through participating in the faith formation program.

Gathering. Gather in a circle for worship and sing a favorite song or two, if desired. Invite the youth to take turns saying aloud one word that describes a new learning or feeling they have experienced as a result of the retreat.

Scripture. Ask a volunteer to read John 1:35–39.

Blessing the journey. After the reading, hold the bowl of water and say:

Water is an essential element to human beings. We use it to nourish and refresh us, to wash and cleanse us. It is a symbol of new life when we use it to baptize followers into a life with Christ. Today I invite you to learn more about God and the church. As I come around and touch your foreheads with water, I will invite you to be a part of a journey of faith that leads to the rite of confirmation. You may wonder what this will mean. You may be certain that you want to be a part of such a journey, or you may have some doubts. You may be ready or willing, or you may be concerned or resistant. Wherever you are, God understands. I speak the invitation and I invite you to respond, "I am a child of God. God will be with me on this journey."

Go around to the youth and adults, touching each on the forehead with a few drops of water and saying, "I invite you on this journey of faith." Invite each person to respond, "I am a child of God. God will be with me on this journey."

Closing prayer. After all have been touched, close with a prayer of thanksgiving such as the following:

O God, we praise you for understanding us and for gathering us into the church, the body of Christ. May we live in the Spirit, building up one another in love, sharing in the life and worship of the church, and serving the world for the sake of Jesus Christ. Amen.[7]

PACK UP, CLEAN UP, AND DEPART (30 MINUTES)

Handout

TIME CAPSULE: MY HOPES FOR THE JOURNEY

Right now, I think of confirmation as . . .

_____

_____

_____

_____

As I begin this journey, my biggest question about God is . . .

_____

_____

_____

_____

When I think about growing in faith, I wonder if . . .

_____

_____

_____

_____

When I think about the ways I can be a part of the church, I . . .

_____

_____

_____

_____

My hopes for the journey are . . .

_____

_____

_____

_____

_____

Handout

REFLECTIONS ABOUT THE RETREAT

Think about all the things you and the group did on this retreat.

◉ List the things you enjoyed.

_____

_____

◉ List the things that were less enjoyable.

_____

_____

◉ What were some things you learned on this retreat?

_____

_____

◉ What do you suppose your leaders and/or mentors learned about you?

_____

_____

◉ What would you like to explore (or what do you have questions) about the faith formation program?

_____

_____

◉ Are there ways that the group became closer to one another during this retreat? If so, how? If not, why not?

_____

_____

◉ Are there ways the group became closer to God during this retreat? If so, how? If not, why not?

_____

_____

SHARING OUR STORIES

Themes

ℯ Our story as the people of God is contained in Scripture, in Christian communities, and in the lives of individual Christians.

ℯ We are to "go and tell" our faith story.

ℯ By sharing our stories, we discover our connections to other followers of Jesus.

Scriptures

MATTHEW 28:1–20—Jesus appears to Mary Magdalene and the other disciples.

LUKE 8:1–3—Women and men go with Jesus to bring good news.

Objectives for This Session

ℯ Recall a time of being lost and found.

ℯ Explore the story of Mary Magdalene.

ℯ Consider our faith stories and the faith stories of others.

Session at a Glance

GATHERING

Experience a guided meditation (10 minutes)

EXPLORING

Learn about Mary Magdalene (10 minutes)

Role-play scenes from Mary Magdalene's story (15 minutes)

CONNECTING

Create a "Life Line" (15 minutes)

Add faith connections to the "Life Lines" (10 minutes)

Discuss "Life Lines" (10 minutes)

Hear the faith stories of God's people (15 minutes)

GOING

Worship together (5 minutes)

Biblical and Theological Background

Sometimes we think of the Christian story as appearing mainly in the Bible. The educator Thomas Groome defines the Christian story as "the whole faith tradition of our people however that is expressed or embodied."[1] That means the Christian story is found not only in Scripture but also in *everything* that Christians have experienced in all of history!

The Christian story can draw us in and change us in amazing ways. By hearing about others—their faith and doubts, their encounters with God, and what it means for them to live life as Christians—we become part of the story too. We want to know a loving God who understands us and accepts us as we are. We want to be in covenant with God and with others through Jesus Christ. We want to become part of the vision of the reign of God. As we become engaged in the story, we become part of it.

Our experience with the Christian story comes from at least three different places in the context of Christian community: the Bible, the worshiping congregation, and the witness of Jesus' followers throughout history to the present. When the good news of the story is told, lives may be transformed and God's love may be known.

When we look to the Bible, we discover the story of our relationship with God. There we find the history of salvation: how we, as God's people, go through cycles in our covenant with God, failing to live up to our promises to be faithful, often by forgetting God and worshiping false gods. When we realize our failure and repent—have a change of heart, mind, attitude, and habit—God's mercy and forgiveness are ours. The covenantal relationship with God is based on the promise that God is our God and we are God's people. The Bible is our primary source for this story. It tells us what kind of people we are as the people of God.

The worship life of a congregation is another important source for the retelling and remembering of our story. Through prayers, praise, proclamation of the Word, and sharing of the sacraments, worship is a joyful response of God's people to God's redeeming love in Christ. The whole Christian year, with its seasons, colors, symbols, and holy days, helps to tell the life of Christ, the central figure in our story. This is especially true when the *Revised Common Lectionary*, a three-year cycle of scripture readings, is used in worship. Each cycle is centered on one of the Synoptic Gospels (Matthew, Mark, and Luke). Texts from the Gospel of John are spread over all three years. The readings follow a sequence that is intended to lead worshipers to a deeper understanding of Christ's life, death, and resurrection and encourage a faithful response to God's saving grace.

We also need to share the Christian story as it has been lived out in history and is being lived today. We need to hear the stories of children, youth, and adults of all ages. We need to hear the testimonies of people who are different from us, who are from different cultures, or who have different abilities. We need to be open to the witness and movement of the Holy Spirit in our lives and in the lives of others. Being part of a faith community with people who are willing to share their faith helps to remind us of the covenantal relationship God seeks to have with us. It guides us into the future. Hearing the stories of people of faith gives richness and dimension to our story and helps us to find our identity as followers of Christ. It help us to appreciate the diversity in our own local church and the Christian church as a whole.

Hearing scripture, worshiping together, sharing personal faith stories, and hearing the stories of others whom we may never meet face to face helps us to believe that God loves each of us and will work in our lives too.

One story from scripture that has the power to change lives is the story of Mary Magdalene's encounter with the resurrected Christ. In Luke's Gospel we read that Mary once had seven demons cast out of her by Jesus (8:1–2). Luke is not specific about her problems; but somehow when she meets Jesus and follows him, her life changes dramatically. Not all change is that decisive, but in ways both great and small, God meets us in the midst of our lives. As we learn about Mary and others who followed Jesus, it is not hard to conclude that if Jesus could make such a difference in their lives, then he can in ours too.

Materials Needed

- Bible for each participant (various translations, if possible)
- *Confirmand's Journal* for each participant
- Crayons, markers, pens, and pencils in a variety of sizes, colors, shapes   paper

Preparing for This Session

Using the suggestions in the "Exploring" section of this session, study the Bible with the other leaders on your team. Complete the "Life Line" exercise found in the *Confirmand's Journal* for yourself. Reflect upon your own faith story and be prepared to share with the youth.

Choose a meeting room that is comfortable and inviting to lead a guided meditation and discussion. Provide a table where the youth can work in their journals. Assemble the materials needed for this session. Pray silently for each young person and leader (including yourself) in the group.

Gathering

EXPERIENCE A GUIDED MEDITATION (10 MINUTES)

Welcome the confirmands. Indicate that you will be leading them in a guided meditation. They may sit on chairs or cushions, put their heads down on the table, or lie on the floor. They need to spread out so that they have their own space. If this is your group's first experience with a guided meditation, explain that it is a way to pray using our imagination as a leader guides us along.

Speak softly and slowly, asking them to close their eyes if they wish. Those who are uncomfortable with this may keep their eyes open. Ask them to be aware of their breathing. You may say:

Take in a long slow breath, hold it, then release it slowly. As you breathe out, imagine you are letting go of all your worries and cares. As you breathe in, imagine that God is entering into your whole self. [Pause]

Now recall a time when you became lost. Perhaps as a child you were in a store and lost sight of your mother or father or the person caring for you. Maybe it was your first day at a new school and you couldn't find your classroom. Maybe you were hiking or biking or driving and lost your way. Take a few moments to think about that time and how you felt when you were lost or alone.

Give them one or two minutes to reflect upon this. Then say:

Our faith is a journey in which we sometimes become lost and then find our way again. It can be scary, even terrifying, when we feel lost or alone. Sometimes we find our own way back to where we need to be, or maybe we meet someone who can point us in the right direction. Think about ways in which you have been helped when you were lost or alone. [Pause]

Sometimes we find ourselves in a place where others we trusted have let us down. But God knows us and loves us and will help us make it through the "lost" times. Be still and be open to the love God has for you, a love that calls you by name and will not let you go. [Pause]

Listen to your breathing again. Perhaps it is slower and calmer now. Take a deep breath in and slowly let it out. When you are ready, you may open your eyes.

Exploring

LEARN ABOUT MARY MAGDALENE (10 MINUTES)

If the group has more than eight members, form groups of four or five. Tell the group(s) that in this session they will be looking at the story of Mary Magdalene, a woman who was healed by Jesus and became a faithful disciple.

Read aloud the reference to Mary Magdalene in Luke 8:1–2. Explain that meeting Jesus changed her life. She had been troubled with many demons. This was the way the people at that time explained the presence of some physical or mental illnesses. It did not mean that someone was morally or ethically corrupt. Luke tells us that Mary Magdalene was cured. Luke also puts her first among the list of women who traveled with Jesus and the disciples, bringing the good news of God's reign. Sometimes she is mistakenly identified as the woman from Luke 7:36–50 who anointed Jesus' feet, but there is no evidence to connect her to that story.

Ask for volunteers to read Matthew 28:1–20, where Mary meets the resurrected Christ. (Be aware that not all youth read well aloud, so ask for a volunteer who is comfortable with the task.) Read the story more than once from different translations of the Bible, if possible.

Identify some of the major points in this story, such as:

- Mary Magdalene and the other Mary went to Jesus' tomb.
- An angel, or messenger, appeared to them and told them that Jesus was not to be found in the tomb, but had risen.
- They were directed to go and tell this to the other disciples.
- When the disciples met the Risen Christ, Christ told them to go into the world to spread the good news and to teach God's ways to others.
- Jesus promised to be with them as they went about doing this.

ROLE-PLAY SCENES FROM MARY MAGDALENE'S STORY (15 MINUTES)

both stories

Engage in the following role play. Ask the group to reenact the scenes from Matthew 28. Encourage creativity with this role play. For example, it may be done in the format of a news report, pantomime, or a play in several acts. Following the role play of the scripture, encourage discussion using these questions:

- How do you think Mary Magdalene and the other Mary felt when they saw Jesus?
- How do you think the other disciples felt when they heard that Jesus appeared to these two women?
- How do you think the disciples may have felt when Jesus came to them and gave them instructions to go out to continue Jesus' ministry?

Ask the group to do the role play again. This time, have the group improvise a contemporary scene in which someone is telling about an incredible event he or she witnessed and the listeners do not believe it. Ask:

- How do we know when we can believe someone else?
- Are we more likely to believe someone because we have come to know and trust them?

Connecting

✓ CREATE A "LIFE LINE" (15 MINUTES)

For Mary Magdalene, meeting Jesus was a significant, life-changing event. Invite the group to examine some significant events in their own lives through the activity "Life Lines." Give these instructions:

In your journal (page 11), find the "Life Line" and mark on it the significant events that are part of your life history. They can include events such as when you were born, started school, learned a new skill, met an important friend, faced losses, and so forth.

Be aware that some youth may not feel they have lived long enough to make a "Life Line," but reassure them that they have and give them additional examples if necessary.

✓ ADD FAITH CONNECTIONS TO THE "LIFE LINES" (10 MINUTES)

Continue by saying:

Look at your "Life Line" again, and, using a different color, mark the times in your life where you sensed God's love and presence in some way. The marks may indicate important dates, such as your baptism or a time when someone helped you with a problem. They may indicate times of faith, doubt, unbelief, or times when you were (or were not) a part of a church or community of faith. They may reflect times when you felt close to (or distant from) God or times when you felt courage, strength, or inspiration coming from some place beyond yourself. You may want to use the questions in your journal to help you recall these times and the people or circumstances around the events.

✓ DISCUSS "LIFE LINES" (10 MINUTES)

When the youth have completed this step on their "Life Line," form groups of no more than six, if possible, including the leader(s). In these groups, invite persons to share the parts of their "Life Line" that they are comfortable talking about. If the youth have trouble getting started, the leader(s) may begin. Use the following questions (also in the journal) to guide the sharing:

- ℮ What are some of the times when you have been aware of God's presence with you?
- ℮ What experiences, events, or people have helped you to know of God's presence?
- ℮ How have your family, friends, or members of the church helped you in your faith journey?
- ℮ What qualities or traits might someone else see in you that show your faith?

❷ What qualities or traits do you hope God will help you develop as your faith grows?

❷ Even though our faith journeys and experiences are unique, have you discovered ways your story connects to the stories of others?

Questions may be asked by the others in the group, but the person telling the story is to be the focus. Allow dialogue and discussion, but be sensitive to the personal nature of the sharing.

Have the group imagine the future and add things they anticipate will happen in life such as relationships, education, careers, and retirement.

✓ HEAR THE FAITH STORIES OF GOD'S PEOPLE (15 MINUTES)

Invite the group to look at the quotes in the *Confirmand's Journal* from various people in the United Church of Christ who have shared why they believe in God and are disciples of Jesus. Have the confirmands and leaders use the instructions and the space provided in the journal to reflect on the quotes.

Going

✓ WORSHIP TOGETHER (5 MINUTES)

In a closing circle, invite confirmands to name at least one way that they see God at work in their lives or the lives of others in the congregation or community. Close the session with this prayer or any prayer of thanks for those who have shared their faith and for the ways in which God empowers us to spread the good news:

God, thank you for all the people you have touched with your power. Thank you for Jesus Christ and the men and women who followed him. Thank you for our church and the way it witnesses to the good news Christ brings. Thank you for the ways in which you have already touched our lives. Please continue to be with us, heal us, bless us, and empower us in all we say and do. In Jesus' name, amen.

Do questions assign. for next time - 2 people, one can be a parent, can do it over phone

Connecting with the Congregation

CONDUCT INTERVIEWS OR WRITE LETTERS

Invite the confirmands to conduct interviews or write letters to persons in the congregation and ask them
about their faith journeys and stories. Make assignments during this session and designate the deadline.
Mentors may accompany the confirmands on the interviews or the confirmands may go on their own.
This is a good way to help youth make connections with others in the congregation. Suggest that they
use a tape recorder to record the interview (with permission, of course!) and take a picture of who they
interviewed, if possible.

Ask confirmands to develop a list of questions before they conduct the interview. Examples are:

- Were you baptized? Where? How?
- Were you confirmed? If so, what was the process like?
- What do you remember about church if you attended when you were a child?
- What kind of influence did your family and upbringing have on your faith?
- How do you imagine God?
- What sustains your faith during hard times?
- What events in your life and in your faith have affected you most profoundly?

Alternatively, you may ask the whole group to spend time developing other questions.

Thinking About This Session

How did the confirmands respond to the "Life Line" activity? Were they able to think of times when they
felt God's presence? For some this is a new question to consider. Don't assume that all the youth have
had some faith experience thus far. This kind of exploration may be new for some. Be aware of times
that are challenging or uncomfortable for individuals in the group. Try not to single anyone out because
his or her experience is different from others.

Planning Ahead

Gather together worship bulletins and other materials needed for the next session. Make necessary arrangements for the group to meet in the church's worship space. Ask worship planners how confirmands can
assist in leading worship and report the response to the group.

WORSHIP

Themes

@ Worship is the way God's people offer praise and thanksgiving to the living God.

@ Worship is the way God's people respond to God's grace and God's initiative in our salvation.

@ Worship gives order to the church's life, linking the past to the present and the future.

@ Worship is not limited to any particular place or time.

Scriptures

JOHN 4:21–24—True worship may happen anywhere if we worship God in spirit and truth.

PSALM 100—Worshipers are called to praise God in joyful celebration.

ACTS 2:22–42—Peter speaks of God's saving love through Jesus Christ.

ACTS 10:34–48—Peter preaches to the Gentiles and many receive the gift of the Holy Spirit and are baptized in Christ's name.

Objectives for This Session

@ Explore purposes and elements of Christian worship.

@ Explore their own congregation's worship practices.

@ Experience worship together.

Session at a Glance

GATHERING

Look at the Elements of Worship (15 minutes)

EXPLORING

Look at the Worship Practices in Your Congregation (45 minutes)

CONNECTING

Look at a Poem about Worship (15 minutes)

GOING

Worship Together (15 minutes)

Biblical and Theological Background

Worship is central to the life of Christians and grows out of the practice of Jewish worship, which gave it form and substance. As the *United Church of Christ Book of Worship* affirms in its introduction, "Like worship in Judaism, Christian worship is the glad response of total individuals—through 'heart, soul, strength, and mind'—to the saving acts of God in history."[1] Worship throughout Christ's church reflects the church's diversity and often defies definition. Yet it is the best and most effective way we have of regularly renewing our faith and continually forming and reforming our ideas about what it means to be a Christian.

Think of your worship experience; how much of it do you connect with a particular day, time, group of people, or place? For example, many would think of worship on Sunday morning, in their local church, surrounded by people they know.

In John 4:20–26, we read a portion of the conversation Jesus had with a Samaritan woman at the village well. She takes this opportunity to ask Jesus to describe the reasons why the Jews would think that Jerusalem is the place where people should worship. We learn that her sense of worship as a Samaritan is also connected with a particular place, namely Mount Gerizim, the mountain where her ancestors worshiped.

The reference to Jerusalem as the proper place to worship calls to mind a time one thousand years before, when the Hebrew king David brought the ark of the covenant to Jerusalem (2 Samuel 6:12–19) and later built an altar to hold the ark (2 Samuel 24:18–25). This site then became the place where King Solomon, David's son, built the Temple. Just as the Samaritan woman's ancestors began at some point to worship on the mountain, Jesus' ancestors began to center worship around the Temple in Jerusalem, which, by their tradition, was a place of God's presence.

In this conversation, Jesus overturns her thinking and frees worship from a particular place and group of people. Jesus tells her that, with his presence, now is the time when there will not be just one place in a temple or on a mountain where God's presence may be found and celebrated. In this teaching of Jesus we find a new idea: *who* worships and *where* worship occurs are not as important as worshiping God in spirit and truth.

So often when we think of worship, our thoughts are too limited. We may envision only that one hour, on Sunday, surrounded by those familiar faces. But worship can happen anywhere, anytime, in a group of any size. The possibilities and situations for worship to occur are endless—from singing songs to God on a wooded hillside to gathering with others at work or play to pray, praise, and thank God.

The word *worship* actually comes from the old English word *weorthscipe*—literally, *weorth*, which means "worthy," and *scipe*, which means "ship."[2] The combination of words refers to the way we place worth and value on things and persons. While a service of Christian or Jewish or Muslim worship assumes that it is God who is the one we give value and worth to above all, it is important to remember that almost anything can be worshiped, as the Israelites did with the golden calf and as we do with all kinds of things. Another word used often, *liturgy,* comes from the ancient Greek and means literally "the people's work."[3]

Within the United Church of Christ, worship may take many forms and occur in a variety of places with groups of any size, but its purpose is still to provide us with the opportunity to praise and give thanks to God, our Creator, Redeemer, and Sustainer. This is our task as God's faithful people.

This work is described in Psalm 100. (The Psalms were the hymnbook of the Hebrew Scriptures and have been used in worship by Christians from the beginning of the church.) The worshipers are invited to "make a joyful noise," to "worship with gladness," and to "give thanks." This is a call to let loose and, with delight and freedom, celebrate God.

Worship may take on a variety of forms. For the purposes of this session, we focus on corporate, communal worship—where two or more are gathered. It is important to recognize that small group gatherings and private devotions are also an integral part of a Christian's worship life. Worship is not simply confined to one hour on Sunday morning, just as it is not confined to one place we call "church."

Christian worship invites us to approach God by bringing our whole selves to the experience. To help believers worship, certain practices have evolved over the centuries. Christian worship today is a melding of Jewish worship practices in the Temple and synagogue with contemporary understandings of how, as a gathered people, we may approach God, celebrate God's presence, and embrace the Holy Spirit's activity. Worship helps us become aware of the spiritual gifts God gives the faithful. Worship helps us renew and ready ourselves for God's service in the world.

One way some churches organize themselves for worship is through the liturgical year patterned on Jesus' life. It begins in late November or early December with Advent and the anticipation of Christ's birth and second coming; it moves through Christmas, Epiphany, Lent, Easter, Pentecost, the Sundays following Pentecost; and it concludes with Reign of Christ Sunday (also known as the Festival of Christ the Sovereign).

In worship, there are many opportunities for God to meet us. Through the sermon, prayers, assurances, hymns, offering, and sacraments, God may speak to our hearts that we "may speak in living echoes"[4] of God's tone.

In this session we will look at how your congregation praises and thanks God and how it is fed and renewed as it follows Christ. We will also look at how the physical surroundings and design of the worship setting assist in that task.

Materials Needed

- Bible for each participant
- *Confirmand's Journal* for each participant
- Video of an event with an audience (optional)
- Newsprint and markers
- A calendar of the church year
- *Revised Common Lectionary* (if possible)
- Worship bulletins from your congregation
- Clergy stoles, paraments, and banners
- *United Church of Christ Book of Worship*
- Hymnals

Preparing for This Session

Gather the needed supplies and place them in the room where you will be meeting. Your congregation's place of worship is the recommended setting for at least part of this session, so you will need to make the necessary arrangements to reserve the space. Become familiar with all the ways worship occurs in your local church. Who is responsible for planning worship? Do you have a worship committee, or is this one of the pastoral tasks? Who makes the decisions about the order of service and liturgy? Speak with these worship planners to determine how the worship is designed. Ask the planners what guidelines they use and what commitments they honor as they plan worship.

Review your congregation's order of worship, and be prepared to go over this with the confirmands.

Gathering

LOOK AT THE ELEMENTS OF WORSHIP (15 MINUTES)

Welcome the youth and leaders. Ask the group to think about events where there are audiences or show a video segment of such an event. They might name a play, a sports event, a concert, or a construction crew building a house. If worship is compared to one of these events, who is the audience? Who are the players? Who is the director, coach, or supervisor? Take some time to consider these questions and formulate answers. If we would compare worship to one of these events, we might say that the congregation is the audience, the pastor(s) and worship leaders are the players, and God is the one in charge, telling the actors what to say and do. Does this metaphor fit with the idea that our worship is our response to God?

Now suggest a different view. In what ways are the pastor(s) and other worship leaders like the ones in charge, leading the players (the congregation) through their parts? Who is the audience? [God.] What difference might it make in worship to remember that we are doing this for God?

Exploring

LOOK AT THE WORSHIP PRACTICES IN YOUR CONGREGATION (45 MINUTES)

Using four sheets of newsprint, label each with one of these headings: "What Is Worship?" "Where Is Worship?" "Who Worships?" and "What Is Required?" Have confirmands brainstorm answers from their own experience. Record their responses on the newsprint. Make sure the discussion includes, but is not limited to, Sunday morning services. Point out that worship refers to persons or things that we value above others. Ask the confirmands:

Where and at what times during the week do you think about God? When and where is God most important to you? How are those times worshipful?

If possible, move as a group to your congregation's primary place of worship. Hand out samples of your congregation's worship bulletin and invite the confirmands to take a few moments to look at the worship outline (liturgy). If your congregation does not use a bulletin, create an average Sunday's worship flow on a sheet of newsprint. Notice the progression of elements. Are there examples of what was written earlier on the newsprint? Discuss:

@ Looking at this bulletin, what can you tell about the overall theme or mood of this particular service? What part(s) do you think you would find most meaningful or inspiring? Are there parts that are less helpful or confusing? What parts do you think teach you the most about what it means to be a Christian? How well does this liturgy help you "worship God in spirit and truth" (John 4:23), as Jesus said?

@ How important is "place" in this service? Could this service have occurred in a park or at the beach? If so, would anything need to change?

After this discussion of the elements and their progression in this liturgy, look at the date of this service. In what season of the church year did it occur? The church year, like the calendar year, has seasons too.

Sometimes a different format for the service is used from one season to the next. Briefly review the seasons of the church. Show a sampling of altar paraments and clergy stoles from the different seasons.

If you have additional time you may wish to show the *United Church of Christ Book of Worship* or other worship resources your congregation may use. Point out the variety of liturgies. The *Book of Worship* does not offer rules for worship but provides outlines and suggestions for the content and flow of the various liturgies of the church.

Next, tour the place where your congregation most often worships. Move about the space. Encourage the group to situate themselves in places that may be unfamiliar (such as front pew, balcony, choir area, clergy seats, pulpit, lectern, or communion table). If you have time, you may also wish to look at other spaces where worship occurs for your congregation. Ask:

How does the physical design of this space help worship to happen? How does the space contribute to you feeling close to God? How does this space help you relate to God in spirit and in truth?

Look at the architecture around you. How does it help to create a worshipful atmosphere? Does your worship space have stained glass windows, carvings, or other religious decorative elements? Or is your space simple and plain? In what ways do these elements (decorated or simple) help or detract from worship for you?

What defines this interior space as Christian? What symbols of the faith are visible? What do they call to mind or symbolize? For example, is there a cross, and where is it? Where is the baptismal font? What does its location say about your congregation's understanding of baptism? A font by the entrance to the worship space is a reminder that we are members of Christ's church through baptism, and as we leave it reminds us to live our faith. A font toward the front (chancel) area emphasizes the importance of the act of baptism in worship and reminds us of the ministry to which we are all called as baptized Christians. Where is your font?

Where is the scripture read, sermon delivered, or Holy Communion celebrated? Given that liturgy is the work of the people, how does the placement of each of these activities involve the people? Is there an altar, communion table, or both? What is the difference?

Notice whether or not your worship space is accessible to all persons, including those who live with challenges to mobility, sight, and hearing. Are there ramps, elevators, and doorways designed to accommodate all people? Are large-print bulletins provided? Are there amplification devices for the hearing impaired? Is the service signed?

Connecting

LOOK AT A POEM ABOUT WORSHIP (15 MINUTES)

Have the participants find the poem "What We Bring to Worship" on page 24 in their journals. Take turns reading it aloud. What other ideas about worship and its purpose do you find in this poem? Add these to the lists you created in "Exploring." Sum up the discussion by reviewing the purposes of worship:

    ⎈ to praise God

    ⎈ to confess, repent, and be forgiven

    ⎈ to be healed by God

    ⎈ to be transformed by God's presence

    ⎈ to be called and commissioned for God's service

Going

WORSHIP TOGETHER (15 MINUTES)

End the session with worship using the following outline, or use one patterned after your congregation's order of worship:

Call to Worship—Read Psalm 100 individually or as a group, in unison or antiphonally.

Act(s) of Praise—Sing a hymn, such as "We Are Your People," page 224 in the journal or page 230 in this guide; the Doxology; a Gloria; or other song of praise. Or offer a rhythmic clap or rap that includes expressions of praise to God, or play recorded music and invite each person to offer body movements expressing praise and thanksgiving.

Time of Confession and Assurance of Pardon—Ask participants to write on a piece of paper the completion to this sentence: "Something I am sorry about is . . ." Assure them that no one will read what they have written. Collect these and offer them to God. Afterward, as a sign of being forgiven, the confessions may be burned (outdoor setting recommended), torn into small pieces, or otherwise removed from the tray and destroyed. Conclude with these words in unison: *When we confess our sins, God forgives us. Thanks be to God!*

Scripture Reading—Read John 4:21–24.

Reflection—Ask participants to complete the sentence, "To worship God in spirit and truth means . . ."

Closing Prayer—Invite participants to voice a prayer to God using sentences, a phrase, or just one word. When each prayer has ended, conclude it with: *Thanks be to God!*

Dismissal—Say to the group: *Let us go in the peace of Christ. Amen!*

Do assignment

Connecting with the Congregation

PARTICIPATE IN LEADING WORSHIP

Make arrangements for the confirmands to share in leading worship. They may read scripture, offer prayers, preach, sing, usher, help the clergy distribute communion, and so forth. Look for ways that they may participate in the full worship life of the church. Provide an orientation time to prepare them for these tasks.

Thinking About This Session

Worship is central to the life of a church and its members. How has this session encouraged the confirmands to embrace the experience of worship as an important part of their faith journey? What will the congregation do to make the worship experience inviting and helpful for all ages, especially youth?

Planning Ahead

Secure copies of your church's charter, mission statement, and/or constitution. Research the church's history and collect any materials that would help you to tell its story. If possible, arrange to have a member who knows the church's history make a brief presentation to the confirmands.

GOD'S MISSION AND THE HISTORY
OF OUR LOCAL CHURCH

Themes

@ Our local church has a history.

@ Our local church has a mission.

@ God's mission and our history connect us to the whole Christian church.

Scriptures

ACTS 11:19–26—The first Christian church in Antioch was started.

MATTHEW 22:34–40—Jesus names the two greatest commandments.

LUKE 4:16–21—Jesus reads from the scroll of Isaiah.

ACTS 2:43–47—Life in the first church in Jerusalem is described.

Objectives for This Session

@ Discover the history and mission of your local church.

@ Write a church mission statement.

Session at a Glance

GATHERING

Review the history of the early church in Antioch (5 minutes)

EXPLORING

Research your congregation's history (15 minutes)

Do a role play of a new congregation (30 minutes)

Discuss the role play (10 minutes)

CONNECTING

Review your congregation's mission statement (10 minutes)

Plan a witness and service project (10 minutes)

GOING

Make observations about your congregation's mission

(5 minutes)

Worship together (5 minutes)

Biblical and Theological Background

Members of a local church are part of a wider community called the Christian church. Although each congregation has roots in Jesus Christ and the early Christian church, it also has a unique story to tell of why and how it began. It is interesting to learn about the origins and the missionary vision of local churches. Learning about their histories and reason for being helps to connect the local churches to both God's mission and the whole Christian church.

The story in Acts 11:19–26 tells how the first church in Antioch began. Although this wasn't the first church to form after Jesus' resurrection, it was one of the first churches started among people who were not Jews. It was in Antioch that the disciples were first called "Christians" (11:26).

The other scriptures for this session describe how we are to respond in mission as Christians. Matthew 22:34–40 calls us to love God with all our heart, soul, and mind and to love our neighbor as ourselves. In Luke 4:18–21, Jesus reads the words from the scroll of Isaiah that describe the call he has come to fulfill. Acts 2:43–47 tells how people in the early church shared their possessions.

In this session you will take time with the confirmands to explore God's mission and the history of your local church. Each congregation has a story waiting to be told. What gems of history will you find? What things bind you together with the wider church? What things make your local church unique?

There are many dynamics that come into play when a group of people gather to explore God's mission as expressed in the local church. Our understanding of scripture and what God is trying to say to us helps to shape our response to mission. People bring their experiences and their history in other congregations to the group. Leadership and individual personalities help influence the process. In the end, mission comes about when the Holy Spirit uses the gifts of the members to express God's love to the world.

Materials Needed

- Bible for each participant
- *Confirmand's Journal* for each participant
- Notepaper and pens or pencils
- Copies of your local church's charter, mission statement, or constitution
- Newsprint and markers
- Witness and service project ideas from the opening retreat

Preparing for This Session

To prepare for this session, read Acts 11:19–26, Matthew 22:34–40, Luke 4:16–21, and Acts 2:43–47. Note in your journal what you think each passage says about God's mission.

If your group made plans for any witness and service projects during the opening retreat, take time to assess where each project is. If you did not plan projects at that time, refer now to "A Guide for Witness and Service," pages 271–74, in order to work with the confirmands in this session developing one or more witness and service projects. Enlist the help of others in the church, if necessary.

Investigate the history of your own local church. How and why was it formed? What special and unique events have occurred in the life of the congregation? You may find this kind of information by looking through historical records, old annual reports, or special anniversary booklets. Interview the church historian of your congregation (if there is one) or other persons with an interest in the history of the church. For newer congregations, charter members and founding pastors may be a resource.

If your congregation has a mission statement, obtain the original statement and any revisions. Some local churches refer to their church covenant or statement of purpose to describe the mission. Look in the constitution or charter of your local church for such a statement. You may also refer to the United Church of Christ's Statement of Mission on page 40 of this guide or on page 30 in the *Confirmand's Journal.*

If there is a person knowledgeable in the history of your congregation, invite that person to make a brief presentation during "Exploring." (This person may then remain and participate in the rest of the session.)

Select confirmands to read the scriptures for this session and have Bibles available for all the confirmands to follow along.

Select a room conducive to role-playing and private enough so confirmands will feel at ease.

Gathering

REVIEW THE HISTORY OF THE EARLY CHURCH IN ANTIOCH (5 MINUTES)

Begin by reading Acts 11:19–26 aloud. Ask the confirmands to note how the church in Antioch got started (by the mission activity of nameless Christians, along with Barnabas and Saul). Ask:

@ What significant event is described in Acts 11:26?

[The name "Christian" is used for the first time to refer to believers.]

Exploring

RESEARCH YOUR CONGREGATION'S HISTORY (15 MINUTES)

Share briefly some highlights from your local church's history. If you have invited others from the congregation to do this, introduce them to the group.

DO A ROLE PLAY OF A NEW CONGREGATION (30 MINUTES)

Inform the confirmands that they are to imagine that they are charter members of a newly forming congregation. The charter members are meeting to develop a mission statement to guide the mission and activity of the new church.

Use the following descriptions as roles for the youth to play out the scenario. If you have fewer than five in the group, let each youth choose which role he or she wants to play.

- A person who thinks the congregation needs to focus on children and adults, not just youth.
- A person who wants to make worship the main priority of the congregation.
- A person who is concerned about the church's finances.
- A person who is concerned about justice issues.
- A person who wants the congregation to be like a social club.
- A person who wants contemporary music in all services.

Confirmands may add their own issues and interests to these suggestions. Recruit someone from the group to be the moderator or have the leader moderate. He or she may also take on a role.

Decide what the biblical basis of your mission statement will be. For example, Ephesians 4:11–12 speaks about different callings as Christians. First Peter 2:9–10 speaks about the special calling of Christians in relationship to God. These and other Bible readings make it clear that God calls congregations into life and continues to challenge them to new life.

Brainstorm some key information about this imaginary church and its community. Write these ideas on newsprint. For example, list the size of the church, the varieties of people who are members (age, gender, racial and ethnic background, employment situation, income levels, health concerns), the location of the church, and a description of the church building. Also include some basic information about the community, such as types of businesses and industry, schools, hospitals, social service agencies, and other churches. (To save time, the leader(s) may determine these factors ahead of time and announce them to the group so that they can proceed with the role play in character.)

Spend about thirty minutes on the role play to develop a short mission statement. Explain that a mission statement answers the question, "Why do we exist as a church?" Distribute index cards to each person. Ask them, in their roles, to take five minutes to write their answer to the question above. Their answers can be two or three sentences. The answers can reflect not only what each thinks the church needs to be doing now, but also what the church ought to be doing in the future.

When all have completed their sentences, gather together and share the statements. Now consider this question: What is important for our new local church to do to carry out God's mission within the congregation and the community? Discuss what portions the group wants to include in the final mission statement to answer this question. Work with the whole group for about twenty minutes using newsprint to shape the statement to its final form, about three to four sentences. (They may refer to a sample mission statement in the *Confirmand's Journal*, page 29, for help.) When the mission statement is completed, read it together in unison.

DISCUSS THE ROLE PLAY (10 MINUTES)

When this is completed, summarize as a group what the main focus of the church's mission is as they see it. (This may be put on newsprint.) Then ask:

@ In what ways have you been involved in the mission of this congregation (or other congregations)?

Make a list of what the youth name. Point out that one of the ways God's mission happens in the local church is when people are encouraged to come into the church through baptism or by involvement. All of us are recipients of the mission work of the church. Then ask:

@ In what ways do we want to provide for others who may need or want what the church has to offer?

Connecting

REVIEW YOUR CONGREGATION'S MISSION STATEMENT (10 MINUTES)

Take a look at your congregation's mission statement, charter, constitution, and/or the United Church of Christ Mission Statement. Talk about what your church does and how its activity reflects its mission statement. Consider these questions:

@ What helps the congregation live up to its vision?

@ What keeps the congregation from doing mission work? What might need to change?

@ How does your vision of mission contribute to this?

@ What are the differences in focus between the statement created earlier in the role-play group and that of your congregation?

PLAN A WITNESS AND SERVICE PROJECT (10 MINUTES)

Take time now to introduce (or reintroduce) the idea of expressing God's mission through witness and service using the ideas in "A Guide for Witness and Service" (page 271). Be open to the widest possible interpretations, particularly in light of the confirmands' understanding of mission and their experience in the local church. Develop specific plans for engaging in witness and service as individuals, as a group, or both.

Going

MAKE OBSERVATIONS ABOUT YOUR CONGREGATION'S MISSION (5 MINUTES)

Close the session with the following observations:

Exploring the history and mission of our local church helps us to understand the purpose of our congregation when it began and today. We are all part of the church of Jesus Christ, and we have a unique story to tell. We have been brought together by God, and God asks us to reach out to others, individually and as a congregation. Mission includes loving God and our neighbor, doing as Jesus did, and sharing as the early church shared.

WORSHIP TOGETHER (5 MINUTES)

Form a circle and pause for a moment of silence. Join together for the benediction by reading Luke 4:18–19, reprinted from *The Gospels and the Letters of Paul: An Inclusive-Language Edition:*

The spirit of God is upon me, because God has anointed me to bring good news to the poor, and has sent me to proclaim release to the captives and recovering of sight to those who are blind, to set at liberty those who are oppressed, to proclaim the acceptable year of God.[1]

Additional Activity

GO ON A HISTORICAL FIELD TRIP

The group may want to spend more time discovering the history of your local church. Invite persons who are

knowledgeable about and interested in the history of the congregation to make a presentation to the
youth. Take a field trip to a place connected with the history of your local church. For example, if your
congregation was part of another congregation, you may want to go and visit the church that "birthed"
your congregation and talk with some of the people there. You may want to visit a historical site with
which your congregation is associated, such as Plymouth Rock in Massachusetts, the Amistad Research
Center at Tulane University in New Orleans, Deaconess Hospital in St. Louis, a United Church of
Christ related college or seminary, or the original site where the congregation was founded. The names
of agencies and institutions related to the United Church of Christ are listed in the *United Church of
Christ Yearbook*, published annually (available from the UCC Yearbook Office, 216-736-2113).
Make arrangements in advance with the people and places you plan to visit. Have the confirmands develop
questions to ask the people you meet.

Connecting with the Congregation

PRESENT ROLE PLAY MISSION STATEMENT TO CHURCH LEADERS
Decide how the mission statement you developed in the role play could be shared with an appropriate committee or board of your church.

Thinking About This Session

How well did the confirmands make the connection between the mission and history of your local church
and the history and mission of the whole Christian church? How did they respond to the activity of
writing a mission statement in the role play? Are there ways that their work could be used by your congregation?

Planning Ahead

Read the next session and gather needed supplies, including index cards, various translations of the Bible,
and Bible study helps, such as a concordance, Bible atlas, commentaries, and Bible dictionary, if possible.

Resources

THE UNITED CHURCH OF CHRIST'S STATEMENT OF MISSION[2]

As people of the United Church of Christ, affirming our Statement of Faith, we seek with the Church
    Universal to participate in God's mission and to follow the way of the crucified and risen Christ.

Empowered by the Holy Spirit, we are called and commit ourselves. . .

- to praise God, confess our sin, and joyfully accept God's forgiveness;
- to proclaim the Gospel of Jesus Christ in our suffering world;
- to embody God's love for all people;
- to hear and give voice to creation's cry for justice and peace;
- to name and confront the powers of evil within and among us;
- to repent our silence and complicity with the forces of chaos and death;
- to preach and teach with the power of the Living Word;
- to join oppressed and troubled people in the struggle for liberation;
- to work for justice, healing, and wholeness of life;
- to embrace the unity of Christ's church;
- to discern and celebrate the present and coming reign of God.

AFFIRMING f a i t h

The story of the Christian church tells us about how God works in human history.

Heritage

History

OUR HISTORY AND HERITAGE

THE BIBLE

Themes

❧ The Bible is a collection of stories that tell us of God's actions toward people and creation—creating, loving, judging, and saving.

❧ The Bible tells the story of humankind's experience of God.

Scriptures

PSALM 119:97–106—God's word in Scripture is like honey, sweet to the taste; God's word in Scripture is like a lamp that provides light for our way.

2 TIMOTHY 3:14–17—Paul instructs Timothy to trust Scripture as inspired by God.

Objectives

❧ Explore how the Bible came to be.

❧ Place in order the major events of the Bible.

❧ Identify the place and authority of the Bible in the Christian community.

❧ Experience a simple method of Bible study.

Session at a Glance

GATHERING

Look at various Bible translations (5 minutes)

EXPLORING

Consider how the Bible came to be (20 minutes)

Place the Bible events in order (10 minutes)

Tell the Bible stories to one another (30 minutes)

CONNECTING

Study the Bible (20 minutes)

GOING

Worship together (5 minutes)

Biblical and Theological Background

The Bible is not just one book; it is a collection of sixty-six books that tell the story of God's relationship with humankind and creation. The word *Bible* comes from *biblia*, a Greek word that means "little books." In these books the relationship between God and people is communicated through covenant—the promises God made with humankind to love, care for, and guide us in the way that gives life. In the Hebrew Scriptures (also known as the Old Testament) the covenant is expressed most simply when God said, "I will walk among you, and I will be your God and you shall be my people" (Leviticus 26:12). The covenant was also expressed by Jesus in the early Christian Scriptures (also known as the New Testament) when he made this promise to the disciples at the Last Supper: "This cup is the new covenant in my blood" (1 Corinthians 11:25b).

The Bible has a rich history of how it came to be. At first, over three thousand years ago, the Hebrews, who were nomads, passed on the stories of God's mighty acts through storytelling. Many generations learned the stories through this oral tradition. Then, around 1100 B.C.E., the stories were written down in Hebrew, first on stone tablets, then on animal skins and papyrus. Over time some of the writings took on great importance in the life of the people, and they began to be recognized as special or sacred. Around 400 B.C.E. the Jewish people (Hebrews) began the task of deciding which of the writings should be considered sacred and authoritative. These would be called the canon. The books that were included in the Hebrew canon were books of law, history, poetry, and prophets.

Several generations later, in about 285 B.C.E., as the Jewish people moved and settled in different areas, the Hebrew Bible was translated into Greek. This version was called the Septuagint (SEP–TOO'–A–JINT). In 98 C.E. some Jewish scholars decided that there were seven books of the Septuagint, written in the three hundred years between the Hebrew Scriptures and the early Christian Scriptures, that should no longer be a part of the canon. These books, known as the Apocrypha, are available in some translations of the Bible. The Episcopal and Roman Catholic Churches officially consider them part of the Bible and use them in worship and education. Other Christians sometimes use them for personal reflection and meditation.

The earliest Christian Scriptures were the letters that Paul wrote to various churches and people, the earliest being the letter to the Thessalonians in about 50 C.E. The Gospels were written down much later, and came from the oral tradition of faithful people telling the stories for several generations. The first gospel to be written was Mark, around 70 C.E. The Gospel of Matthew was written around 85 C.E., as was the Gospel of Luke. The Gospel of John was the last one to be written down, sometime around 100 C.E. The writer who wrote Luke also wrote the book of the Acts of the Apostles. Greek was the language in which the Gospels were written.

The canon for the early Christian Scriptures was decided about 400 C.E. after years of discussion and disagreement about which books should be considered sacred and authoritative. Then, around 500 C.E., an official version of the Bible was translated into Latin. It was known as the Latin Vulgate (meaning "to make common").

After the Reformation, in the 1500s, the Bible was made available to the people in many languages, since most people did not read Latin. William Tyndale published the first Bible in English around 1530. In 1611 the King James Version was printed. The American Standard Version was printed almost three hundred years later. The Revised Standard Version (RSV) was published in 1952, and most recently, the New Revised Standard Version was printed in 1989. Today the Bible has been translated into more than one thousand languages.

Materials Needed

- Bible for each participant
- *Confirmand's Journal* for each participant
- Index cards, marker
- Pencils
- Various Bible versions in various languages
- Bible study helps, such as a concordance, Bible atlas, commentaries, and Bible dictionary, if possible

Preparing for the Session

Use the index cards to write the following major events of the Bible on the front and the scripture references on the back, using one card for each major event: The Creation (Genesis 1:1–2:3 and Genesis 2:4b–25); The Rainbow Covenant (Genesis 6:5–9:19); The Covenant with Abraham and Sarah (Genesis 17:1–21); The Exodus (Exodus 1:1–22, 13:17–15:27); The Conquests (Joshua 1:1–11, 23:1–9); The Time of Judges (Judges 2:16–19); The People Demand a King (1 Samuel 8, 9, 10:1–27); The Exile (Jeremiah 39:1, Lamentations 1:1–7, Psalm 137); The Peaceable Kingdom (Isaiah 11:1–10); The Desert Blossoms (Isaiah 35:1–10); The Nativity (Luke 2:1–20); The Good News (Luke 4:16–22); The Crucifixion and Resurrection (Matthew 27:1–44, 28:1–15); The Reign of God (Matthew 6:33, 22:1–11); The Early Church (Acts 2); The New Heaven and Earth (Revelation 21:1–8).

Gather as many versions and language translations of the Bible as possible and display them in a prominent place in the meeting room. Have available a Bible dictionary, concordance, Bible atlas, and commentaries, if possible, for the Bible study time. Read the "Before You Gather" section in the confirmand's journal (page 35) for this session before you meet with the group.

Gathering

LOOK AT VARIOUS BIBLE TRANSLATIONS (5 MINUTES)

Welcome the confirmands and ask them to look at the various Bibles you have collected. If they wish to add their own Bibles to the group to be examined, they may. Have them select an unfamiliar version to look at more closely. If there are not enough for each person, ask the group to share. Give them a few minutes to determine the name of the version, the year it was printed, and the special features it includes, such as maps, indexes, concordances, and study helps. Have them look at the illustrations or drawings, if any. When everyone has had an opportunity to examine the Bibles, ask the group to report back to one another about what they discovered. Ask if there are any surprises in what they found. What features did they find helpful? What illustrations or drawings did they like? Did the illustrations help to portray all of God's people? What changes, if any, would they make to the versions and why?

Complete this experience by asking the youth to find Psalm 119:103 in the Bibles they have been examining. Explain that the writer of this psalm is telling God what the Scriptures are like. Take turns and have each person read the verse aloud, noticing what words are the same and what ones are different in different versions. Ask:

@   Which versions expressed the clearest meaning? Why?

Exploring

CONSIDER HOW THE BIBLE CAME TO BE (20 MINUTES)

Using the information in the "Biblical and Theological Background," talk about the way the Bible came to be. Then, in their journals, have the youth work individually to fill in the blanks in the section "How the Bible Came to Be" with the words and numbers from the accompanying list (page 36). When everyone is finished, review the answers together.

PLACE THE BIBLE EVENTS IN ORDER (10 MINUTES)

Distribute the index cards you prepared earlier. If your group is smaller than the number of cards, give each confirmand more than one, until all are distributed. If your group is larger than the number of cards, have the groups form pairs to share cards.

Point out that important events from the Bible story are printed on the cards. Have the youth work as a group to place the events in the proper sequence by laying the cards on the floor, a large table, or taping them to a wall. The scripture references on the back of the cards tell where the story can be found in the Bible. They may use their Bibles to help them decide the correct order. When they are finished, compare the order to the list in "Preparing for This Session." Make any necessary adjustments to the order. Write numbers on the cards in pencil to indicate the correct sequence. These numbers will be used to indicate the order for telling the Bible stories in the next experience.

TELL THE BIBLE STORIES TO ONE ANOTHER (30 MINUTES)

Redistribute the cards and have each person or group look at the scripture references on the cards and find the story in their Bible. In order, have each person or group tell in their own words what was happening in this story. By the end of this experience the confirmands will have reviewed the major events of the Bible story from the Hebrew Scriptures to the early Christian Scriptures.

Connecting

STUDY THE BIBLE (20 MINUTES)

Introduce the importance of studying the Bible—the stories can help us understand God, ourselves, our faith, our doubts, and how we are to live with others. It is also important to look at the Bible with others so that our insights as individual believers can be tested, shaped, and informed by those who take the Bible and their faith seriously. Review together the steps for Bible study that are found on page 41 of the *Confirmand's Journal*. Then introduce the scripture that you will be studying together, 2 Timothy 3:14–17. Provide the Bible study aids listed above, if possible. Use the "How to Read the Bible" outline with the whole group, taking time to answer the questions that are provided.

Going

WORSHIP TOGETHER (5 MINUTES)

Close this session with a prayer such as:

Thank you, God, for your word that is a lamp to guide us and a light for our path. Help us to love you and live in your ways. Amen.

Connecting with the Congregation

MAKE A "BOOKS OF THE BIBLE" RESOURCE

Collect sixty-six blocks of wood, approximately 2" x 4" x 6" each, or empty cereal or cracker boxes. Cover the wood or boxes with adhesive-backed shelf paper to create a "book." On the spine of the book write each of the books of the Bible. Make these available in the church library, resource room, or children's learning space. They can be used so that children, youth, and adults can learn the names and order of the books in the Bible.

Thinking About This Session

How well were the confirmands able to arrange the Bible events in order and tell the important stories? How can you give support to those who may not have had much experience with the Bible and its contents, yet avoid singling them out?

Planning Ahead

Read the next session and gather needed supplies, including index cards and prizes such as candy, gum, or small novelty toys (if possible).

THE HISTORY OF CHRISTIANITY

Themes

ℓ The Christian church was called into being by the life, witness, death, and resurrection of Jesus Christ.

ℓ The story of the Christian church tells us about how God works in human history.

ℓ The Christian church is more than a human organization, it is a gift from God.

Scriptures

MATTHEW 16:13–20—Jesus affirms Peter's faith as a foundation for understanding God's call.

EPHESIANS 11:11–22—Jesus Christ is the cornerstone of our faith.

HEBREWS 12:1–2—Many faithful people, led by Jesus' example, have gone before us and encourage our faith.

Objective

ℓ Review the history of Christianity.

Session at a Glance

GATHERING

Create a "cloud of witnesses" (5 minutes)

EXPLORING

Create a Christian history time line (45 minutes)

CONNECTING

Play a quiz game (35 minutes)

GOING

Worship together (5 minutes)

Biblical and Theological Background

"Who do you say that I am?" That question, asked by Jesus of Simon Peter, opened the door for Peter to declare unequivocally who Jesus was. Peter's response was simple, only ten words—"You are the Messiah, the Child of the living God" (Matthew 16:16). He didn't seem to spend a lot of time formulating his answer—he simply stated what was obvious to him. But Jesus' reaction to these ten words was to say, "Your name is Peter [meaning rock], and on this rock I will build my church."

The Christian church is built on the rock of Peter's faith, because what it has in common, over the ages and generations, is that those who call themselves Christian do so because they simply *know who Jesus is*. The disciples came to know Jesus as Messiah from their personal contact with him, and from their experience of his impact on their lives. In the early years of Christianity, those who had built their faith on "Christ Jesus . . . as the cornerstone" (Ephesians 2:20) did so at risk of persecution and death. Later Christians watched as their faith became merged with society; and in the Middle Ages, the flickering light of learning was kept alive through the efforts of Christians who deemed it important to maintain the books that recorded the events of their faith. But for Christians across all the ages, bound together by the simple fact of knowing who Jesus was, their connection with those who went before (the "cloud of witnesses" of Hebrews 12:1) allowed them to claim citizenship in a different kind of society altogether. "So then you are no longer strangers and aliens, but you are citizens with the saints and also members of the household of God, built upon the foundation of the apostles and prophets, with Christ Jesus himself as the cornerstone . . . you also are built together spiritually into a dwelling place for God" (Ephesians 2:19–22).

In a very real way, confirmation is about helping persons and communities to become a dwelling place for God. We are invited to join centuries upon centuries of believers who have been willing to claim Peter's simple statement, to say aloud who Jesus is. That dwelling place is built upon a foundation of prophets and apostles, upon stories of the faithful, upon the efforts of a cloud of witnesses to share what has become more than obvious to them in their lives—and yet, a fact worthy of becoming the footing for a church. Hearing the echoes of their words gives us confidence to say them for ourselves: "You are the Messiah, the Child of the living God."

Materials Needed

- Bible for each participant
- *Confirmand's Journal* for each participant
- A roll of butcher paper or newsprint, markers

@ Paper

@ Index cards

@ Prizes such as candy, gum, or small novelty toys, if possible

Preparing for the Session

Before the session prepare a piece of butcher paper or newsprint 12–15' long and at least 12" wide to use for the historical time line. Draw a horizonal line close to the bottom (leaving space to write dates) running the length of the paper. At the left end of the paper, under the line, write 6 B.C.E. Next to it write 0. At the other end of the line write the current year. In the middle write 1000 C.E., then approximate where 500 and 1500 C.E. would be and add marks for one-hundred-year intervals.

Write the quiz show answers and questions (found in the "Connecting" section of this session) including the numbers on the front of index cards to be used when the confirmands play the game. Divide the cards into two piles—even-numbered answers and odd-numbered answers. Cut out cloud shapes from white paper, making at least three for every person in the group.

Gathering

CREATE A "CLOUD OF WITNESSES" (5 MINUTES)

Welcome the confirmands. Briefly introduce the theme for this session, the history of Christianity, using the information in the "Biblical and Theological Background." Then read Hebrews 12:1–2 and invite the group to name people they think of as "saints"—those very special, faithful people who through the ages have expressed God's way in how they lived. Have the confirmands write the names on the "cloud" cutouts and hang them from the ceiling in your meeting room with string. The people they name can be members of your church, living or dead, biblical people, historical figures (especially those in Christian history), or any persons who exemplify God's love and justice in the world. After the clouds are hung, read Hebrews 12:1–2 aloud again.

Exploring

MAKE A CHRISTIAN HISTORY TIME LINE (45 MINUTES)

To help participants visualize and remember many of the events that led to the formation of the Christian church, make a Christian history time line highlighting the events from Jesus' birth to the present day. Find an unobstructed wall on which to hang the paper you have prepared for the time line. Have the youth take turns reading the time line script (on page 45 of the *Confirmand's Journal*) as volunteer scribes take turns writing the bold word or phrase from the script above the time line at the appropriate year.

Connecting

PLAY A QUIZ GAME (30 MINUTES)

Form two teams and arrange the group so that the time line is not in direct view. Explain that each team will take turns giving the other *the answer* to a question. The object for the other team is to state the correct *question* and receive a point. The teams may not look at the time line unless they miss a point. Distribute the index cards with the quiz answers and questions to the whole group, giving the odd-numbered cards to Team One and the even-numbered cards to Team Two. The teams can distribute the cards evenly among their members. Have the person who has the card with question #1 read it aloud. Team Two must decide among themselves the answer without consulting the time line, if possible. If they answer correctly, they get one point. If they answer incorrectly, no point is scored, and the team may consult the time line to state the correct answer. Proceed with the second question, so that the teams take turns giving questions for the answers. At the end of the game, announce the score, thank both teams for playing, and give prizes to everyone, if you wish.

Quiz Game Answers

1. This event marked the beginning of Jesus' ministry. (What is Jesus' baptism?)
2. Coming 40 days after his death, it is the day Jesus' physical body left this earth and rose into the heavens. (What is the Ascension?)
3. It is called Pentecost. (What is the day the Holy Spirit came upon the disciples and the church was born?)
4. He was the first Christian to be killed at the beginning of 300 years of persecution. (Who was Stephen?)
5. He was a Roman Jew who hated Christians and helped to persecute them, but on the road to Damascus he had a powerful, blinding vision of Jesus and was converted. (Who was Paul?)
6. At the conference in Jerusalem in the year 49, it was decided that these two apostles would each lead the building of the church, one among Jewish people, the other among the Gentiles. (Who were Peter and Paul?)
7. This church leader was one of the many who helped Paul start and maintain new churches. (Who was Silas, Timothy, Barnabas, Priscilla, or Aquilla?)
8. It is the book which contains the history of the early church. (What is the Acts of the Apostles?)

9. They were written about 70 C.E. to 100 C.E. and helped to spread the story of Jesus. (What are the Gospels—Matthew, Mark, Luke, and John?)

10. These Christian books were written around the year 100 and deal with the organization and theology of the early church. (What are the Pastoral Epistles?)

11. It is the system of church government that became dominant in the early church. (What is the episcopal system?)

12. It was the year the Christian Scriptures were completed and canonized (within 20 years). (What was 135 C.E.?)

13. In the year 312 C.E., after becoming the new Roman emperor, he made it legal for Romans to be Christian and declared an end to persecution. (Who is Constantine?)

14. It is the way in which the early church decided issues of church administration and theology. (What are councils?)

15. Around the year 800, he rallied the church in Europe after it had been sent into exile by those who attacked Rome. When he became Roman emperor, he gave his subjects two choices, baptism or death. (Who is Charlemagne?)

16. It happened in 1054 between the centers of the church in the East (Constantinople) and in the West (Rome). (What is the Great Schism, the split between the Eastern and Western churches?)

17. They were the violent, unsuccessful attempts by Christians in Europe to win back the Holy Land from the Moslems. (What are the Crusades?)

18. Among the many corrupt practices of the church around 1300, this one provided the only way to have your sins forgiven. (What are indulgences?)

19. During this period of wealth and power of the church (up to 1500), they were the only people able to read Scripture and allowed to sing hymns in church and receive Holy Communion. (Who were the priests?)

20. He translated the Bible into English from the Latin Vulgate. (Who is John Wycliffe?)

21. This priest was among many protestors and critics of the Roman church leadership; he went to the church in Wittenburg, Germany, and demanded 95 reforms. He was driven out, nearly killed, and decided to start his own church. (Who was Martin Luther?)

22. It is the name of the church Martin Luther founded. (What is the Lutheran Church?)

23. Attempting to simplify the church, he led the Reformation movement in Switzerland, creating the Reformed Church. (Who is Ulrich Zwingli?)

24. Another reformer in Switzerland hoped to create a model city based on biblical principles and, in the process, started the Presbyterian Church. (Who is John Calvin?)

25. In the early 1600s, this group separated from the Church of England because it opposed the church's dictatorial, rigid, and oppressive ways. (Who are the Separatists or Puritans or Quakers?)

26. This smaller group within the Separatists came to what is now Massachusetts to find religious freedom. (Who were the Pilgrims?)

27. Coming from Germany and Switzerland, immigrants settled in the middle U.S. Atlantic states and eventually gathered and formed this church in 1710. (What is the Reformed Church?)

28. In 1820, a group of Methodist, Presbyterian, and Baptist churches joined together to form this denomination. (What is the Christian Church?)

29. In Missouri, these German immigrants gathered and formed this church in 1840. (What is the Evangelical Church?)

30. In 1853 this church was the first to ordain a woman into Christian ministry. (What is a Congregational Church?)

31. In the early 1930s, these two new denominations were formed, each from the combination of like-minded, similarly organized churches. (What are the Congregational Christian Churches and the Evangelical and Reformed Church?)

32. This is the year the Congregational Christian Churches and the Evangelical and Reformed Church merged to form the United Church of Christ. (What is 1957?)

Going

WORSHIP TOGETHER (5 MINUTES)

Close this session by singing or reciting together the hymn "For All the Saints" found on page 217 of the journal or page 225 of this guide.

Connecting with the Congregation

Display the time line in a prominent place in the church. Plan a time when the confirmands can tell other members about their discoveries. Plan to play the quiz too.

Thinking About This Session

What parts of this session did the confirmands seem to find most helpful? Was the review of history new information for them? Were they able to make connections with their study of history in school? How can you encourage them to explore this area further through reading, watching videos, or consulting other resources?

Planning Ahead

Read the next session and gather needed supplies, including a potted plant with one main stalk that separates into branches with leaves *or* yarn and construction paper, a globe or map of the world, colored push pins (or other appropriate markers), and videos (optional, see page 64).

If you plan to invite church members to help interpret the United Church of Christ based on their own knowledge or experience, contact them early in the week.

THE HISTORY OF
THE UNITED CHURCH OF CHRIST

Themes

 The United Church of Christ is a uniting church.

 The United Church of Christ is an expression of the universal Christian church.

 The United Church of Christ is organized into settings for ministry and mission.

Scriptures

JOHN 17:20–23—Jesus prays that his followers may all be one.

1 CORINTHIANS 12:4–11—There are a variety of spiritual gifts in the church.

EPHESIANS 4:4–6, 11–16—There is Christian unity amid the diversity of gifts.

Objectives

 Explore the history of the United Church of Christ.

 Review the structure of the United Church of Christ.

 Discover the ministry and mission of the United Church of Christ.

Session at a Glance

GATHERING

Think about the United Church of Christ (10 minutes)

EXPLORING

Look at the parts of the United Church of Christ (50 minutes)

CONNECTING

Reflect on the United Church of Christ (25 minutes)

GOING

Worship together (5 minutes)

Biblical and Theological Background

One is an important word in the New Testament. For example, in the gospels of Matthew and John alone, this word is used nearly three hundred times. In John 17:22, Jesus prays to God for his followers "that they may be one, as we are one." This line expresses an important and frequently encountered theme in the Gospel of John: unity.

Uniting all people through Jesus has been God's plan all along. Jesus' mission was that all could be one. One of the scriptures for this session, John 17:20–23, is a part of Jesus' final prayer, which occurs just before the arrest and crucifixion. This prayer, often called the "high priestly prayer," encompasses all of chapter 17. We may notice at least two things about unity in this passage. First, unity is a result of God's initiative and does not come from our efforts alone. Second, the effect of our oneness and unity is that the world is changed.

Since there is much diversity among those who follow Christ, we might ask, "What does 'being one' mean for us in this day? Must we all be part of the same visible organization or denomination? Do we all need to believe exactly the same things and have a common understanding of mission?" In other words, are the various Christian denominations a sign of disunity, weakness, and brokenness which someday may be "overcome"? Or, are denominations a way to be united in Christ even though we are diverse and different?

The United Church of Christ and the denominations that joined to create it have endeavored to bring about church unity both by uniting organically *and* by honoring the distinctions among the worldwide Christian community. There are many stories that support this inclusiveness in our history. African Americans, Armenians, Asians, European Americans, Hispanics, native Hawaiians, Hungarians, Native Americans, Samoans, and many others have shaped the denomination. Our denomination is the result of a merger in 1957 of two distinct bodies: the Evangelical and Reformed Church and the Congregational Christian Churches. The Evangelical and Reformed Church was a result of a 1934 merger of the Reformed Church in the United States and the Evangelical Synod of North America. The Congregational Christian Churches were formed in 1931, bringing together the General Convention of the South, which included the African American Convention, and the National Council of the Congregational Churches. Since the time of the merger, the United Church of Christ has been in conversation with other Christian churches around issues of unity through the Consultation on Church Union (COCU). Also, the United Church of Christ is joined in a partnership with the Christian Church, USA and Canada (Disciples of Christ), in the Common Global Ministries Board, which coordinates a program of common mission ministries around the world through the United Church Board for World Ministries (UCC) and the Division of Overseas Ministries (CC(DoC)). The United Church of Christ also participates in interchurch bodies such as the National Council of Churches, the World Council of Churches, and the World Alliance of Reformed Churches.

We are the *United* Church of Christ. Our motto is: "That they may all be one." Working for unity yet celebrating diversity is, at times, a difficult balancing act. Paul speaks to this in his letter to the Corinthians, pointing out that while Christians have been given different gifts, "to each is given the manifestation of the Spirit for the common good" (1 Corinthians 12:7). While there are necessary and important differences among denominations and church members, all are united in Christ.

In the letter to the Ephesians, Paul affirms that there is "one Sovereign, one faith, one baptism, one God of all" (4:5–6). Note that Paul makes this claim in a time, the first century after Christ, when the church was already divided into many different factions. His appeal is just as important now as it was then: the church, though divided into many denominations, is still one in Christ.

Similarly, our forebears in the United Church of Christ were concerned with both a *personal faith* as guided by the Holy Spirit and the Scriptures and the *social responsibility* of continuing Jesus' ministry of healing, feeding, comforting, and freeing. While ultimate authority is lodged in Christ as the head of the church, we rely on the inspired and informed word of individual members, local churches, associations, conferences, the General Synod, and national offices and instrumentalities. Just as a local church or conference is organized for ministry and mission, so it is with the national offices and instrumentalities of the church. Many of these offices are located in Cleveland, Ohio, while some of the regional offices are located around the country. A chart outlining the functions of these offices can be found in the *Confirmand's Journal,* page 68.

The church in all its settings must continually be renewed by the power of the Holy Spirit to meet changing times. What the church has been in its history is important and valuable, but what the church will yet become is just as important and valuable.

Materials Needed

- Bible for each participant
- *Confirmand's Journal* for each participant
- Potted plant with one main stalk that separates into branches with leaves (or yarn and construction paper to create a plant on a bulletin board or posterboard)
- Globe or map of the world
- Newsprint, markers
- Colored push pins (for map) or other appropriate markers

@ A current copy of *In Mission: A Calendar of Prayer for the United Church of Christ,* or photocopies of pages 67–69

@ Videos (optional—see suggestions on page 64)

Planning for This Session

Become familiar with the history and mission of the United Church of Christ. *The United Church of Christ: History and Program* booklet provides an excellent overview. It is available by calling United Church of Christ Resources at 1-800-325-7061. If there is someone in your congregation who has particular knowledge or experience with the history of the United Church of Christ, spend some time learning from this person, and consider inviting him or her to attend the session as a leader. If there are United Church of Christ congregations nearby that have backgrounds different from your own (e.g., a different racial or ethnic constituency, a mission focus different from your church's), consider visiting them or inviting their members to visit your church. Strive to make the meeting an opportunity to join together as brothers and sisters in Christ by leading worship together, planning a joint witness and service project, or sharing some confirmation sessions or retreats. Attend a meeting of your association, conference, or an event of the national church. Read the newsletter of your conference and *United Church News,* the monthly newspaper published by the United Church of Christ; view videos that tell about the denomination.

As a person with a unique faith history, your own church experience is a valuable asset in sharing with the confirmands what being a part of the church has meant to you. Think about your past and present experiences of church and what the United Church of Christ means to you. Sharing your insights about the value in being connected to a faith community at appropriate times during the session will be a positive witness to the youth. At the same time, be open to learning for yourself more about what the United Church of Christ is and is becoming.

Place a potted plant in the center of your seating arrangement. (Or you may create a plant using colored yarn for roots and stems and construction paper for leaves and mount it on a bulletin board or posterboard.) This plant should have one main stalk that separates into branches with leaves.

If other church members will be present to help interpret the United Church of Christ based on their own knowledge or experience, make sure that these persons are invited ahead of time.

Secure a current copy of *In Mission: A Calendar of Prayer for the United Church of Christ.* (A copy is mailed to every United Church of Christ congregation each spring. Order additional copies from United Church of Christ Resources, 1-800-325-7061.) Photocopy the pages for the current week. As an alternative, copy the sample pages of this resource, found on pages 67–69.

Place the globe or map of the world in a visible place in the meeting room. Have markers to use with the globe or colored push pins available if you are using the map on a bulletin board.

Write the questions for the activity "Look at the Parts of the United Church of Christ" on newsprint before the session begins.

Gathering

THINK ABOUT THE UNITED CHURCH OF CHRIST (10 MINUTES) ✓

Ask the participants to look at the plant in the center of your seating arrangement. Note the parts of this plant: roots, stem, branches, and leaves. Then say:

These are all important, but there is another part just as important: the new growth that is about to appear. Without it, the plant will stagnate and die. This plant has a history—where it came from. Because of its history it is now poised to produce its most important product—its future!

Explain that in this session you will look at the forming of the United Church of Christ, its roots, the main stem, branches, and leaves that have sprung from it over the years. Like this plant, our church's roots are very important; they have brought us to the place where we are today. Given those roots, our most important task now is to tend to our growth into the future.

Offer the following prayer or one in your own words:

Holy God, you have called people to be the church in the name of Christ and in the power of your Spirit. Be with us this day as we trace the roots and branches of the United Church of Christ. Help us to understand the ministry and mission of Jesus in our time. We pray in the name of the one who prayed that we might all be one. Amen.

Review tree diagram briefly

Exploring

LOOK AT THE PARTS OF THE UNITED CHURCH OF CHRIST (50 MINUTES) ✓

Refer confirmands to their journals, page 58, to find "The Roots of the United Church of Christ." Divide the group into four smaller groups and assign each group one of the denominations that formed the United Church of Christ. (If there are fewer than four persons in your group, do not divide the group but work on all four together.) Have each group, or the group as a whole, review their assigned story and take notes, paying attention to the questions on the newsprint (and in their journals):

@ Where did this denomination begin?

@ What was happening in history when this church began?

@ What were its main beliefs?

@ What special mission focus did it have?

When all the groups have completed their research, bring them together and, one at a time, have them share with the other groups their findings. Point out the box on the journal page that shows when the four denominations became two. Then say that in 1957 in Cleveland, Ohio, the United Church of Christ was born out of the merger of these two denominations. This is the "trunk" of the tree.

Point out the heritage of your particular congregation, recognizing that some congregations are young enough to have been born into the United Church of Christ, and that some came to the United Church of Christ from other traditions or continue as federated or "yoked" churches (i.e., United Church of Christ and the United Methodist Church).

Point out to the group that each of the four predecessor denominations was committed to freeing people as much as possible so they could follow God. This came from the theological belief that Jesus Christ alone is the head of the church and each person is called into relationship with Christ. This understanding was also reflected in the United Church of Christ's commitment to work in society. Consequently they worked to found schools, hospitals, relief organizations, and overseas missions. Point out that the United Church of Christ and its predecessor denominations also have a long history in social justice: helping to abolish slavery, advocating the rights of women (including ordination), opposing racism, establishing ethnic congregations, advocating justice for persons who are gay and lesbian. Name other justice issues that you may be aware of or that your own congregation or conference is currently involved in. Note that these could be considered the "fruit" on the United Church of Christ tree.

Now refer to the "Chart of Relationships and Functions in the United Church of Christ" in the journals, page 68. Give the group time to look this over, then briefly outline how the national church is organized.

Hand out the copies of the current week from *In Mission: A Calendar of Prayer for the United Church of Christ*, if possible, or distribute copies of pages 67–69. Give the group a few minutes to read through the week. Then ask for volunteers to read a few of the daily sections aloud, including the prayer for Sunday. Using the colored push pins or some other marker, locate on the globe or world map the place where these ministries are happening.

See Film

Connecting

REFLECT ON THE UNITED CHURCH OF CHRIST (25 MINUTES)

As a group, discuss one or more of the following:

- Looking at the history of the United Church of Christ, how does our local church continue to benefit from the history and heritage of our forebears in faith?

- Looking at the United Church of Christ or our local church, how do we respect the differences of others while at the same time seeking to be united?

- In what ways are we united in spite of our differences?

- How might the United Church of Christ best live out its motto "That they may all be one"?

- What signs are there in the United Church of Christ that it has tried in its history to be inclusive of God's people from a variety of cultures and races?

- Often these histories are hidden stories. Sometimes a preference for one story or point of view hides the fact that many people from various cultures and races have been involved in the history all along. How can we find a way to tell the rich and varied history of the United Church of Christ?

Note: For a fuller treatment of "hidden histories" within the United Church of Christ tradition, see Hidden Histories in the United Church of Christ, 2 volumes, by Barbara Brown Zikmund (United Church Press, 1984, 1987).

Going

Close w/ statement of faith

WORSHIP TOGETHER (5 MINUTES)

Gather around the plant. Invite the confirmands to name something about one of the roots or branches of the United Church of Christ that was a new learning for them or that holds special meaning for them. Then invite the group to name their hopes for the fruit—what the church might become in their lifetime. Ask:

- In what ways can you and our local church prepare for God's future?

Conclude with a prayer, using the one for the current Sunday from the *Calendar of Prayer* (if appropriate), one in your own words, or the following:

God, we give you thanks for the church you have created which is scattered about the face of the earth. Gather us in unity and preserve us in truth. Empower us for the mission you have given us. In Christ's name, amen.

Additional Activities

VIEW A VIDEO

View video materials from your conference, the United Church Board for Homeland Ministries, the United Church Board for World Ministries, or another instrumentality. Some examples are:

- ℮ "To Walk Together" (21 min.)—The history of the UCC adapted from a film-strip presentation. $18.00.
- ℮ "Bridging the Divides, Seeking Transformation" (four segments approximately 10 min. each)—The four segments are: The Amistad Event; Ministries of Justice; The United Church of Christ and the Board for Homeland Ministries Today; and Facing the Twenty-first Century. The video and accompanying guide were created in conjunction with the 150th anniversary of the American Missionary Association in 1996. Free.

Order these videos from United Church of Christ Resources at 1-800-325-7061.

INVITE A SPEAKER

Within many United Church of Christ congregations there are persons who have experience in and knowledge about the ministry and mission of the denomination. If there is not such a person in your local church (and don't assume there isn't!), check with neighboring congregations or your association or conference office.

ATTEND A NATIONAL EVENT

Assemble a group from your congregation, cluster, or association to attend and participate in the next National Youth Event, General Synod, or other gathering of our wider church.

VISIT OTHER CHURCHES

Visit other congregations of the United Church of Christ in your area that have a heritage different from your own, such as a difference in racial or ethnic makeup or a difference in mission and ministry. Invite youth or other persons from these congregations to worship with you. (For additional help, see "A Guide for Field Trips," page 289.)

DISTRIBUTE OTHER RESOURCES ABOUT THE UNITED CHURCH OF CHRIST

Order the various identity resources such as:

- "About the United Church of Christ" (Channing L. Bete Co., 1980)
- Robert C. Burt, ed., *Good News in Growing Churches* (Pilgrim Press, 1990)
- David Dunn et al., *A History of the Evangelical and Reformed Church* (Pilgrim Press, 1990)
- Louis H. Gunnemann, *The Shaping of the United Church of Christ: An Essay in the History of American Christianity* (United Church Press, 1977)
- Louis H. Gunnemann, *United and Uniting: The Meaning of an Ecclesial Journey* (United Church Press, 1987)
- Charles E. Hambrick-Stowe and Daniel L. Johnson, eds., *Theology and Identity: Traditions, Movements, and Polity in the United Church of Christ* (Pilgrim Press, 1990)
- *History and Program: The United Church of Christ* (United Church Press, 1991)
- *Inquiring and Exploring: The Meaning of Membership in the UCC* (United Church Board for Homeland Ministries) (also available in Spanish)
- Eric Lincoln, *The Black Church in the African American Experience* (Duke University Press, 1990)
- Allen O. Miller, *The United Church of Christ Statement of Faith: A Historical, Biblical, and Theological Perspective* (United Church Press, 1990)
- Robert S. Paul, *Freedom with Order* (United Church Press, 1987)
- Roger L. Shinn, *Confessing our Faith: An Interpretation of the Statement of Faith of the United Church of Christ* (Pilgrim Press, 1990)
- *United Church of Christ* (pamphlet) (United Church Press, 1990)
- John von Rohr, *The Shaping of American Congregationalism* (Pilgrim Press, 1992)
- Williston Walker, *The Creeds and Platforms of Congregationalism* (Pilgrim Press, 1991)
- Barbara Brown Zikmund, *Hidden Histories in the United Church of Christ*, 2 vols. (United Church Press, 1984, 1987)

Pilgrim Press or United Church Press items can be ordered by calling 1-800-537-3394. For additional items, check the resource section of the current *United Church of Christ Desk Calendar and Plan Book* for ordering information.

Connecting with the Congregation

SPONSOR A HISTORY AND HERITAGE EVENT

Adapt this session to be used with the whole congregation. Have the confirmands lead others in the activities.

Planning Ahead

Read the next session and gather needed supplies. If you decide to make the banner, you will need fabric (3' x 6'), smaller assorted pieces of fabric, scissors, fabric adhesive or fusible webbing, an iron, two dowels (3' each), two eye screws, and heavy cord (6' long).

Handout

A CALENDAR OF PRAYER[1]

Sunday

Loving God, we pray that you will be with Ian and the students of Kodaikanal International School this week. Help them become acquainted with their new home, and help them build a community in which all feel accepted. We give you thanks for bringing them together.

In July, according to Ian Oliver, UCC/Disciples missionary serving at Kodaikanal International School (KIS) in Kodaikanal, India, the monsoon season brings clear, crisp mornings and the certainty of rain every afternoon. This week, it also brings new students to the school. KIS was originally founded as a school for the children of missionaries who served in India. Ian, who is chaplain at the school, has been at "Kodai" since 1990.

"People in the States often ask me what kind of students we have and how we are connected to the Indian churches," he writes. "Yesterday, a good example walked into my office here. He was the Rev. Dr. Devamani, who had just returned to India after five years in the U.S., three of which were spent as a pastor in the Eastern Association of the Illinois Conference, UCC.

"He is returning to India after completing his doctor of ministry degree at Chicago Theological Seminary to become Ecumenical Officer of the Church of South India, a critical post in a church whose ecumenical spirit has sometimes waned since its formation in 1947. He has four girls, two of whom were old enough to have spent five years in American schools. He had hoped to put them in schools in Madras, but the girls found the transition very difficult. Many Indian schools are strictly hierarchical, where teachers are distant authority figures. Also, an Indian language is required, which the girls didn't know.

"So, a bit desperate, Dr. Devamani bought a train ticket to Kodaikanal and came up to the hills, hoping we might be the answer. I was not encouraging. KIS is a hard school to get into. But Mrs. Rocky Nichol, our admissions officer, surprised me by saying she would find openings and that a scholarship would be available.

"In a global church like ours, where our churches are encouraging the exchange of personnel and the movement of church leaders around the world, a school like KIS can fill a small but important gap. KIS hopes to be a home and a haven for children whose parents' moving from one country to another has left them not really fitting into any educational system. We hope to be an educational community where we build on the diverse experiences of our students and encourage them to share them, rather than trying to force everyone into a mold of what the 'best' culture is or what the 'right' way of being Christian is. Please keep KIS and our work in your prayers."

Monday

"As a community organizer, advocate, pastor and pioneer in the UCC, I am challenged," writes Lynice
Pinkard, a member of City of Refuge Community Church in San Francisco, California. Lynice received
a Charles Shelby Rooks Fellowship for Racial and Ethnic Theological Students from the UCBHM to
assist her in her studies at the Pacific School of Religion. Her aim is to proclaim "this transforming
movement called Christianity, which is constantly breaking down walls, creating an inclusive, inter-
social, multicultural, intergenerational, multigender, multisexual, international *living* church."

The UCC/Disciples/Global Ministries also assist theological students. The Rev. Elias Isaac is a student in
social ethics at Christian Theological Seminary in Indianapolis, Indiana, and the Rev. Luciano Chianeque
is at the University of Durban-Westville in South Africa. Both are members of the Evangelical
Congregational Church of Angola and are harnessing their visions of ministry to help rebuild their war-
torn country.

Tuesday

Jeanette Samter is a UCC/Disciples missionary in Lesotho teaching at Masianokeng High School at the
invitation of the Lesotho Evangelical Church. "My calling," she has written, "is to help children when
and where I can."

Helping young people understand AIDS is an increasingly important part of education both in Africa and in
the United States. The AIDS ministry of First Church in Cambridge, Massachusetts, supports Cambridge
Cares about AIDS, Inc., a local AIDS service organization that exchanges sterile syringes for contami-
nated ones. Staff members build trusting relationships with injecting drug users by letting them know
that their lives matter. Gay Harter, the co-chair of the church's Social Action Committee, said, "It was
important that we demonstrate to the city of Cambridge that as an institution we are committed to the
struggle to stop the spread of HIV."

Wednesday

The Illinois Conference is made up of 314 churches. "We are a multiracial and multicultural church and are
in the process of learning how to celebrate and understand that reality," said the Rev. Jeffrey Nichols,
Conference Minister. On any given Sunday morning, services are held in at least ten difference languages, including English, Spanish, Korean, German, Chinese and several different Filipino dialects.
"We are grateful for the support we receive from our churches, and give thanks for all those who have
contributed to the Make a Difference! campaign," said Jeff. He requests prayers that the Conference will
be able to focus on ministries that celebrate both the common ground of Jesus Christ and the many varieties of witness and service found in the churches of the Conference.

Thursday

LaTonyia Johnson, administrator at the UCC-related Greencastle of Kenwood low-income housing residence knows the importance of extending hospitality and service to the residents. Regular Bible studies and worship services involve residents, local clergy and seminary students from Chicago Theological Seminary. "Residents find this pastoral support helps to create a haven for them in the midst of Chicago's south side where crime, poverty and violence are a part of their daily environment," writes the Rev. Julie Ruth Harley, chaplain at Lifelink/Bensenville, which manages Greencastle.

Mary Ann Ezell, UCC/Disciples missionary working with students at Marshall Christian High School in the Marshall Islands, goes out of her way to help the students feel at home. Students come to Rongrong from the 1,225 islands and 28 atolls of the Marshall Islands. "Many from the outer islands are sponsored by the church on their island," she writes. She considers it a "teacher's dream" to give them a foundation in English and feels that "this is the place I should be."

Friday

HOPE is an outreach program of Heritage United Church of Christ in Baltimore, Maryland, which models a Christian response to AIDS. "Our outreach is a ministry to relatives, caregivers and friends of people who are living with or have died as a result of HIV/AIDS," writes Yvonne M. Leacock, director. "Our primary mission is to care for the children who are sad, angry, confused or frightened by the illness or death of one or both of their parents. Most of our services are to children between 6 and 12 years of age. We ask God to make us instruments of healing as we lovingly and faithfully serve families touched by HIV/AIDS."

In the Philippines, Renate Rose, professor of New Testament at Union Theological Seminary in Cavite, focuses her preaching and teaching on the children who will "rule the planet in God's good time."

Saturday

The Katpadi Family Village Farm is one of the sites of the UCBWM Child Sponsorship Program. Through this program, churches or individuals may "adopt" a child, such as Michael.

When Michael's mother died in childbirth, the husband's family, distraught over the loss, performed a hideous act of revenge. They dowsed the newborn with battery acid, leaving him almost totally blind. Michael was given emergency treatment by Vellore Christian Medical Hospital and then brought to Kapadi. Five years later, Michael is a child who knows joy and love. And hope. One of his eyes was not totally blinded, leaving open the possibility of a corneal transplant. Michael will also have the opportunity to learn at a special school for the visually impaired. Without Kapadi, none of this would have been possible.

THE STATEMENT OF FAITH

WE BELIEVE IN YOU, O GOD, ETERNAL SPIRIT, GOD OF OUR SAVIOR JESUS CHRIST AND OUR GOD, AND TO YOUR DEEDS WE TESTIFY.
                                                                    —STATEMENT OF FAITH

Themes

- The United Church of Christ Statement of Faith affirms God's deeds and encourages our faithful response.
- There are many ways to express our faith.

Scriptures

ACTS 10:34–43—Peter tells the good news of Jesus Christ.

JOHN 3:16–21—God's saving love is for the whole world.

ROMANS 12:9–21—Paul provides guidelines for Christian living.

Objectives

- Explore the meaning of the Statement of Faith.
- Discover the beliefs that define who we are.
- Examine possible responses to the Statement of Faith.
- Experience the Statement of Faith as a prayer.

Session at a Glance

GATHERING

Consider the concepts in the Statement of Faith (10 minutes)

Read the Statement of Faith in unison (5 minutes)

EXPLORING

Look at the "Seven Declarations" of the Statement of Faith

(50 minutes)

CONNECTING

Examine possible response to the Statement of Faith

(15 minutes)

GOING

Pray the Statement of Faith (10 minutes)

Biblical and Theological Background

What does the United Church of Christ hold in common with other Christian churches? This question may
be just as important as its partner, "What makes the United Church of Christ distinctive?" Yet both
questions relate to what it means to be a community of faith and how faith in Jesus Christ is expressed.
To be active participants in the church of Jesus Christ, it is important to know who we are and what we
believe. There are many things that unite us in the United Church of Christ. One of them is the
Statement of Faith.

The Statement of Faith, first written in 1959 and rewritten in its more prayerful and doxological form in
1981, tells the glorious deeds of God. Its very form is more evangelical, more worshipful, than creedal. It
is more a testimony than a test of faith. It testifies to the activity of God in Jesus Christ, the Holy Spirit,
and the church, and it outlines the promises made to those who enter a trusting relationship with God.
It originated as a statement of common beliefs written to celebrate the birth of the United Church of
Christ in 1957, uniting the Congregational Christian Churches and the Evangelical and Reformed
Church. The Uniting General Synod, which met in Cleveland, Ohio, in 1957, elected thirty people, fifteen each from the two founding denominations, to develop a Statement of Faith. Allen O. Miller refers
to the Statement of Faith as "the wedding vows of our two unifying churches"[1] which brought together
diverse histories and traditions.

The United Church of Christ Statement of Faith was born out of dedicated study and prayer. Many parts of
the Bible helped form the foundation for the statement:

*The faith which unites us and to which we bear witness is that faith in God which the Scriptures of the Old
and New Testaments set forth, which the ancient church expressed in the ecumenical creeds, to which our own
spiritual [forebears] gave utterance in the evangelical confessions of the Reformation, and which we are in duty
bound to express in the words of our time as God . . . gives us light.*[2]

From the very beginning of the United Church of Christ, the Statement of Faith and other historical creeds
were seen as ways to express faith in a given time and place. The Statement of Faith was presented as a
testimony to the faith of the whole church, not as a test of faith for individual members.

After its adoption by the Second General Synod in 1959 at Oberlin, Ohio, the Statement of Faith was offered
to the whole church. The newly formed church encouraged freedom of conscience in practices of worship
and education, and local churches, associations, and conferences immediately began to use the statement
in creative ways in worship, study, and sermons. Since the original version was adopted, there have been
two major revisions. In 1977, General Synod XI recommended a revision by Robert V. Moss Jr. to use

inclusive language, and in 1988 General Synod XIV affirmed a revision in the form of a doxology, addressing God as in prayer. It is this form that is used in *Affirming Faith*.

The Statement of Faith reaches beyond our denomination. It has been included in a collection of resources for worship by the World Council of Churches. Christians in Europe and in Latin America have used its German and Spanish translations.[3] In addition, the statement provides words that speak to those outside the church about the meaning of the Christian faith. It has been used by many congregations as a basis for educating those who wish to become members of the church for the first time.

Overall, the statement is a recital of the mighty acts of God, expressing the covenantal drama of the Bible. In Acts 10:34–43, Christians are directed to tell others about Jesus. In the early church, reaching beyond the Jewish community was an act of radical faith. Since Jesus and most of his early followers were Jewish, some early Christians wondered if it would be possible for someone who had not come to know God through the teaching and laws of Judaism to understand Jesus. But Peter reminds his readers that Jesus commanded his followers to testify that Jesus was the one chosen by God (Acts 10:42). Having faith and speaking faith go hand in hand. Mature faith must be expressed in words and actions. The Statement of Faith of the United Church of Christ provides a way for the church to reach beyond itself with the good news of God's action in the world.

Another of the scriptures for this session, John 3:16–21, is part of a conversation between Jesus and Nicodemus. Here Jesus emphasizes God's action not as judgment and condemnation, but as salvation for the whole world. This action is reflected in the words of the statement, "reconciling the world to yourself." This line serves to remind us of the importance of remembering that God's saving action is not just for one sect or denomination. God's intentions are for the whole world.

Romans 12:9–21 lists some of the signs of Christian living and gives background for the statement. The list ends with the instruction, "Do not be overcome by evil, but overcome evil with good" (Romans 12:21). The Statement of Faith of the United Church of Christ provides a way of declaring the intention of the church to overcome evil with good. Its words have provided guidance for the faith of the United Church of Christ in its early years and will continue to provide a way to proclaim faith for years to come.

The Statement of Faith of the United Church of Christ is the focal point for this faith formation program because of its unique role in the life of the church. The statement is a powerful expression of God's saving acts and our invited response. Challenging Christians to "accept the cost and joy of discipleship, to be God's servants in the service of others, to proclaim the gospel to all the world and resist the powers of evil" are important steps in discovering what it means to be a follower of Christ and a member of Christ's church.

Materials Needed

- Bible for each participant
- *Confirmand's Journal* for each participant
- Blank paper
- Pencils
- Newsprint and markers
- Materials for a banner (optional): fabric (3' x 6'), smaller assorted pieces of fabric, scissors, fabric adhesive or fusible webbing, iron, 2 dowels (3' each), 2 eye screws, heavy cord (6' long)

Preparing the Session

Review the Statement of Faith of the United Church of Christ found on page 239. Be sure to read both the revision in inclusive language by Robert Moss Jr. (page 79 of the journal) and the version in the form of a Doxology, which addresses God directly, as in prayer. Read the "Biblical and Theological Background" and the scriptures for this session. Then think about your own beliefs. What words or phrases in the Statement of Faith are most meaningful to you? What words or phrases are most challenging? Take a few minutes with a blank sheet of paper and jot down some notes about what you have discovered.

Give yourself time for prayer before meeting with the confirmands. Use the Statement of Faith if you wish. Remember the youth individually in prayer as well.

Arrange the meeting room with a table where the participants can sit and write or draw. Choose a well-lit room and provide ample space for each learner. Have the Bibles and writing and drawing materials at hand.

If you choose the optional experience of making a banner, make sure that you have the appropriate materials available. You may want to prepare the fabric ahead of time by sewing a seam at the top and bottom and inserting dowels to make it easier to hang.

Gathering

CONSIDER THE CONCEPTS IN THE STATEMENT OF FAITH (10 MINUTES)

Ask the youth to find the Statement of Faith (doxological form) in the *Confirmand's Journal*, page 78. Ask a volunteer to read aloud the Statement of Faith. Then have the group name words or phrases that are most meaningful to them and list them on newsprint.

READ THE STATEMENT OF FAITH IN UNISON (5 MINUTES)

When the list is complete, lead them in reading the Statement of Faith in unison. Encourage them to be expressive as they say the words aloud.

Exploring

LOOK AT THE "SEVEN DECLARATIONS" OF THE STATEMENT OF FAITH (50 MINUTES)

Give a brief historical overview of the Statement of Faith using the information in the "Biblical and Theological Background" section. Then refer confirmands to the "Seven Declarations" of the Statement of Faith in the *Confirmand's Journal*, page 74. Point out the following information about its content:

The Statement of Faith begins with a statement that we believe in God. This statement is followed by seven declarations of the deeds of God. They are: 1) God creates; 2) God seeks to save; 3) God judges; 4) God comes to us in Christ; 5) God bestows the Holy Spirit; 6) God calls to discipleship; and 7) God promises.[4] The Statement of Faith ends with a concluding statement of praise to God. Each declaration is drawn from the experiences of many Christians over a long period of time. Each declaration has roots in the Bible as well as in the history of the Christian church.

After you have given this information to the group, ask individuals to take a pencil and a piece of paper and find a place to work. The group will be looking at the Statement of Faith together, and will be asked to respond to each declaration of the Statement of Faith with some words or a sketch. Refer the youth to their journals (page 74). If you have more than seven learners, have them share the declarations in groups of two. If the group has fewer than seven learners, ask each to select one declaration and leave the remainder undistributed.

Ask the participants to read their declaration and look up the biblical references listed. Then ask them to reflect on the accompanying question(s) and the meaning of the declaration for their life. They can do so by writing poetry or narrative, or by sketching on the paper. As an example, point out that the first declaration talks about God as creator. Its biblical reference contains at least two long narrative stories. There are other stories of God creating as well. Perhaps the youth can tell the story of God's creative activity in their life, or draw a picture of a place where God's creative activity has been apparent to them.

As the youth work, circulate among them to provide help and keep them on task. If one member of the group finishes before the others, allow that individual to work on a different declaration. Some youth may have difficulty understanding the task. Encourage them to talk about their declaration and the accompanying question(s) and what it means to them as a way of developing ideas for writing or for a sketch.

Give a five-minute warning before bringing the group back together. When the group has reconvened, go through the Statement of Faith one more time. Have the group read the opening confession together. Then ask those who have been working with the first declaration to share their writing or sketch if they are willing. If no writing or sketch is available for a particular declaration, read that declaration aloud and go on to the next declaration. If more than one youth has the same declaration, make sure that each is given the invitation to show his or her creation to the group. After completing the seven declarations, read the concluding doxology in unison.

When the group has completed reviewing the writing and sketches, say the following:

For the thirty members of the committee who wrote the Statement of Faith, each word was important. Imagine you were one of the members of the committee. Being a part of the process of writing the Statement of Faith was far more than reaching intellectual agreement. It was an exercise in expressing the deepest and most important beliefs of the United Church of Christ.

Take a minute now to think about what beliefs define who you are. Ask yourself the question, "What is the one thing that is absolutely necessary for my life to have meaning?"

Allow a full minute of silence. (Use a watch to assure that at least one minute is allowed.) Ask each participant to look at the Statement of Faith for some connection between the one thing that is most important to him or her and the words of the Statement of Faith. Perhaps that one thing is only one word: love, trust, or compassion. Perhaps it is one of these statements: "God seeks to save," "Christ shared our common lot," or "God promises forgiveness." Ask the question,

@   Where does your most important belief intersect with the Statement of Faith?

Some youth will be more interested in the questions than in coming to an answer. For them, time to reflect and individual time with others who will listen to their thoughts, like a parent or mentor, might help them to make connections. Perhaps the questions in their minds can keep the search active. It may take years of exploring and maturing in faith for the connection to be made. Others in the group may see some connection. For them the reading of the Statement of Faith may be a celebration of their own beliefs. Words on paper that seem to be lifeless can become an expression of their deepest faith.

Connecting

EXAMINE POSSIBLE RESPONSES TO THE STATEMENT OF FAITH (15 MINUTES)

Ask participants if they can name ways the Statement of Faith is used in your congregation. (Many congregations read the Statement of Faith in unison during worship. Some read it every Sunday, others on special occasions.) After discussing how it is used in your congregation, ask the participants to think of places where they have seen the Statement of Faith written. Perhaps they have seen it in a hymnal or on a certificate. If they have not seen it, or it is not used in your congregation, take a minute to talk about how it could be used.

Now point out the section of the Statement of Faith that describes what God's call into the church means. These assertions speak of the direct actions of believers. Ask the group to look at that declaration once again. Make a chart on newsprint that lists each one of the parts to this declaration in the left column. In the right column have the group list ways the church might respond to each of the calls to action. For example, have them consider what it would mean for the group to accept the cost and joy of discipleship, be servants in the service of others, proclaim the gospel to all the world, resist the powers of evil, share in Christ's baptism, eat at Christ's table, and join in Christ's passion and victory. Allow for discussion of the ways in which the Statement of Faith calls for action in the lives of the members of your group.

Going

PRAY THE STATEMENT OF FAITH (10 MINUTES)

Gather the group in a place where they have shared worship before. This may be the sanctuary of the church or a place in your usual meeting room. Ask each to find a comfortable place to sit where they can see the faces of each person in your group. Find the doxological Statement of Faith (The Revision of 1981: A Doxology) in the *Confirmand's Journal*, page 78.

Point out to the group that this form of the Statement of Faith is a prayer. One way to express faith is to remind ourselves that God is a witness to all that we do and say. When we say our beliefs aloud, we offer them to God. When we remind ourselves that God is listening, we open ourselves to a deepening relationship with God.

Ask the youth to join you in praying this version of the Statement of Faith to close the session.

Connecting with the Congregation

RESPOND TO THE STATEMENT OF FAITH

Make a banner of the Statement of Faith to display in the church. Invite other groups in the church to help. You will need a large piece of fabric for a banner and smaller pieces of cloth to make the symbols on the banner. You may want to prepare the background cloth ahead of time by sewing a seam at the top and bottom so that dowels can be inserted. You may also want to cut letters for words at the top and the bottom of the banner. Fasten eye screws to the ends of one of the dowels and thread the ends of the cord through the screws for hanging.

The group can form smaller groups to work on the different symbols or work as a large group on the banner. Individuals may cut individual pieces of fabric. If you use fusible webbing or an iron-on adhesive, the material is cut the same size as the cloth you wish to attach to the banner (ironing may need to be done outside the group session). Other adhesives, such as white glue, can also be used. If you choose to sew the banner, the sewing may need to be done outside the group session.

Be creative with the banner, but make sure that it has one item for each of the nine sections of the Statement of Faith. The sections include: the Confession of Faith Prologue, God Creates, God Seeks to Save, God Judges, God Comes to Us in Christ, God Bestows the Holy Spirit, God Calls to Discipleship, God Promises, and the Concluding Doxology.

After the banner is completed, it can be used as a visual aid to assist in memorizing the Statement of Faith. Even if it is not memorized by the learners in your group, the banner will increase their familiarity with the outline and structure of the Statement of Faith.

Thinking About This Session

What parts of the Statement of Faith were most helpful to the confirmands? What parts were most challenging? Did they connect the words and meaning of the statement to the reality of their own lives? If not, how might you help them make this connection in future sessions?

Planning Ahead

Read the next session and gather needed supplies, including a bowl of moist soil, a bowl for water, towels, and newspapers for a floor covering.

The creation of the whole universe and humanity is the work of God, the Eternal Spirit. All that God creates is good.

GOD

GOD CREATES

YOU CALL THE WORLDS INTO BEING, CREATE PERSONS IN YOUR OWN IMAGE, AND SET BEFORE EACH ONE THE WAYS OF LIFE AND DEATH.

—STATEMENT OF FAITH

Themes

@ The creation of the whole universe and humanity is the work of God, the Eternal Spirit.

@ All that God creates is good.

@ Humanity is made in the image of God.

@ God gives humankind the capacity to choose the way of life.

@ God calls humankind to be stewards of the Earth and part of the ongoing miracle of creation.

Scriptures

GENESIS 1:1–2:4A—At God's word the universe and humanity are created.

GENESIS 2:4B–25—God creates humankind from dust and gives the breath of life.

DEUTERONOMY 30:11–20—God sets before humankind the way of life and death, and calls people to choose life.

Objectives

@ Explore the power of God's creative word that brought the worlds into being.

@ Discover the gift of life that God offers humankind.

@ Consider that creation is a never-ending miracle.

@ Explore our responsibility as stewards of creation.

Session at a Glance

GATHERING

Make a mural of the creation stories (30 minutes)

EXPLORING

Think about the creation stories (10 minutes)

Hear a poem (5 minutes)

Brainstorm ways to be stewards of the Earth (10 minutes)

CONNECTING

Create a "web of life" (20 minutes)

GOING

Worship together (15 minutes)

Biblical and Theological Background

The creation stories from Genesis 1:1–2:4a and Genesis 2:4b–25 are two of the most familiar texts in the
Bible, but they are frequently misunderstood. The confusion seems to arise from the fact that the stories
are, at times, viewed as historical fact rather than as an affirmation of the creative power of God, the
Eternal Spirit. There are no particular historical references in the texts. Instead, the stories tell of the
unfolding drama of the relation of the Creator to creation.

The power of God's word calls the worlds into being. God's sovereignty is supreme. God is active, birthing land,
sea, and creature. "God's word is an act, an event, a sovereign command, which accomplishes a result. The
creation story affirms that God's word, mighty in history, is also the very power which brought the creation
into being."[1]

God takes dust and forms humankind. God breathes into humanity and gives the gift of life. Life is a gift,
fashioned and molded, formed and created, valued and blessed by God. Humanity is a part of creation
and yet is made uniquely in the image of God. God issues the call to humanity to live in God's world, to
live with other creatures, and to live on God's terms.[2]

In Deuteronomy 30:11–20, we hear more, through God's prophet Moses, about what those terms are. "See, I
have set before you today life and prosperity, death and adversity. . . . Choose life so that you and your
descendants may live" (Deuteronomy 30:15, 19b).

As God's creation, made in God's image, we live with unique qualities: our *creatureliness and dependence* and,
in contrast, our *freedom and creativity*. One shows us our dependence on our Creator for the gift of life.
The other points to our capacity for choice in God's creation. With the gift of choice comes responsibility
—as children of God, we are given creative powers to be stewards of creation and servants of peace and
justice.[3] As stewards, we are to care for God's good creation with humility, reverence, and concern for
the whole of creation.

For God, creation is an ongoing process with covenantal implications. God is known through acts of salva-

tion, justice, and freedom. God creates, saves, and loves. God is at work daily, renewing creation.
As those called to trust in God's purposes, we, too, can be renewed daily by God's creative Spirit. God calls
us to life-giving actions, resisting the powers of death, so that creation will not be diminished. Even when
we forget our call and turn away from God, God does not abandon us, but says, through the prophet
Isaiah, "Do not fear, for I have redeemed you; I have called you by name, you are mine" (Isaiah 43:1).

Materials Needed

- Bible for each participant
- *Confirmand's Journal* for each participant
- Newsprint, markers
- Construction paper, crayons, pencils, scissors, tape, yarn
- A bowl of moist soil, a bowl of water, towels, newspapers for floor covering

Preparing for the Session

Select a room that has a large wall space where the mural of the creation stories can be hung. Provide table
space for drawing, cutting, and assembling the mural. For the "Going" activity, have available towels and
bowls of water and moist soil for the affirmation ritual. Provide a floor covering to prevent damage if
spills occur.

Gathering

MAKE A MURAL OF THE CREATION STORIES (30 MINUTES)

Welcome the confirmands and divide the group into two. (If your group is smaller than eight, work
together on each story as one group.) Give each group a creation story from the Bible (Genesis
1:1–2:4a and Genesis 2:4b–25) to read to themselves. Then have them create illustrations of the story
with construction paper cutouts. Encourage them to convey the essential parts of the story while
working quickly to make the cutouts. Explain that after the cutouts are made, a volunteer will read
each story aloud, pausing at appropriate times to allow the groups to hang the illustrations that depict
the parts of the story.
When the groups are finished, read aloud each of the stories from Genesis and construct the murals.

Exploring

THINK ABOUT THE CREATION STORIES (10 MINUTES)

When the murals are completed, take time to look at the display. Use these questions to start the discussion:

- What did you like best about these stories?
- What parts were the most challenging to you?
- How are these stories different from a scientific theory of creation?
- What do you suppose are the most important parts to remember about these stories?
- What kind of love might God have for all that God has created?
- What hopes might God have for creation?
- What part do you think God wants humankind to play in making those hopes real?

HEAR A POEM (5 MINUTES)

Ask the confirmands to turn to page 89 in their journals. Have a volunteer read aloud Chief Seattle's poem about the web of life as the rest of the group follows along.

BRAINSTORM WAYS TO BE STEWARDS OF THE EARTH (10 MINUTES)

Distribute index cards and ask the group to think of ways to care for the Earth, the people of the Earth, and all of creation (examples might be recycling, working for justice, conserving water). Have them write each idea on a separate index card. After some time for writing, ask the group, one at a time, to read their cards and tape them somewhere along the border of the creation stories mural. Do this until all the cards are displayed. Then review the cards as a group and invite the youth to think of more ideas. Continue this process for fifteen minutes, allowing time for their ideas to be exhausted.

Connecting

CREATE A "WEB OF LIFE" (20 MINUTES)

Next remind them of the Chief Seattle poem and the stories of creation that call upon humanity to be stewards, that is, ones who care for God's good creation. Have them make symbols that represent themselves to tape onto the creation stories mural. They can write their names on the symbols and make them look realistic or abstract. Then have all the youth take long pieces of yarn and create a "web of life" by choosing at least five different ways they will try to care for God's creation and attaching pieces of yarn from their symbols to the index cards listing their choices. After all have made their selections and attached the yarn, take time to look at the web that was created. Have each one in the group name the commitments to God's creation he or she will be making and how each expects to carry them out.

Going

WORSHIP TOGETHER (15 MINUTES)

If possible, move outdoors for this experience. If you are indoors, take precautions to protect the floor from spills during this experience. Gather in a circle around the container of soil.

Using the moist soil, take turns and ask each person to make the sign of the cross on the back of the hand of the person to his or her right. As they make the sign they may say, "You are created in God's image and called to be a steward of God's creation." Then have a volunteer read aloud Deuteronomy 30:19.

Sing "Wakantanka Taku Nitawa (Many and Great, O God, Are Your Works)" from the *Confirmand's Journal* (page 232) or this guide (page 237). If your group prefers not to sing, have them read the words together.

Close with the following benediction:

Living God, we give thanks for your creation. Thank you for creating us in your image and calling us to choose the way of life. Fill us with your love. Amen.

Connecting with the Congregation

Decide how your group could sponsor an event that would focus on caring for God's creation. You may want to lead a recycling effort for the congregation or plan a clean-up project in your community that would involve the whole church.

Thinking About This Session

Did the confirmands understand the idea of being a good steward of God's creation? Did they commit themselves to realistic ways to care for creation? How can you encourage them to honor their commitments?

Planning Ahead

Read the next session and gather the needed supplies, including meditative music, a cassette or CD player, and an offering plate.

GOD SEEKS AND SAVES

YOU SEEK IN HOLY LOVE TO SAVE ALL PEOPLE FROM AIMLESSNESS AND SIN.

—STATEMENT OF FAITH

Themes

@ God seeks us in holy love, calling us into relationships based on wholeness and shalom.

@ Sin is a state of human life in which we are separated from one another, from ourselves, and from God.

@ Salvation is the gift of God's grace that frees us from sin, guilt, and the powers of death.

Scriptures

ROMANS 5:12–21—Righteousness and life come from God's saving grace.

MARK 10:35–45—James and John seek honor.

MATTHEW 26:31–35, 69–75—Peter denies knowing Jesus.

JEREMIAH 2:4–13—God, through the prophet Jeremiah, accuses the people of turning against God.

Objectives

@ Explore the nature of aimlessness and sin.

@ Discover stories of sin and wholeness in the Bible.

@ Make a personal covenant with God.

Session at a Glance

GATHERING

Consider how God calls us (15 minutes)

EXPLORING

Dramatize stories from the Bible (50 minutes)

CONNECTING

Respond to God's call to wholeness (20 minutes)

GOING

Offer your covenants to God (5 minutes)

Biblical and Theological Background

God seeks us in holy love, calling us into relationship. God has a call for everyone. God's call, first and foremost, is to enter into a relationship—a deep, abiding connection to God. Too often people respond to God as a distant being who has little interest in them and who dictates rules and punishes them when they do wrong. But as the Statement of Faith reminds us, God seeks in holy love to save us from aimlessness and sin. Such a desire and movement on God's part does not imply God is a stern and distant disciplinarian, but rather a God who wants to save us from this brokenness through relationship.

The aimlessness and sin from which God seeks to save us cannot be seen as behaviors to avoid, nor as a list of immoral actions never to be done. Rather, God desires that we live in *shalom*. *Shalom* is the Hebrew word meaning wholeness, health, and deep and abiding peace. It is both a personal and corporate experience. A shalom person acts in ways that show God's love and grace. A shalom society expresses God's justice and righteousness in its way in the world. Sin is the absence of shalom.

Paul Tillich, in his powerful sermon "You Are Accepted,"[1] suggested a simple definition of sin that may be helpful to discuss with youth: sin is separation.

There are three kinds of separation to which the word *sin* refers: separation between people, separation of a person from him/herself, and separation of all people from God. This threefold separation is one of the realities of life—it is a universal fact, it is the fate of every life. To be human is to experience this separation. Before sin is an action, it is a way of being.

Look at how biblical people such as Abraham, Miriam, Moses, Jacob, Ruth, Elizabeth, Mary, Peter, Paul, Anna, and Phoebe dealt with God—speaking, negotiating, wrestling, even arguing in the most intimate ways. They knew God to be as close to them as their closest friend.

God's call to us is not only to believe in God, but also to *love* God. This call does not come to us as a demand, but as an invitation. We are called to enter into a loving relationship with God, not because God will love us any less if we don't, but precisely because God has loved us first, and will always love us, no matter what we may do. Such unconditional love invites our love in return.

When we enter this relationship of love with God, it is likely that we will find ourselves beginning to value the very things God values and treasuring those God loves. Being in relationship with God leads us to want to do the things God finds pleasing. Consequently, in responding to God's love and saving grace, we become sensitive to God's concerns, and respond to them so that God's own desires for justice and compassion are our desires too. We want to extend ourselves in holy love to those suffering the consequences of aimlessness and sin. Jesus, who experienced the closest relationship possible with God, illustrated how he saw this relationship being lived out: he would "bring good news to the poor . . . proclaim release to the captives and recovery of sight to the blind, [and] let the oppressed go free" (Luke 4:18).

Discernment is a key here. Many people discover God's call within their lives and in their communities through an inner "pulse." An experience in this session will help the confirmands explore the thoughts and feelings that may reveal the ways God is calling them to greater faith, love, and service. The session concludes by offering each confirmand the opportunity to write a personal covenant.

Think about Paul Tillich's definition of sin: "Sin is separation." Reflect on ways you or your faith community has experienced being separated from other people, from your own best intentions, and from God. Read the scriptures for this session and think about the ways these stories help to interpret the nature of sin separation or the absence of shalom.

Materials

- Bible for each participant
- *Confirmand's Journal* for each participant
- Newsprint and markers or chalkboard and chalk
- Cassette tape or CD of meditative music
- Cassette tape or CD player
- Pencils, paper
- Offering plate

Preparing for the Session

Write the two sets of suggested questions to be used in "Exploring" (found on page 91) on newsprint. Decide if you will provide accompaniment for "Amazing Grace" when it is sung during the closing worship.

Gathering

CONSIDER HOW GOD CALLS US (15 MINUTES)

Welcome the youth. Put this definition on newsprint or on a chalkboard for the group to see: "Sin is separation." Say that the Statement of Faith affirms that God seeks to save us from aimlessness and sin.

Ask the group to help make three lists in their journals of some of the ways we sin that separate us as we live our lives.

@   We separate from other people.

@   We separate from our own best intentions.

@   We separate from God.

Ask group members to suggest examples in each category. List them on newsprint. Point out that the Bible is full of stories of people being separated from one another, themselves, and God.

Exploring

DRAMATIZE STORIES FROM THE BIBLE (50 MINUTES)

Divide the group so that each smaller group may look more closely at one of the following Bible stories. (If your group is three or less, do not divide, but work together as a group.) These stories are examples of the brokenness we may experience as a result of the separation of sin. Provide the following background for each text.

Mark 10:35–45—James and John seek honor. (We separate from other people.)

In this story, James and John ask Jesus if they may sit at Jesus' right and left, the most favored positions, when Jesus reigns in glory. Jesus promises only the suffering that will come if they follow him, but he cannot guarantee the positions of honor. When the other disciples hear about these two disciples' request, they are indignant. This expression of anger gives Jesus an opportunity to teach the group about the importance of service, saying that true greatness comes not from power and position, but in service to others.

Matthew 26:31–35, 69–75—Peter denies knowing Jesus. (We separate from our own best intentions.)

After vowing to Jesus that he would never deny him, Peter is confronted after Jesus' arrest by someone who says he is a follower of Jesus. Peter, fearing association with Jesus, denies knowing him three times. When Peter realizes what he has done, he cries bitterly.

Jeremiah 2:4–13—God, through the prophet Jeremiah, accuses the people of turning against God. (We separate from God.)

This scripture is somewhat different from the others because the sin of separation is the act of a whole group of people. The basic issue is that Israel, God's chosen people, has not been faithful in its devotion to God. The people have turned away from God to "worthless things," forgetting the first commandment, "I am the Sovereign, your God, who brought you out of the land of Egypt, out of the house of slavery; you shall have no other gods before me" (Exodus 20:2–3).

Assign each group a Bible story and have them read it together. Ask the group(s) to retell the story in a modern-day setting. They may write it or act it out. Then ask them to consider the following questions:

@ What was the sin that occurred in this story?

@ Was wholeness achieved? How?

Invite the individual groups to read the Bible stories aloud to the whole group and to share their modern-day versions. Then explore the questions above for each story. Then ask:

@ Think of a promise you have made or that was made to you. Was it kept or broken?

@ How does it feel to keep a promise? to break a promise? to get another chance?

@ Can you think of ways God has been with you in the past?

@ What is God calling or inviting you to do now in your life?

@ In what ways do you think God offers us help to live in relationships that are whole and loving?

Encourage the youth to think about God's unconditional love and forgiveness, as well as the power that comes from the Holy Spirit to help us "make things right" when we separate from others, ourselves, and God. Talk about the meaning of the word "reconciliation": God's action through Christ to break down the barriers of hate, greed, jealousy, indifference, intolerance, and prejudice that divide the human family. Have the youth write or draw their own definitions of reconciliation in their journals (page 95).

Connecting

RESPOND TO GOD'S CALL TO WHOLENESS (20 MINUTES)

From biblical times onward, a covenant has sealed the relationship between God and those who would follow God. A covenant is a specific agreement of commitment to one another that two parties enter.

Ask group members to consider once more that God calls us each to wholeness in our relationships with others, ourselves, and God. Give them some time to think and write about this question in their journals (page 96):

@ How would you be the same or different if you took seriously the call to covenant with God?

Through this discernment exercise, the confirmands may imagine themselves in touch with the need the world has for wholeness, shalom.

Ask the confirmands to write in their journals (page 98), completing the following idea:

@ Because of the great love God has shown toward us, I hereby covenant to show my love for God by . . .

Encourage them to be as concrete and specific as possible, considering possibilities both for themselves and for the group. They can read the covenant poem by Elizabeth S. Tapia in their journals (page 96) as an example of such a covenant. Ask them to write their covenants on separate slips of paper as well. They will present them as an offering in the "Going" experience.

Going

OFFER YOUR COVENANTS TO GOD (5 MINUTES)

Gather in a circle with the offering plate placed in the center. Tell the story of John Newton and the song "Amazing Grace" as follows:

John Newton, the author and composer of "Amazing Grace," was born in London, England, in 1725 and died there in 1807. As the son of a shipmaster, John was at sea by the time he was a teenager. As an adult, he became the captain of a slave-trading ship. Converted by powerful preachers and his own reading about Christ, Newton gave up slave-trading and became an abolitionist, working to end slavery. Later he became a parish minister and hymn-writer. The hymn "Amazing Grace" is autobiographical, telling how the love of God came into his life and changed him. John Newton requested the following words on his tombstone: "John Newton, Clerk. Once an Infidel and Libertine, A servant of slaves in Africa, Was, by the rich mercy of our Lord and Savior, JESUS CHRIST, Preserved, restored, pardoned, And appointed to preach the Faith He had long labored to destroy. . . ."[2]

Teach the song if it is new to the youth (page 228 in the journal; page 234 in this guide). Then invite the group members to come forward and place their covenants in the offering plate as they sing "Amazing Grace." Continue by inviting them to join in the prayer found in the *Confirmand's Journal* (page 99).

Connecting with the Congregation

Find a time during worship or fellowship when the confirmands can present their dramas of the Bible stories to the congregation. Have a discussion around the meaning of the section of the Statement of Faith used in this session: "You seek in holy love to save all people from aimlessness and sin." End with an invitation to the congregation to write their own covenants with God.

Thinking About This Session

Did the concept of God's holy love become more than an intellectual idea for the confirmands? Do you think they were able to explore ways of separation that seem like sin? Were the confirmands able to articulate their ideas about aimlessness and sin? How might you help them continue to explore their covenant with God?

Planning Ahead

Read the design for the next session and gather needed supplies, including a large candle, matches, small pen flashlights, cloth the color of the liturgical season, and objects or symbols of both just and unjust relationships (such as friendship bracelets, peace signs, paper hearts, letters, newspaper or magazine pictures, and chains).

GOD LOVES AND JUDGES

YOU JUDGE PEOPLE AND NATIONS BY YOUR RIGHTEOUS WILL DECLARED THROUGH PROPHETS AND APOSTLES.

—STATEMENT OF FAITH

Themes

@ God is a saving God who judges.

@ God judges relationships with God, one another, ourselves, and the world by God's righteous will.

@ There are times when we fail as individuals and as a church to be just and loving.

Scriptures

MICAH 6:6–8—Faithfulness to God is shown in acts of justice, kindness, and humility.

MATTHEW 25:31–40—What we do for others we do for Christ.

PSALM 130—God's love redeems.

Objectives

@ Hear what God requires.

@ Explore the meaning of God's unconditional love.

@ Discover God's offer of forgiveness.

Session at a Glance

GATHERING

Recruit volunteers for the session (5 minutes)

EXPLORING

Consider what God requires (30 minutes)

Explore God's unconditional love (20 minutes)

CONNECTING

Relate scripture to our lives (25 minutes)

GOING

Worship together (10 minutes)

Biblical and Theological Connection

Micah 6:6–8 and Matthew 25:31–40 were written in different centuries and in times that were very different from our own, yet they address relationships in a way that is contemporary and real to adolescents today. Micah 6:6–8 tells us that God is more concerned with how we treat one another, ourselves, and God than in beautiful rituals or formal liturgies. The prophet Micah lived in the eighth century B.C.E. It was a time filled with personal and political excess and corruption. He proclaimed that individual actions and relationships could make or break the entire realm. He also affirmed that the people would eventually make loving and life-giving choices, and their world would again be filled with joy. Eight centuries after Micah lived, Jesus' words in Matthew 25:31–40 echo the words of the prophet. Jesus tells us that the way we treat friends, family, and strangers is, in effect, the way we treat God.

Psalm 130 reminds us of God's unconditional love for us. Nothing we have done or ever could do will change that love. It also voices a prayer for deliverance, a cry for help and forgiveness in the midst of personal trouble. This scripture passage reminds us that, although we may make unhealthy choices, God's choice is to love and care for us. God gives us the courage and strength to repair and restore our relationships. This is wonderful news in the life of youth whose day-to-day relationships are full of change and uncertainty.

When you engage in conversation with youth, you will find that their relationships, especially with peers, are a top priority. Thinking about their friends, talking to them, and living through the ups and downs of relationships consume much of their energy. Sometimes these relationships are sustaining and fulfilling. Other times they may be in conflict with the wholeness God desires for each person. This session will lead confirmands on a journey that explores relationships in Scripture and will help them relate their learnings to their own lives and the life they live in community with others. The journey is one that connects us to God's love and judgment. The journey begins with God calling us to accountability in our relationships with God, one another, and creation. Throughout the biblical story and our personal journeys we are faced with choices about how to answer that call. God is constantly encouraging us to make healthy and loving choices in our interactions with our world and God. Healthy choices in our relationships with God and one another must also include healthy choices in our relationships with the natural world, ourselves, and our communities. God encourages us to repair and rebuild relationships that are damaged. The journey is ongoing and the choices are always there for us to make. God's way offers hope for reconciliation.

Materials Needed

- Bible for each participant
- *Confirmand's Journal* for each participant
- One large candle and matches
- Small pen flashlights
- Cloth the color of the liturgical season
- Objects or symbols of human relationships both just and unjust:

  JUST—friendship bracelets, peace signs, paper hearts (whole), letters, newspaper or magazine pictures of peace or reconciliation

  UNJUST—chains, paper hearts (torn), newspaper or magazine pictures of war or distress
- Pencils or pens
- Small slips of paper (one for each participant)

Preparing for This Session

The content of this session is the interweaving of scripture, a role play, questions for reflection, and time for personal sharing. As a leader, you are encouraged to read the scriptures for this session: Micah 6:6–8, Matthew 25:31–40, and Psalm 130. Read through the "Exploring" section (pages 98–99) and think about how you would respond to the questions there. Read over the scenarios and become familiar with the instructions for their use.

Select a meeting room that will lend itself to the full effect of candlelight and subdued lighting. In the middle of the room, place a low table (or designate a place on the floor) around which the group may sit in a comfortable circle. Chairs may be used or, for more intimacy, use floor pillows (with some back support). This activity could also be done effectively outside on a warm night under the stars.

Create a worship center on the table with items that are meaningful and appropriate. For example, arrange on the cloth some symbols that remind you of human relationships, both just and unjust (see "Materials Needed"). Place the candle in the midst of the symbols on the worship center. Place Bibles around the edges of the worship center.

Gathering

RECRUIT VOLUNTEERS FOR THE SESSION (5 MINUTES)

As the confirmands come in, ask them to volunteer to do one of the following during the session:

- Read Micah 6:6-8 aloud.
- Read Psalm 130 aloud.
- Read Matthew 25:31-40 aloud.
- Light the candle at the appropriate time.
- Blow out the candle at the appropriate time.

When all the volunteers have been recruited, describe the "Exploring" activity and the use of a scenario. Invite the confirmands to sit in a circle around the table and turn down the lights.

Exploring

CONSIDER WHAT GOD REQUIRES (30 MINUTES)

Explain that from the beginning of creation God called us into relationships with God, one another, ourselves, and the world. Share that you will be exploring how God judges those relationships.

Ask the volunteer to read Micah 6:6–8. Then describe the scenario:

Two friends are shopping. One decides to buy a new pair of sunglasses. The other friend says that they are too expensive and suggests that instead of buying them he/she should hide them and walk out of the store. A store clerk overhears this conversation.

Explain that the activity will be to role-play this scene twice, coming to a resolution each time. The first time through they are to use their imaginations to make the interactions as real as possible. The essential characters are the two friends and the store clerk. You may also include a friend, parent, security guard, minister, and teacher in the role play. Make role assignments as needed for the size of your group. Each group should include no more than eight people.

The second time through the role play, give the instructions that the first friend and the clerk (as well as the minister and security guard) are to let their words and actions be guided by the scripture from Micah 6:6–8. Have the players act out the role play to some resolution. If your group is large, you may wish to take turns, having half the group perform the first scenario, then the other half perform the second scenario.

When both role plays are completed, ask the whole group:

- What differences were there in the two versions of this scenario?
- What do you think contributed to those differences?
- What would you have changed in either one?
- How did the words from Micah 6:6–8 affect the outcome of the role play?
- How could those words from scripture affect your own life and the relationships you have or the choices you make? Explain.

EXPLORE GOD'S UNCONDITIONAL LOVE (20 MINUTES)

Note that even when we have acted in an unkind fashion and damaged our relationships, if we are truly sorry (repentant), God forgives us. Remind the youth that there are all kinds of reasons for relationships to fail or become damaged. Whatever the reasons, God is always there to help us "pick up the pieces." Sometimes a relationship becomes so damaged or damaging to us or the other person that the most healthy and loving thing to do is to end the relationship. God is also present to help us heal from this kind of hurt.

Paradoxically, it is also true that knowing that God will love us and forgive us no matter what we do may lead us to a change of heart (repentance). Experiencing God's gift of forgiveness can also be healing. Yet sometimes we have more trouble "forgiving ourselves" than God does.

Ask the volunteer to read Psalm 103. Then discuss these questions:

- What would it be like to have a friend who would never stop loving you no matter what?
- Have you ever been in a situation where someone hurt you and you were able to forgive him or her? What was that like?

Connecting

RELATE SCRIPTURE TO OUR LIVES (25 MINUTES)

Take some time to reflect on the experiences in this session. Ask the volunteer to read Matthew 25:31–40. Then ask the following discussion questions:

- What do the words *judgment* and *repentance* mean to you?
- How are the meanings different now than they were before this session?
- How do you suppose one would live to show God's righteous will?

Invite the confirmands to look at the "Questions to Consider" and to write their responses in their journals (page 103). Then ask them to think about a relationship in their life or a situation in the world that needs God's healing or God's forgiveness. Invite them to complete the sentences that are in their journals (page 105). Tell them that no one else will see their responses. Then ask them to look at the items in the worship space that symbolize just and unjust relationships. Have them pick one from each category (just and unjust) that expresses the brokenness and the hope for healing they wrote about in their journals.

Going

WORSHIP TOGETHER (10 MINUTES)

Light the candle in the center of the worship space and turn down the lights in the room. Form a circle and sing or say together "Be Still and Know That I Am God" (see page 225 in the *Confirmand's Journal* or the music section on page 231 of this guide). Then have a minute of silence, followed by a reading of Psalm 130. Ask the confirmands to think about the sentences they completed in their journals and pray about the relationship or situation they wrote about. Following the time of silence, ask them to lay their objects on the worship table as an act of hope for forgiveness and healing of these places. Then bless the group with this benediction:

May the love of God, the saving power of Christ, and the strength of the Holy Spirit go with you from this place. May you live God's call to just and loving relationships, and may you forgive others, even as God forgives you. Amen.

Extinguish the candle.

Connecting with the Congregation

Have the confirmands participate in the worship service by reading scripture, sharing a "moment for mission," or performing some other appropriate expression of leadership.

Thinking About This Session

Did the confirmands understand the broader, global dimension of what God requires the community of faith to do together, as well as what each individual is called to do to express God's righteous will? What witness and service projects are they undertaking that will help with this understanding?

Planning Ahead

Read the next session and gather needed supplies, including a large candle (preferably white), two taper candles, candle holders, and matches.

God became
one of us in
the person
of Jesus of
Nazareth.

Jesus Christ

JESUS CHRIST

JESUS CHRIST,

HUMAN AND DIVINE

IN JESUS CHRIST, THE MAN OF NAZARETH, OUR CRUCIFIED AND RISEN SAVIOR, YOU HAVE COME TO US AND SHARED OUR COMMON LOT.

— STATEMENT OF FAITH

Themes

@ Throughout history God has sought to relate to human beings.

@ God became one of us in the person of Jesus of Nazareth.

@ Jesus' life expressed God in the world.

Scriptures

JOHN 1:1–18—The Divine became human in Jesus Christ.

LUKE 22:63–23:46—Jesus was physically hurt.

MARK 4:35–38—Jesus slept.

MATTHEW 21:18—Jesus was hungry.

JOHN 11:28–36—Jesus wept for a friend.

MARK 6:30–32—Jesus spent time with his friends.

JOHN 2:1–11—Jesus celebrated.

JOHN 2:13–16—Jesus got angry.

LUKE 2:41–51—Jesus upset his parents.

MATTHEW 15:30–38—Jesus felt sorry for someone else.

Objectives for This Session

@ Discover the joys of being human.

@ Explore the meaning of the incarnation.

@ Reflect on what Jesus Christ means to us.

Session at a Glance

GATHERING

Name what you like about being human (15 minutes)

EXPLORING

Look at the humanity and divinity of Jesus (30 minutes)

Consider the meaning of the Incarnation (20 minutes)

CONNECTING

Name the importance of Jesus to us (20 minutes)

GOING

Meditate on John 1:1–18 (5 minutes)

Biblical and Theological Background

The Gospel of John, especially in the powerful and poetic opening words, affirms that Jesus was both fully human and fully divine—that God became incarnate in Jesus of Nazareth. From the early church to the present day, Christians have struggled to understand how Jesus could have been fully human and fully divine simultaneously.

Roger Shinn, in his book *Confessing Our Faith* about the United Church of Christ Statement of Faith, describes what was at stake for the early church:

Christians, attempting to state this belief, sometimes made fumbling compromises. Sometimes they said that Jesus was God, pretending to be human. Or that Jesus was truly divine and almost human. Those beliefs were soon declared heretical (although they survive occasionally today). Sometimes Christians said that Jesus was really human and almost God. Or that Jesus was an in-between being, almost divine and almost human. Those beliefs were soon ruled out.

The early church, living in a world filled with stories of gods masquerading as human beings, wanted to say that Jesus was genuinely a human person, one who prayed, "Abba, . . . not what I want, but what you want" (Mark 14:36), one who cried out from the cross, "My God, my God, why have you forsaken me?" (Mark 15:34). Yet it wanted to declare also that in Jesus—in his demands, his love, his judgment—it had met the demands, the love, the judgment of the one true God.[1]

Many biblical scholars believe that John's Gospel was probably written at the end of the first century or near the beginning of the second. Jesus' death and resurrection had occurred at least a half-century earlier. The author of this gospel wants the reader to know the theological meaning of the birth, life, teaching, death, and resurrection of Jesus. Christians in the community in which this Gospel was written wanted Jesus to make sense to people of their day living amid the confusing mixture of Greek philosophy, Roman oppression, and the myriad of Near Eastern and Mediterranean religions and factions. All these influences were already represented within the young Christian church. (There are many parallels to the environment surrounding the church today.) Far from being a historical text in the modern sense of the word, the Gospel of John is a theological work looking back at the person Jesus through the early church's experience of the risen Christ. For a fuller exploration of this concept you may want to read Marcus Borg's book *Jesus: A New Vision* (HarperSan Francisco, 1993).

Christians of all ages participate in the ongoing struggle to understand the mystery of the incarnation. Youth in the church bring their own deep spiritual experiences and questions and have a need to sort out their own beliefs as they journey toward adulthood. Youth are perhaps at a unique place to explore what it means for Jesus to have been human and divine. They are themselves experiencing a personal awareness of their own humanity as their bodies change almost daily during the adolescent years. Whether consciously self-reflective or not, they feel hunger, thirst, pain, sexual energy, joy, and growth on emotional, physical, and spiritual levels. Youth also have a great capacity for mystical spiritual experiences and often move to and from firm belief to questioning unbelief with some frequency.

Materials Needed

- Bible for each participant
- *Confirmand's Journal* for each participant
- Posterboard and markers
- Pens or pencils
- Newsprint
- Low table
- Large candle, preferably white
- Two taper candles, holders, and matches

Preparing for This Session

Spend time reflecting on how you feel and what you believe about the incarnation of Jesus Christ. Read over the discussion questions and be prepared to share your opinions and beliefs during the session.

You will need to make the signs for the "Human Like Me" activity. On separate pieces of paper or posterboard write, draw, or paint the following phrases and scripture citations:

- Jesus was physically hurt (Luke 22:63–23:46)
- Jesus slept (Mark 4:35–38)

- Jesus got hungry (Matthew 21:18)
- Jesus wept for a friend (John 11:28-36)
- Jesus spent time with his friends (Mark 6:30-32)
- Jesus celebrated (John 2:1-2)
- Jesus got mad (John 2:13-16)
- Jesus upset his parents (Luke 2:41-51)
- Jesus felt sorry for someone else (Matthew 15:32)

Read the passages of scripture that correspond to each phrase.

Display the signs in the meeting room. Place the large candle, to symbolize Christ, on a low table in the center of the conversation space flanked by two other candles. Also, recruit someone with a sense for dramatic reading, either a confirmand or leader, to read "The Parable of the Birds," found on page 111, during "Exploring."

Gathering

NAME WHAT YOU LIKE ABOUT BEING HUMAN (15 MINUTES)

As the confirmands gather, distribute index cards and pens or pencils and ask them to write on it at least one thing they like about being human (eating, seeing the sunset, listening to music, and so forth). When all have finished, ask them to share their response with the group and place their cards on the low table next to the large candle in the center of the meeting space.

Exploring

LOOK AT THE HUMANITY AND DIVINITY OF JESUS (30 MINUTES)

Draw the confirmands' attention to the two taper candles in the center of the space. Tell them that many congregations have two candles on their communion table or altar. These two candles symbolize the humanity and the divinity of Jesus. Have one of the confirmands light one of the candles and tell the group that it is a reminder of the humanity of Jesus.

Invite the confirmands and leaders to look at the "Human Like Me" signs that are displayed around the room. Invite everyone to choose an experience Jesus had that parallels one they have experienced in the past week. Ask them to go and stand by the appropriate sign. When everyone has chosen, ask each group member to share briefly why he or she chose that sign. Ask the group if anyone knows the story about Jesus indicated on the sign. If so, have him or her tell the story. If not, read the appropriate passage aloud.

Repeat the exercise several more times, asking each person to choose a different sign. When they are
finished, ask if anyone can tell the story behind any phrase that has not already been discussed.

At the end of the discussion light the other candle, pointing out that it is a symbol of the divinity of Jesus
Christ.

CONSIDER THE MEANING OF THE INCARNATION (20 MINUTES)

Introduce the concept of incarnation to the youth by saying:

*An important teaching to understand when we explore the humanity and divinity of Jesus Christ is the incar-
nation. It comes from a Latin word, incarnatio, and means "in the flesh." The incarnation means that God
became a human, historical person in Jesus Christ. It also means that in Jesus Christ, the authority and power
of God is present.*

Now tell the group that they will hear a story that attempts to explain why God chose to become human.

Ask the volunteer to read the "Parable of the Birds" by Louis Cassells found on page 111.

Ask two people to light the larger Christ candle in the middle of the circle using the other two candles. Tell
the group that the candle is a symbol that reminds us of the presence of Christ.

Ask the group to consider the following two questions, listing their answers on two separate sheets of
newsprint:

@   Why is it important to you that Jesus is truly God?

@   Why is it important to you that Jesus was truly a human person?

Connecting

NAME THE IMPORTANCE OF JESUS TO US (20 MINUTES)

Read aloud the following observation by Roger Shinn:

*The Statement of Faith says: "In Jesus Christ, the man of Nazareth, our crucified and risen Savior, you
[God] have come to us." That is, in this person Jesus, a genuine human being, you, the true God, have
entered into our midst. You have not simply sent a messenger, a representative, but you . . . have entered the
life of this person and through him the life of humankind.*[2]

Ask the youth to complete the following sentences. Have them write their answers in the *Confirmand's Journal* on page 113.

☙   When I think about God coming to us and sharing our common lot I . . .
☙   When I think about Jesus Christ as a Savior I . . .

Discuss together your thinking about Jesus.

Going

MEDITATE ON JOHN 1:1–18 (5 MINUTES)

Invite group members who want to read aloud to each read one verse of John 1:1–18. Then ask the youth to pick up the index cards they placed on the table earlier. This time ask them to write what they like best about being "a child of God" (from John 1:12). Examples might be "I can pray for others," "I look for signs of God in ordinary events," "I am able to love even my enemies," and so forth. Do not ask them to say what they wrote. Affirm these offerings by singing or saying together the spiritual "I Thank You, Jesus," on page 216 in the journal or page 224 in the guide.

Close with this benediction:

Loving God, you came to us in Jesus Christ to show us your way. Thank you for calling us your children and sharing our common lot. Go with us now, we pray. Amen.

Connecting with the Congregation

Decide how the story "The Parable of the Birds" might be shared with the congregation at an appropriate time during a worship service or fellowship gathering. It could be told, dramatized, or depicted in drawings or sculpture. Look for ways to sing the spiritual "I Thank You, Jesus" in worship. Have the confirmands teach it to the congregation if it is new to them.

Thinking About This Session

What parts of this session were most helpful in supporting the objectives? What evidence do you have that the confirmands grasped the meaning of the incarnation? How might you help them if the concept is still vague?

Planning Ahead

Gather art that depicts the arrest, trial, crucifixion, and resurrection of Christ. Check your church or public library for appropriate books. A helpful resource would be *Imaging the Word: An Arts and Lectionary Resource*, volumes 1, 2, and 3 (United Church Press).

Resources

THE PARABLE OF THE BIRDS[3]

Once upon a time there was a man who looked upon Christmas as a lot of humbug. He wasn't a Scrooge. He was a very kind and decent person.

But he didn't believe all that stuff about an incarnation that churches proclaim at Christmas. And he was too honest to pretend that he did. He simply could not understand the claim that God became a human being. It didn't make any sense to him.

On Christmas Eve, his wife and children went to church for the midnight service, but he stayed home. It began to snow. "If we must have Christmas," he thought, "it's nice to have a white one." He sat down by the fire to read the newspaper. A few minutes later he heard a thudding sound, followed by another and another. Birds, caught in the storm and in a desperate search for shelter, had tried to fly through his window. Now they lay huddled miserably in the snow. "I can't let the poor creatures lie there and freeze," he thought. "But how can I help them?"

He thought of the barn. It was a warm shelter. He put on his coat and overshoes and tramped out through the deepening snow to the barn. He opened the doors wide and turned on a light.

But the birds didn't come in.

"Food will bring them in," he thought. So he sprinkled a trail of bread crumbs from the birds to the sheltering barn.

To his dismay, the birds ignored the crumbs and continued to flop around helplessly in the snow.

He tried shooing them into the barn. They scattered in every direction—except the warm, lighted barn.

"They find me a strange and terrifying creature," he said to himself, "and I can't seem to think of any way to let them know they can trust me. If only I could be a bird myself for a few minutes, perhaps I could lead them to safety."

Just at that moment, the church bells began to ring. He stood silently for a while, listening to the bells pealing the glad tidings of Christmas.

Then he sank on his knees in the snow. "Now I do understand," he whispered. "Now I see why you had to do it."

JESUS CHRIST,

CRUCIFIED AND RESURRECTED

IN JESUS CHRIST, THE MAN OF NAZARETH, OUR CRUCIFIED AND RISEN SAVIOR, YOU HAVE COME TO US AND SHARED COMMON LOT. —STATEMENT OF FAITH

Themes

@ Jesus lived among us.

@ Jesus was crucified and resurrected.

@ Jesus' life and resurrection are central to the Christian faith.

@ Jesus Christ is present today in relationship.

Scripture

JOHN 18:1–20:31—The story of the crucifixion and resurrection is told.

Objectives for This Session

@ Explore the meaning of the passion and resurrection of Jesus Christ.

@ Assess beliefs about Jesus.

@ Consider Christ's presence with believers.

Session at a Glance

GATHERING

Pray together (5 minutes)

EXPLORING

Look at the Passion and resurrection of Jesus (50 minutes)

CONNECTING

Review the events of the Passion and resurrection of Jesus

(10 minutes)

Decide what you believe (15 minutes)

GOING

Worship together (10 minutes)

Biblical and Theological Background

Whether one is considering the Christian faith for the first time or one has been a Christian from earliest memory, there are few events more important or more difficult to understand than the crucifixion and resurrection of Jesus. Why did Jesus die? What is the resurrection? What proof do we have in these matters? What does it mean that Jesus died for my sins and the sins of the world?

Martin B. Copenhaver, in his book *To Begin at the Beginning*, says:

Some things are so familiar that we cease to see them for what they are. Even the strangest realities can become so familiar that our sense of their strangeness needs to be refreshed. No symbol is more familiar to Christians than the cross. We are accustomed to seeing the cross displayed in places of worship, and it is often prominently situated outside church buildings because this symbol identifies them as Christian churches. This same symbol is found on the covers of hymnals and Bibles and embroidered on the vestments worn by clergy. We make the sign of the cross on the forehead of someone being baptized. Sometimes a cross is worn on a chain around the neck, either as a statement of Christian faith or simply as a piece of jewelry. "In the cross of Christ I glory," Christians sing is but one of the many hymns that extol the centrality of the cross in Christian devotion. Everywhere we turn, there is that stark and simple symbol.

But what a strange symbol the cross is. It is strange that a means of execution should become a cherished symbol for those who follow the one who was executed. Its strangeness can be refreshed if we consider that, if Jesus had been executed by other means, Christians today might identify their places of worship with electric chairs atop their steeples.[1]

Today, Christians who look at the cross see love and life, rather than a brutal instrument of hate and death. But those first confronted with the reality of Jesus nailed to a cross were not drawn to the sight but repelled by it. On Good Friday all their hopes that Jesus would fulfill God's promises and usher in God's realm were dashed. Jesus seemed so helpless, nailed to a cross, dying like a common criminal, scorned by those who executed him. Jesus' followers saw their hopes dragged into death with him. They scattered and hid, afraid that those who executed Jesus might put them to death also.

It was only later, after the resurrection, that the followers of Jesus were able to proclaim that on the cross, when things seemed most hopeless, when God seemed absent, and when God's purpose seemed thwarted, God was most surely present and God's ways most truly manifest. The Gospels tell of the many experiences of Jesus' followers that compelled them to say, "Christ is risen." They experienced the presence of the Christ, enabling them to live and act as disciples in ways they never dreamed would be possible. The resurrection enables Christians to live fully—with God's grace—in an imperfect world.

Over the past twenty centuries, a variety of explanations of the resurrection have been offered. There were some who believed that Jesus' disciples had secretly gone to the burial cave and stolen the body so they could claim that Christ had risen from the dead. There were others, called Gnostics, who claimed that Jesus was not really a human being like the rest of us. They said that his spirit was the only thing real about him, and, since he wasn't alive in the same way that human beings are, he didn't experience death as human beings do. Another common belief in the Greco-Roman world was that the body and soul were separate, with the body serving merely as a house where the soul would live. This led to the idea for some that Jesus' spirit was resurrected, leaving his body behind.

None of these views were proclaimed by the early Christians. They simply told what they knew: the continuing presence of the risen Christ among them brought them out of hiding, freed them from their fears, and enabled them to proclaim God's love. As the Statement of Faith affirms, through the cross and the resurrection they experienced God sharing their "common lot, conquering sin and death." They proclaimed Jesus' resurrection as a unique event that demonstrated God's power over death once and for all.

John reports that the resurrected Jesus appeared to the fearful disciples, who had hidden themselves away from the Roman authorities and religious leaders. The disciples were afraid that the authorities might come seeking to execute them also because they were followers of Jesus. The disciple Thomas, who was not present the first time Jesus appeared to the disciples, refused to believe Christ was risen until he could see Jesus with his own eyes and touch Jesus' wounds. Once Thomas was convinced, however, he cried, "My Lord and my God!" (John 20:28). And Jesus' response to him underscores the mystery of the resurrection for the early church and for succeeding generations: "Have you believed because you have seen me? Blessed are those who have not seen and yet have come to believe" (John 20:29).

Materials Needed

- @ Bible for each participant
- @ *Confimand's Journal* for each participant
- @ Copies of different artists' renditions of the arrest, trial, crucifixion, and/or resurrection (for example, see *Imaging the Word: An Arts and Lectionary Resource*, volumes 1, 2, and 3, United Church Press)
- @ Newsprint and markers
- @ Candles, matches, and drip guard
- @ Bread

Preparing for This Session

Read John 18:1–20:31. You may wish to read the crucifixion and resurrection accounts in Matthew and
Mark as well (Matthew 27:32–28:10, Mark 15:21–16:8).

The Statement of Faith says, "In Jesus Christ, the man of Nazareth, our crucified and risen Savior, you have
come to us." The mystery of what this means and how this could be is at the heart of this session.

Reflect on the crucifixion and resurrection with other leaders. This will enhance your understanding and
self-confidence as you engage in dialogue with the confirmands about your own convictions. The following questions are offered to help you reflect on the texts. How do you respond to the report in the
Gospels that everyone abandoned Jesus during the trial and crucifixion? What is your feeling about why
Jesus was crucified? Even though the Gospels present Pontius Pilate, the chief priests, scribes, Pharisees,
Judas, and even Peter as the "villains" in this drama, is it possible to understand or even justify the part
they played in the crucifixion?

Arrange seating in a circle or semi-circle with a candle on a table in the center or in view of the entire group.
Place on a nearby table several different examples of artwork depicting the arrest, crucifixion, and resurrection.

Prepare four large pieces of newsprint with the following scripture verses as titles: John 18:1–27, John
18:28–19:16, John 19:17–42, and John 20:1–30. Down the left side of each newsprint sheet, write the
following: "Who?" "What?" "When?" "Where?" and "Why?" These will be used in "Exploring."

Gathering

PRAY TOGETHER (5 MINUTES)

Ask a youth to light the candle and say an opening prayer:

*We rejoice, mighty God, that you have raised Jesus Christ from the dead. We praise you and glorify your
name. New life blossoms where dead hopes were buried. The world is made new. Be known among us in resurrection power; through Jesus, our crucified and risen Savior. Amen.* [2]

Place the candle either in the center of the circle or in front of the group as a reminder to the group that the
light of God was revealed to humanity in the person of Jesus of Nazareth.

Extinguish the candle.

Exploring

LOOK AT THE PASSION AND RESURRECTION OF JESUS (50 MINUTES)

Ask participants to look at all of the artwork and choose one that is meaningful to them. Ask them to examine it closely and decide what they think it communicates about how Jesus felt and how his followers and family may have felt at the time of the passion—Jesus' arrest, trial, crucifixion—and resurrection. Ask each person to share with the group the chosen art and what it expresses to him or her.

Although we were not present at the time, we can get a sense of the intensity by telling the story of the Passion as reported in the Gospels. For this session we will use the story recorded in the Gospel of John. Display the four sheets of newsprint for all to see. Ask for volunteers to record the responses following the readings. Ask one or more narrators to read the passages using these narrative segments:

@ John 18:1-27

This scene depicts Judas betraying Jesus into the hands of Roman soldiers and Temple guards; Peter attempting to protect Jesus by cutting off the ear of the high priest's slave; and Peter's denial that he was one of Jesus' followers. Jesus is interrogated by Caiaphas before the Temple leaders, known as the Sanhedrin.

@ John 18:28-19:16

Jesus is led away from the Sanhedrin to the praetorium where Pilate asks Jesus' accusers what charge they bring against him and then interrogates Jesus before giving into the crowd's demand that Jesus be crucified.

@ John 19:17-42

This passage describes the crucifixion and burial of Jesus.

@ John 20:1-31

These verses describe Jesus' resurrection and the appearance of Jesus to the disciples, including his encounter with Thomas.

Ask the first reader to read John 18:1–27. Work as a group to determine what was happening in the story using the categories of who, what, when, where, and why. The recorder may write the group's responses on the newsprint. Repeat this process for the other three sections from John.

Connecting

REVIEW THE EVENTS OF THE PASSION AND RESURRECTION OF JESUS (10 MINUTES)

Ask the group to think about the following questions:

- Why do you think everyone abandoned Jesus during his trial and crucifixion?
- Why do you think Jesus was crucified?
- Do you feel any sympathy for Pontius Pilate, the chief priests, scribes, Pharisees, Judas, Peter, or Thomas? If so, why? If not, why not?
- What do you think Jesus meant when he said to Thomas, "Blessed are those who have not seen and yet believe" (John 20:29)?

DECIDE WHAT YOU BELIEVE (15 MINUTES)

This is an exercise that combines physical activity with choosing what one believes. It will use the crucifixion and resurrection texts as sources for statements that will require the group to respond by placing themselves somewhere on an imaginary line between "strongly agree" and "strongly disagree." Ask the confirmands to position themselves on the continuum in response to each statement. Designate one side of the room "strongly agree," the other side "strongly disagree"; have the youth move to the center of the imaginary line connecting the two sides. This experience provides an outlet for kinetic energy and, at the same time, empowers the youth to express their beliefs, feelings, and attitudes toward questions of faith. It is also a fairly nonthreatening activity for those youth who are reluctant or less able to put their thoughts into words when in a group.

Read each statement and have the youth move quickly to the place on the line that indicates their response. When everyone is in place, pause so they can see where everyone is, but do not make comments or have a discussion about their choices.

- Jesus was a human person like me.
- Jesus was divine.
- Jesus was a great teacher.
- Jesus is the child of God.
- Jesus was a Jew.
- Jesus knew that he was the child of God.
- Jesus was a spirit in human disguise.
- Jesus never did anything wrong.

- Jesus felt pain.
- Jesus always did what his parents expected.
- Jesus liked to party.
- Jesus was always meek and mild.
- Jesus was never sad or depressed.
- Jesus' life expressed God in the world.

After the group has made their decisions, underscore the idea that Jesus Christ is present to us today. Jesus Christ is the real expression of God in the world and lives in relationship with individuals and communities. Talk about the way Jesus' life—the teaching, healing, and ministry—as well as his death and resurrection reveal God to us.

Going

WORSHIP TOGETHER (10 MINUTES)

Relight the candle. Close the session by asking the person who lit the candle and offered the opening prayer to hold the candle with the drip guard and say to the group:

Jesus Christ is our crucified and risen Savior. Now we are the body of Christ. Carry the light of Christ to all you meet along the way.

The next person takes the candle and says, "May the light of Christ shine in all I do." Continue passing the candle and have each person repeat that phrase until the candle comes back to a leader who says, "Christ is risen." Ask the group to respond, "Christ is risen, indeed!"

Connecting with the Congregation

PLAN A GREAT EASTER VIGIL WORSHIP SERVICE

Another way for youth to experience the resurrection stories from the Bible is to prepare them to participate in the Great Easter Vigil worship service in the *United Church of Christ Book of Worship*, pages 225–43. This liturgy, which begins with the "Lighting of the New Fire," recounts the resurrection stories in dramatic form. Take time to practice the various parts of this service and then involve confirmands in the leading of the liturgy.

Thinking About This Session

How well did the confirmands grasp the idea of Jesus Christ as the expression of God in the world through his life, death, and resurrection? What did you observe during the "beliefs" activity? Are there some in the group who are uncertain, confused, or resistant to affirming their faith? It will be important to be supportive of their faith journey without expecting them to have answers to all their questions. Explore with them the idea that faith continues to be shaped and formed throughout one's life.

PLANNING AHEAD

Gather the materials that you will need for the next session, including posterboard, Post-It Notes, and current newspapers and newsmagazines. Make a large cross from the posterboard.

JESUS CHRIST, RISEN SAVIOR

IN JESUS CHRIST, THE MAN OF NAZARETH, OUR CRUCIFIED AND RISEN SAVIOR, YOU HAVE COME TO US . . . CONQUERING SIN AND DEATH AND RECONCILING THE WORLD TO YOURSELF.

—STATEMENT OF FAITH

Themes

@ Jesus Christ is Sovereign and Savior.

@ Jesus Christ delivers the world from sin, death, and oppression.

@ Jesus Christ restores a right relationship between humanity and God, among persons, and with all of creation.

Scriptures

JOHN 1:29–34—Jesus takes away the sin of the world.

2 CORINTHIANS 5:16–21—God calls us to be reconcilers.

Objectives for This Session

@ Explore the meaning of reconciliation.

@ Discover God's intentions for us in Christ.

@ Consider the questions asked during the rite of confirmation.

Session at a Glance

GATHERING

Explore the meaning of reconciliation (15 minutes)

EXPLORING

Discover the cross as a symbol of reconciliation (45 minutes)

CONNECTING

Create "before and after" pantomimes (20 minutes)

GOING

Worship together (10 minutes)

Biblical and Theological Background

Jesus was born into a mix of despair, frustration, fear, and confusion. He grew up when times were difficult and uncertain. Most people were poor. Many who were well-off did little to help the less fortunate. Many people suffered from mental or physical illness or disabilities; others were homeless and hungry. In those days there were few cures; people died from diseases and malnutrition. Some of the religious leaders taught that people were sick or poor because they did not live according to God's law or will. Some believed that people were to blame for their situations.

The Jewish people lived under the rule of the Roman Empire—they were oppressed, heavily taxed, and treated cruelly. The vast majority of the people were looked down upon by those who were wealthy and had power. Ordinary citizens, Jews and Gentiles (non-Jews), young and old, were afraid of both government officials and religious leaders. They felt helpless and hopeless. They had no power—economically, socially, or politically. They lived at the margins of society and yearned for freedom and dignity.

Many of the people longed for a savior, someone who they hoped would rescue them from their lowly status. During his ministry, Jesus taught about the reign of God that would transform peoples' lives. Some people, then as now, believed this meant social reform and a politically dominant religious government. Others longed for a place of peace and tranquility. Still others recognized that Jesus offered a new way to live in the midst of all that worked against them, even while maintaining hope for the future.

Jesus taught that the reign of God comes as a miracle and as a gift. Signs of God's reign included healing, offering forgiveness and blessing, and having fellowship with outcasts. Jesus' actions demonstrated that God's reign was present: he healed people who were sick, lame, blind, and possessed by evil spirits; he ate with sinners, gluttons, and tax collectors, who were despised by most people; he listened to women and others who were given few opportunities or power in his society to express their ideas and perspectives.

One of the most important signs of God's reign was the forgiveness of sin. As we discovered in earlier sessions, sin is anything that separates us from God's purposes for creation. Sin is present throughout the world, enslaves humanity, and corrupts creation. All sin is an act of idolatry—replacing God with gods of our own making, like being obsessed with money and material things or preoccupied with self, envy, hatred, oppression, injustice, or refusing to develop and use the gifts and talents God gives. The Gospels proclaim the good news that Jesus is the one who takes away the sin of the world (John 1:29).

In 2 Corinthians 5:16–21, the apostle Paul claims that there is a new reality for everyone who is in Christ. This present age is radically changed and the love of God in Christ is now the foundation and standard for everything. Paul describes the transformed reality as the "new creation" (2 Corinthians 5:17). He equates the new creation with the reconciliation of all people and all creation to God. Jesus has shown us how to live and has drawn us back to God and God's will.

One of the greatest signs of God's reign was God saying no to the powers of death through the resurrection. In Christ's death and resurrection God met death and exposed its weakness. Christ's resurrection says that death has no lasting power and that people are free to live a new life. The resurrection was God's great act of salvation for the entire universe.

In the Statement of Faith, the verbs *conquering* and *reconciling* are in the present tense. This was done intentionally to indicate that, through Christ, God continues to conquer sin and reconcile creation and calls us through the ministry of reconciliation to "become the righteousness of God" (2 Corinthians 5:21).

Materials Needed

- Bible for each participant
- *Confirmand's Journal* for each participant
- Posterboard and masking tape
- Markers
- 3" x 3" Post-It Notes
- Pens or pencils
- Newsprint
- Current newspapers and news magazines and scissors

Preparing for This Session

Read John 1:29–41 and 2 Corinthians 5:16–21. Think about what reconciliation means to you. Look at the definition of the word in the glossary on page 251. What else would you add from your own experience to elaborate on its meaning? Reflect on your experience of being "in Christ," as 2 Corinthians 6:17 describes. How would you characterize your relationship with Christ? Reflect on your experiences of harmony and discord in relationships with others and with the earth. Recall experiences of forgiveness and reconciliation. Be prepared to share some of these with the confirmands, if appropriate, during the session. It helps the youth to know that they are not alone as they struggle with similar issues.

Prepare a large cross out of posterboard, about 2' x 3'. Any color will do, but it needs to be light enough so that writing can be seen. Display it on a wall in the meeting room. Arrange chairs so that all can see the cross and move to it quickly and easily.

Have a stack of Post-It Notes available. The confirmands will be writing on them and attaching them to the cross during "Exploring."

Gathering

EXPLORE THE MEANING OF RECONCILIATION (15 MINUTES)

Welcome the group. Have a volunteer read aloud 2 Corinthians 5:16–21. Invite the confirmands to think about the word *reconciliation*. Have them refer to the definition in the glossary on page 247 of their journal and write a definition of reconciliation in their own words in the space provided in the journal.

Allan Boesak, a leader in the movement that ended apartheid in South Africa, reflected on the cost of discipleship in the context of the church in South Africa and defined reconciliation this way:

> *Reconciliation is not feeling good; it is coming to grips with evil. In order to reconcile, Christ had to die. We must not deceive ourselves. Reconciliation does not mean holding hands and singing: "black and white together." It means rather, death and suffering, giving up one's life for the sake of the other.*[1]

Ask the group to consider the following questions:

- What does it mean to you to show reconciliation?
- What is most difficult about reconciliation?
- What makes reconciliation important?
- How did Jesus show reconciliation?
- How would you go about the process of reconciliation?

As a leader, offer one or more of your own stories about what reconciliation means to you.

Exploring

DISCOVER THE CROSS AS A SYMBOL OF RECONCILIATION (45 MINUTES)

Draw attention to the large cross taped to the wall. Tell the group that the cross has two parts: a vertical part (up and down) and a horizontal part (side to side). The vertical axis of the cross can symbolize our relationship with God. The horizontal axis can symbolize our relationship with other human beings and all of creation. Explain that the Bible teaches us that when we separate from our fellow human beings, we have separated from God. The horizontal and vertical meet in the cross.

Invite the youth to write on the vertical axis those things that separate us from God; they can be both personal and corporate and reflect both attitudes and actions. Responses could include things like rebellion, disobedience to God's will, oppressing or mistreating others, apathy, abusing creation. Next invite them to write on the horizontal axis those things that separate us from other people and the created order. Responses could include things like jealousy, envy, greed, lying, stealing, bigotry, prejudice, polluting the environment, wasting food, and using more water than is needed. Invite those who wish to name some of what they have written and why they believe it separates us from God and one another.

On the Post-It Notes, ask the group to write down what they believe God wants for us and all creation. Responses could include things like treating others fairly, confronting wrongs, standing up for others, being willing to forgive, spending time in worship and prayer, recycling, and participating in mission projects, clean-up projects, and work camps. Have them place their Post-It Notes on top of the things that separate us from God, one another, and creation. After all have had an opportunity to add their notes to the cross, review what was written.

Tell them that placing the Post-It Note expressions of God's hopes for us over the sins is a symbolic way to show what Christ has done. Christ has "covered," or taken away, our sin and fully expressed God's intentions for us, for others, and for the world. Christ expressed how much God loves us and assures us that we have nothing to be afraid of. Christ makes a way for us to live as God intended.

Connecting

CREATE "BEFORE AND AFTER" PANTOMIMES (20 MINUTES)

Give the group ten minutes to look through newspapers and news magazines for headlines, illustrations, words, or phrases that indicate a problem or tension spot in their community or the world where they think God's ministry of reconciliation is needed. If your group has more than five members, work in smaller groups of three. Have them cut out at least three examples for each group. When this is completed, have the whole group review all of the clippings. Take turns, letting each group select one of the clippings and create a "freeze frame" pantomime of the problem. For example, if the headline says, "Rebels carry a wounded comrade away from the frontline," then they could freeze in place with two people struggling to hold a "wounded" person. If they need more people to create the scene than are in the small group, they can use others. This would depict the scene before reconciliation. Then have them imagine what a "freeze frame" would look like after some kind of reconciliation had occurred. Ask them to imagine and depict a scene after reconciliation. The rest of the group can join in by providing suggestions to the small group to develop the scene. Let the groups take turns. If there is time, each group can have another turn and create "before and after" pantomimes of the other clippings as well.

Explain that God has done something radical—trusting us to help bring about reconciliation. Ask them how many ministers are in the congregation. Then say that everyone who follows Christ is asked to be a minister—including them! Have them list what contribution they can make to bring God's reign to its fullness. This list could serve as preparation for another witness and service project (see "A Guide for Witness and Service," page 271).

Going

WORSHIP TOGETHER (10 MINUTES)

Direct the confirmands to "Litany: Questions of the Candidate" on page 127 of the journal (see next page). Explain that these are the questions that will be asked of them during the rite of confirmation. Read through them as a "reverse" litany. That is, let youth read the questions, and have the leaders respond. Point out that these questions address our loyalty to Christ, who invites us to live as new and transformed people. End the session by saying together the words from 2 Corinthians 5:17, also printed in the journal (page 127): "So if anyone is in Christ, there is a new creation: everything old has passed away; see, everything has become new!"

Connecting with the Congregation

Look for ways to help with special mission projects, offerings, or other important work of the congregation. Make arrangements with the appropriate committee or leader in your church.

Thinking About This Session

Were the experiences in this session helpful in conveying the meaning of reconciliation and God's intentions for us through Christ? What are the signs of "new creation in Christ" and faith formation that are happening in your group? How can you acknowledge and celebrate these important signs? Look for ways to encourage the members of your group on their journey.

Planning Ahead

Begin collecting objects or pictures that symbolize the Holy Spirit, such as a dove, flames, wind, eagle, or other items to use in the next session.

Litany: Questions of the Candidate[2]

Confirmands: *Do you desire to affirm your baptism into the faith and family of Jesus Christ?*

Leader(s): *I do.*

Confirmands: *Do you renounce the powers of evil and desire the freedom of new life in Christ?*

Leader(s): *I do.*

Confirmands: *Do you profess Jesus Christ as Lord and Savior?*

Leader(s): *I do.*

Confirmands: *Do you promise, by the grace of God, to be Christ's disciple, to follow in the way of our Savior, to resist oppression and evil, to show love and justice, and to witness to the work and word of Jesus Christ as best you are able?*

Leader(s): *I promise, with the help of God.*

Confirmands: *Do you promise, according to the grace given you, to grow in the Christian faith and to be a faithful member of the church of Jesus Christ, celebrating Christ's presence and furthering Christ's mission in all the world?*

Leader(s): *I promise, with the help of God.*

The Holy Spirit creates, nurtures, and helps us use our gifts for the good of all creation.

THE HOLY SPIRIT

GUIDED BY THE SPIRIT

YOU BESTOW UPON US YOUR HOLY SPIRIT, CREATING AND RENEWING THE CHURCH OF JESUS CHRIST.

—STATEMENT OF FAITH

Themes

- The Holy Spirit is a part of the great mystery of the Trinity.
- The Holy Spirit creates, nurtures, and helps us use our gifts for the good of all creation.
- The Holy Spirit works through the church.

Scriptures

JOHN 16:1–7—Jesus promises that the Advocate (Holy Spirit) will come to the disciples.

JOHN 20:19–23—The risen Christ offers peace to the disciples and gives them the gift of the Holy Spirit.

GALATIANS 5:13–26—Living by the Spirit produces fruit of the Spirit.

1 CORINTHIANS 12:4–11—There are varieties of gifts, but the same Spirit is in everyone for the common good.

Objectives for This Session

- Compare the wind and the Spirit.
- Complete a gifts inventory.
- Name symbols of the Spirit.
- Experience a centering prayer.

Session at a Glance

GATHERING

Compare the wind to God's Spirit (10 minutes)

EXPLORING

Consider what it means to be led by God's Spirit (10 minutes)

Identify symbols of the Spirit (20 minutes)

Explore the presence of God's Spirit (20 minutes)

CONNECTING

Create an expression of the work of the Holy Spirit

(20 minutes)

GOING

Pray together (10 minutes)

Biblical and Theological Background

The reality of the Spirit permeates most religious traditions. The Chinese believe in Ch'i (breath, vital force). Native Americans refer to the Great Spirit or Wakan-Tanka (Lakota). The Hebrew Scriptures speak of God's creating spirit as Sophia or Wisdom. The psalmist affirms that this Spirit is everywhere (Psalm 139:7). Christians use the name Holy Spirit, which we believe to be the third person of the Trinity—both the spirit of God and the spirit given by Christ. This Spirit is both inside us and all around us. The Holy Spirit strengthens and sustains us and empowers the work and worship of the church.

The Hebrew word *ruach* or *ruah*, like the Greek word *pneuma*, can mean "wind" or "breath" as well as "spirit." In the beginning, the spirit or wind of God swept over the face of the waters (Genesis 1:2) and gave us the breath of life (2:7). Continuing this word play, Jesus says to Nicodemus, "wind blows where it chooses, and you hear the sound of it, but you do not know where it comes from or where it goes. So it is with everyone who is born of the Spirit" (John 3:8).

The scriptures for this session show how the Holy Spirit comes in many different forms and works through the lives of people in a variety of circumstances. Youth are often curious about spiritual experiences, diverse faith traditions, and other religions. This session on the Holy Spirit can foster and inform that curiosity.

In the conclusion to his letter to the young Christian communities in Galatia, Paul addressed the issue of freedom. What does it really mean to be "free" in Christ? That was also a primary question in Paul's first letter to the Corinthians. In both letters he describes a freedom of mutual responsibility and accountability based on a vision of the church as a body with many parts (1 Corinthians 12). Each part of the body, that is, each person, bears gifts of the Spirit for the common good of the whole body (12:7). Paul goes so far as to urge that "through love [we] become slaves to one another" (Galatians 5:13c)—a disturbing idea in our time, but for Paul it was an idea firmly rooted in the law of love given to us by Christ Jesus. That law of love, affirmed over and over by Jesus in the Gospels, calls upon us to serve one another

(John 13:12–17) and even to lay down our lives for one another (15:12–17), following Jesus' own teaching and example.

In the letter to the church in Galatia, Paul used another metaphor to describe these same ideas. When we give ourselves to one another to satisfy the law of love, we reap together what Paul calls the "fruits of the spirit" (Galatians 5:22–26), drawing us closer and more strongly toward one another and toward God. These "fruits" are similar to the "gifts" or "works" of the Spirit that Paul describes in 1 Corinthians 12.

The Holy Spirit enables Christians to experience kinship with, and respect for, all people of faith. Every human being has access to the Holy Spirit, and that Spirit "blows where it chooses" (John 3:8), often where we least expect it. Christians, including Saint Francis of Assisi and many Christians of native traditions, stress that the Spirit nurtures and directs all of creation; therefore, we are sisters and brothers in the Spirit. In the scriptures for this session, we also experience the Holy Spirit as the one who creates, renews, and empowers the church for ministry.

Materials Needed

- Bible for each participant
- *Confirmand's Journal* for each participant
- Electric fan (optional)
- Meditative music for reading (optional)
- Objects that symbolize the Holy Spirit
- Crayons, markers, and pencils

Preparing for This Session

Read the scriptures for this session: John 16:1–7, John 20:19–23, Galatians 5:13–18, 6:1–2, and 1 Corinthians 12:4–11. Think about each text. Pray for yourself, your church, and the confirmands by name. Consider these questions: When have you been aware of the presence of the Holy Spirit with you? What were the circumstances surrounding these times? What impact do these experiences have on your faith? How might you put this into words? Write your responses in your journal.

Gather objects or pictures that symbolize the Holy Spirit, such as a dove, flames, wind, eagle, or other items that you identify with the nature of the Holy Spirit; display them in the meeting space.

Gathering

COMPARE THE WIND TO GOD'S SPIRIT (10 MINUTES)

Welcome the group. Go outside or, if you stay inside, turn on a fan. Be quiet. Invite the group to close their eyes and listen for the movement of the wind. Actually, the wind doesn't make "sound." Instead the sound is the result of the action of the wind in relation to other objects. Similarly, we can't see the Spirit, yet we can see and hear and feel the action of the Spirit. How does one feel God's Spirit? experience it? How is wind like the Spirit of God?

Read together the following prayer from the *Confirmand's Journal* (page 133):

O Great Spirit, whose voice I hear in the winds, and whose breath gives life to all the world, hear me! I am small and weak, I need your strength and wisdom. . . . Make me always ready to come to you with clean hands and straight eyes. So when life fades, as the fading sunset, my spirit may come to you without shame.

—Traditional Native American Prayer[1]

Exploring

CONSIDER WHAT IT MEANS TO BE LED BY GOD'S SPIRIT (10 MINUTES)

Read aloud the stories from John 16:1–7 and John 20:19–23 in which Jesus first promises the Spirit to the disciples and then gives the Spirit to them. Then ask the youth:

- Have you ever felt led by the Holy Spirit?
- Was it a time of crisis? loneliness? quiet? confusion?
- What was the experience like?

IDENTIFY SYMBOLS OF THE SPIRIT (20 MINUTES)

Look at the displayed objects that are used as symbols of the Holy Spirit. Discuss how the Holy Spirit is symbolized, visualized, and imagined. Talk about the symbols and the qualities each has that helps to convey the nature of the Holy Spirit. Then discuss these questions:

- What are some traditional places where people go to experience the presence of the Holy Spirit?
- Where have you experienced the presence of the Spirit?
- How do you sense the Spirit moving within you?

EXPLORE THE PRESENCE OF GOD'S SPIRIT (20 MINUTES)

Explore how the Spirit is present in our lives by reading Galatians 5:16–26 and 1 Corinthians 12:4–11. Talk about the following ways the community of faith helps each of us know what gifts the Spirit has given us and how we can use them. The Spirit's gifts in us need to be *identified, called forth, and confirmed.* Then they need to be *owned, accepted, offered, and received.*[2] Give examples from your own experience to illustrate these steps. Then complete the "Gifts Inventory" found in the *Confirmand's Journal,* page 134. After the inventory is completed, discuss your answers together.

Connecting

CREATE AN EXPRESSION OF THE WORK OF THE HOLY SPIRIT (20 MINUTES)

Ask confirmands to spend some time working in their journals. Tell them that at the end of the session those who wish may share their work. Suggest that they might choose one of the following options:

- Write a story or poem about a time when you felt the Holy Spirit was with you.
- Draw a picture that represents the Holy Spirit bringing unity in diversity.
- Write a prayer that asks the Holy Spirit to address a concern you have for the world.

Going

PRAY TOGETHER (10 MINUTES)

Invite the confirmands to close their eyes and listen to their breathing. Ask them to think about how the action of their breathing feels as air fills their lungs. Have them take several breaths in and out, slowly and consciously. Point out that many Christians use this kind of exercise as a "centering prayer." Then say:

As you breath in, imagine the Spirit of God filling your life. As you breath out, imagine the Spirit of God going out into the world through you and other Christians.

Ask the youth to try this kind of centering prayer for several minutes, focusing on their breathing and imagining the Spirit filling them and going into the world.

End the session by singing or saying together "Spirit of the Living God," found on page 222 in the *Confirmand's Journal* and page 228 in this guide.

Additional Activities

WATCH A VIDEOTAPE

There is an excellent video on the Holy Spirit called *What's the Holy Spirit?* (25 minutes, VHS). It is the fourth part of a series, *Questions of Faith*, and may be found in your local resource center, conference office, or ordered from EcuFilm, 1810 12th Avenue South, Nashville, Tennessee 37203 (1-800-251-4091 or 615-242-6277).

Connecting with the Congregation

Make plans with the confirmands to do the "Gifts Inventory" activity with the congregation. Perhaps the activity could happen during a fellowship time, retreat, or leadership training.

Thinking About This Session

Did the confirmands grasp the idea that the Holy Spirit nurtures and supports the church and the world through the gifts that are given to them to share with others? How might you continue to encourage them to discover and share their gifts?

Planning Ahead

Read the next session and gather needed supplies, including red paper to make "flames."

BOUND BY THE SPIRIT

YOU BESTOW UPON US YOUR HOLY SPIRIT, . . . BINDING IN COVENANT PEOPLE OF ALL AGES, TONGUES, AND RACES.

—STATEMENT OF FAITH

Themes

@ The Holy Spirit works in and through each of us.

@ The Holy Spirit unites us in our diversity.

Scriptures

JEREMIAH 31:31–34—God's covenant is written on human hearts.

1 CORINTHIANS 11:23–25—Paul describes the new covenant in Christ's blood.

ACTS 2:1–24—Jesus' followers were filled with the Holy Spirit and began to speak in many languages.

ACTS 2:37–47—Peter called the people to repentance, and the early Christians became a community.

Objectives for This Session

@ Review the story of Pentecost.

@ Explore the meaning of covenant.

@ Experience being bound together in covenant.

Session at a Glance

GATHERING

Put the story of Pentecost in order (15 minutes)

EXPLORING

Learn about covenant (10 minutes)

Role-play a committee meeting (30 minutes)

CONNECTING

Discuss the role play (10 minutes)

Consider the meaning of being bound together by the Spirit

(15 minutes)

GOING

Share writings or drawings (10 minutes)

Biblical and Theological Background

The church is made up of a covenant people. A covenant is "a binding and solemn agreement made by two or more individuals or parties."[1] The church has understood covenant as an agreement between God and God's people.

The concept of covenant was fundamental to the faith of the Hebrew people, and it remains important for Christians as well. The significance of covenant is rooted in the Hebrew Scriptures, which tell of God's covenants with Noah, with Abraham and Sarah, and with Moses, Miriam, and the children of Israel. The prophets repeatedly called on people to be true to the covenant made with God. Jeremiah spoke about the hope of God's covenant being so ingrained in the people that it would be as if it were written on their hearts (Jeremiah 31:31–34). The apostle Paul tells us that Jesus on the night of betrayal said, "This cup is the new covenant in my blood" (1 Corinthians 11:23–25).

Roger Shinn, in discussing the way in which the Holy Spirit draws the church into covenant, says, "It is important for the church to remember the nature of its belief about the covenant. The Christian covenant is not simply an agreement between consenting people, who are free to break it by mutual agreement. It is a covenant between people of faith and God, the Creator and Renewer of the church."[2]

It was not easy for the early church to be God's people in covenant. The mission of preaching the good news in the context of the Greek and Roman world required a great deal of adaptability. In almost all of the letters he wrote to churches, the apostle Paul emphasized the need for early Christian communities to live creatively in a pluralistic world. Paul used all of his persuasive power to encourage Christian people, both those of Jewish heritage and those from the Gentile world, to recognize their differences without assuming that their particular group was superior to others. Paul's persistent reminder can apply to the church today.

According to Luke, the author of Acts, the followers of Jesus experienced a baptism of the Holy Spirit during the celebration of the Feast of Weeks, also known as Pentecost. During this festival, many Jews from many parts of the ancient world had come to the holy city of Jerusalem. There they listened to God's wonders being proclaimed in many different languages ("tongues") by Jesus' followers.

The different "tongues" in the Pentecost story are not only vehicles of communication among human beings but are also symbols of a different way of looking at life. The story of Pentecost affirms that the reality of God cannot be expressed in just one way.

In spite of this reality, the church has not always recognized diversity as a gift of the Spirit. Some Jewish followers of Jesus preferred in the beginning of their mission to keep the good news inside the confines of Judaism. Later when the message started spreading into the Gentile world, there were ardent conflicts about what it was to be a loyal Christian. However, the gift to the church on that Pentecost was the Spirit that could break down the separations among them. The Spirit of God does not tolerate religious and social segregation. When we truly receive God's blessings, we find that human differences—between men and women, young and old, those served and those who serve, differently abled persons, those with various racial and ethnic backgrounds—no longer control our relationships with one another in negative ways.

It is in this way that the early church found its solidarity. These first Christians, opening their lives to the mission prompted by God's Spirit, shared their material goods and were concerned for the well-being of all members of the community of faith. It could not be any other way since through the quiet and imperceptible work of the Spirit of God they experienced themselves as one body. The early church learned it was necessary to affirm the diverse gifts and characteristics of each member, and that each part of the body is indispensable and cannot claim any kind of superiority over any other part.

The Holy Spirit leads us to encounter and to identify with other human beings, particularly those who are from groups different from our own. When Christians experience God's radical diversity and our understandings and actions are changed, the Spirit of God is at work.

Materials Needed

- Bible for each participant
- *Confirmand's Journal* for each participant
- Red paper for "flames"
- Newsprint and markers or chalkboard and chalk
- Paints, crayons, markers, and paper

Preparing for This Session

Read the scriptures for this session—Jeremiah 31:31–34, 1 Corinthians 11:23–25, Acts 2:1–24, and Acts 2:37–47. Make notes to yourself about your impressions while reading these passages. Gather with other leaders, if possible, to share your impressions. Think about the differences that exist among the members of your congregation and among the members of your community. What do you think is the message of these texts for your congregation and your community? Pray for each member of the group and ask guidance from the Holy Spirit as you lead this session.

Make fourteen flame shapes about 5" x 5" from the red paper and write out on each a different verse or verses from the Pentecost story in Acts 2:1–24 as follows (omit the verse reference numbers)—verses 1–2, verses 3–4, verses 5–6, verses 7–8, verses 9–11, verses 12–13, verse 14, verses 15–16, verse 17, verses 18–19, verses 20–21, verse 22, verse 23; verse 24. These will be used in the "Gathering" activity.

Gathering

PUT THE STORY OF PENTECOST IN ORDER (15 MINUTES)

Welcome the group. Distribute the flames on which are written the verses from Acts 2. Ask group members to work together and, without looking in the Bible, arrange the flames in order. They may wish to attach the flames to a wall or place them on the floor or large table. When the task is complete, read the story of Pentecost aloud by taking turns reading the verses from the flames. Make adjustments in their order if some are out of place. Point out that the miracle on that Pentecost was that the disciples were filled with the Holy Spirit and were empowered to speak in a variety of languages that were quite different from their own. When the crowd, made up of people from many nations and languages, was able to understand them, they were bewildered; but Peter preached and explained to them what was happening. This experience made it clear that God's revelation in Jesus Christ was for all people, not just a chosen few. God's message was for all ages, tongues, and races. The work of the Holy Spirit enabled this to happen.

Exploring

LEARN ABOUT COVENANT (10 MINUTES)

Read aloud Jeremiah 31:31–34 and 1 Corinthians 11:23–25. Ask the group to help make a list (on newsprint or chalkboard) of the promises God makes to us that we might "write on our hearts" (see Jeremiah 31:33).

Call their attention to the quote by Roger Shinn included in the "Biblical and Theological Background" and
also printed in their journals on page 140. "It is important for the church to remember the nature of its
belief about the covenant. The Christian covenant is not simply an agreement between consenting people, who are free to break it by mutual agreement. It is a covenant between people of faith and God, the
Creator and Renewer of the church."[3]

Ask the group to think of the signs or evidence of God's covenant binding together a group of people of
faith.

ROLE-PLAY A COMMITTEE MEETING (30 MINUTES)

Ask the group to role-play a church committee meeting where the task is to plan a worship service to celebrate the fiftieth anniversary of the church. Have each person in the group take one of the following
roles. Include the leaders in the role play, if desired. The roles are:

- a person who wants everything in worship to be the same as it has always been
- a person who is concerned about the church's financial state and does not want to spend any money
- a person who wants the worship to be lively and creative
- a person who is always criticizing the committee process
- a person who wants to make decisions quickly
- a person who wants to make decisions slowly
- a person who insists on taking control of the process

The committee's task is to plan the anniversary worship and decide who will take part, how the church will
be decorated, and what the parts of worship will be. Have each person in the role play assume one of the
roles and stick to it throughout the experience. Give them about fifteen minutes to play out the scene. If
you have a small group, use the first several roles that are described. If the group has more than seven,
give the same role to more than one person or make up your own.

Connecting

DISCUSS THE ROLE PLAY (10 MINUTES)

Following the role play ask:

- What was the experience like? What surprised you about the role play?
- If you could do it again, with the instructions to think about the Holy Spirit binding all of you together, what
  would you have said or done differently? What would you keep the same?

CONSIDER THE MEANING OF BEING BOUND TOGETHER BY THE SPIRIT (15 MINUTES)

Have a volunteer read the quote from Daniel Romero in the *Confirmand's Journal*, page 141. Then ask:

- What does it mean to you to be bound together by the Spirit?
- How could you express this in a letter, a poem, a song, or a drawing?

Have available paint, crayons, markers, and paper for the group to write or draw.

Going

SHARE WRITINGS OR DRAWINGS (10 MINUTES)

Invite confirmands to share the work from the last experience. Not everyone needs to share. Close with a
prayer of your own or say the following:

*O Holy Spirit, who refreshes us like the wind, and refines us like a fire: unite us is our diversity that we may
celebrate the many expressions of your love for the world. Amen.*

Connecting with the Congregation

Find stories that show God's love at work in the world in the various publications of the United Church of
Christ, such as *United Church News, In Mission: A Calendar of Prayer and Connections,* and *Common Lot,*
and share them with the congregation. You may wish to take a "moment for mission" in the worship service to tell the stories or make a visual display on a bulletin board or wall.

Thinking About This Session

How did the group respond to the roleplay? Were they able to grasp the meaning of covenant and being
bound together in the Spirit? How are they expressing their understanding of these concepts in the
group?

Planning Ahead

Read the next session and gather needed supplies.

What is the church?
The church is the
body of Christ,
with individual
members working
together as one
body.

The Church

THE CHURCH

THE BODY OF CHRIST   16

YOU CALL US INTO YOUR CHURCH . . .

—STATEMENT OF FAITH

Themes

- The church is the body of Christ.
- Christians participate in ministries of worship, teaching, and service.

Scriptures

1 CORINTHIANS 12:12–27—The church is the body of Christ.

ROMANS 12:1–8—Paul outlines the way believers are to live as the body of Christ.

1 TIMOTHY 4:11–16—Paul instructs Timothy in the way to teach about Christ.

EPHESIANS 4:1–16—Unity in the body of Christ is the ideal.

Objectives for This Session

- Explore the ministries of the church.
- Discover the gifts needed by the body of Christ.
- Consider how the body of Christ functions.

Session at a Glance

GATHERING

Paraphrase 1 Corinthians 12:12-27 (10 minutes)

EXPLORING

Recall a worship experience (15 minutes)

Consider how the church is the body of Christ (20 minutes)

CONNECTING

Respond as the body of Christ (30 minutes)

Affirm the gifts of the body of Christ (10 minutes)

GOING

Worship together (5 minutes)

Biblical and Theological Background

What is the church? The church is described by the apostle Paul in 1 Corinthians 12:12–27 as the body of Christ, with individual members working together as one body. The phrase "body of Christ" is a metaphor, in which members of the church are described as being parts of a body. This metaphor helps us know that as members of the body of Christ, we are different and have different gifts to offer the church. When all are contributing their gifts, the body is healthy and whole. When one or more of us does not participate as we are able, the whole body suffers.

The church is that body of people who believe in God and seek to help others gain an understanding of and belief in God through Jesus Christ. The body has been inspired and transformed by the life, death, and resurrection of Jesus Christ, the Holy Scriptures, the history and traditions of the church, and personal revelations inspired by God's Spirit. The body is called to live as Christ did, spreading a gospel of love, peace, and justice.

The church has many ministries carried out by its members. Three essential ministries are: a ministry of worship (*leiturgia*), a ministry of teaching (*didache*), and a ministry of service (*diakonia*). These three ministries provide a foundation for seekers of the faith to explore, deepen, and live out their understanding of God.

Worship means acknowledging there is a source of life, an eternal power beyond ourselves. In the book of Romans, the apostle Paul said, "I appeal to you therefore brothers and sisters, by the mercies of God, to present your bodies as a living sacrifice, holy and acceptable to God, which is your spiritual worship. Do not be conformed to this world but be transformed by the renewing of your minds, so that you may discern what is the will of God—what is good and acceptable and perfect" (Romans 12:1). Through worship of God, our minds can be renewed to know what is the will of God—what is good, acceptable, and perfect.

A second ministry of the church is the ministry of teaching. Teaching is more than learning about who Christ was and is. It is about enabling people to think and act as Christ did. In 1 Timothy 4:11–16, the writer suggests that a good minister of Jesus Christ is one who teaches and lives with all godliness. "Do not neglect this gift that is in you" (1 Timothy 4:14).

A third ministry of the church is the ministry of service. Paul, in Ephesians 4:1–16, calls us to live worthy of a calling to which we have been called, to live with humility, gentleness, and patience, bearing with one another in love. We have been given gifts and we are called to use these gifts to build up the body of Christ (the church) and the world. Believing and following Jesus Christ includes striving to minister not only within the Christian community, but also in the world. Through worship, teaching, and service, we may begin to discover that our lives are a part of a larger whole related to a source of power beyond ourselves. We may gain a better understanding of who God is and what God is calling us to be and do in the world. And we may be able to witness God's love more fully.

Materials Needed

@ Bible for each participant
@ *Confirmand's Journal* for each participant
@ Large sheet of newsprint or butcher paper
@ Markers

Preparing for This Session

Youth are a part of the church for a variety of reasons. Some youth are present because their friends come and they want to be with them. Still others come because of expectations from parents or guardians. But some youth come to church not only for social reasons or because they are required, but also because they are interested in developing their faith and knowing more about God. One way God is made known is through the church. Explore the scriptures and themes for this session. Make notes of your thoughts and the questions you have as you explore each passage and theme.

How do you respond to the metaphor of the church as the body of Christ in 1 Corinthians 12:12–27? What gifts do you bring to the body of Christ? What gift are you to the body of Christ?

Romans 12:1–8 affirms worship as a life-changing, transforming experience. How is worship in your congregation transforming or life-changing for you and others? How is it not? What could be done to make worship a more life-changing, transforming experience?

First Timothy 4:11–16 relates to education—the teaching ministry of the church. Think about the teaching ministry of your church. What are the signs in your local church that show teaching is or is not important?

Ephesians 4:1–16 relates to how we do Christian ministry in our own setting in community with others in the church. Think about examples of when you felt connected to the body of Christ while doing Christian ministry. What particular gifts do you bring to the ministry you are doing now?

Select a meeting room that is comfortable and quiet enough to allow discussion. Hang the newsprint or butcher paper for the activity in "Exploring."

Gathering

PARAPHRASE 1 CORINTHIANS 12:12–27 (10 MINUTES)

Welcome confirmands as they gather. Begin your time together by inviting the confirmands to listen to a
passage from a letter the apostle Paul wrote to a congregation that was struggling with conflict within
the church.

Ask one of the confirmands to read aloud 1 Corinthians 12:12–27. Then ask the group how they would paraphrase this scripture in their own words in a sentence or two. Have them work as a whole group or in
smaller groups to rewrite this passage on newsprint. Then ask them how they see this scripture coming
to life in your congregation. List those ways on newsprint as well.

Exploring

RECALL A WORSHIP EXPERIENCE (15 MINUTES)

Take some time to review the three ministries of the church as described in the background material. Then
ask the group members to recall a time they attended worship or were otherwise involved in the life of
the congregation. In pairs, ask group members to interview each other by discussing the following:

℮ Tell about an experience in worship that was meaningful for you. What happened that made it meaningful?
How did it connect you with other Christians?

℮ Name at least three things that you have learned about faith while you have been involved in a church-sponsored
activity.

℮ What have you taught others about God or faith, either formally or informally, at church?

℮ What have you taught others about God or faith, either formally or informally, in some setting other than the
church?

℮ Name the talents or abilities church members are encouraged to share no matter where they are because
they are followers of Christ.

Ask pairs to share the results of their interviews.

CONSIDER HOW THE CHURCH IS THE BODY OF CHRIST (20 MINUTES)

Direct the group's attention to the large piece of newsprint or butcher paper posted on a wall. Have a volunteer stand with his or her back against the paper and trace the outline of his or her body on it. Read
aloud Romans 12:1–8. Talk about the seven gifts that are named: prophecy, ministry, teaching, exhorting,

giving, leading, and being compassionate. Then ask the confirmands to think about the gifts they have
to offer and how they can express themselves in the body of Christ.

Explain that the outline of the human body on the wall represents the body of Christ. Distribute Post-it
Notes, then give them five minutes to write as many gifts and qualities they can think of that are important to bring to the body of Christ and have them place the notes somewhere within the outline of the
body. For example, they may name caring, creativity, patience, honesty, love of music, teaching, preaching, leading, following.

Have them return to the group, then ask:

@ What do you think you have to offer to others at this point in your life?

@ What do you need from others to help you?

Invite those who are willing to discuss their responses. Affirm each person and respect each response given.

Connecting

RESPOND AS THE BODY OF CHRIST (30 MINUTES)

Now invite the confirmands to think of the church as a community that can help us learn how to express
love and care. Sometimes the church struggles to express that love and care to one another because, as a
community that is made up of human beings, it is not perfect. As human beings, we are prone to make
mistakes or make wrong choices. The church is a community where we can learn how to care for one
another even in the middle of disagreements and conflicts. Offer the following situations for the group
to discuss. Ask the group to think about how they might respond as the body of Christ.

*Jenny has volunteered to be the treasurer of the account for the offering your youth group makes to the home-
less shelter. She usually collects the money turned in to her and records it on a sheet of paper before turning it
over to the leader. One Sunday, you discover that Jenny is "pinching" some of the money and is not recording
or turning it over. What should the body of Christ do?*

*Andy, who uses a wheelchair, has started to attend the church. He has expressed interest in the youth meet-
ings, but knows they are in the basement and the only way to get there is down a steep flight of stairs. What
should the body of Christ do?*

Bob is a friend you invited to be a part of a youth activity at your church. He is a show-off who enjoys being in the spotlight of all the discussions. You notice other members complaining behind his back about this problem. What should the body of Christ do?

The youth group is always having to wait for Angela. She shows up late for group activities and excursions. One day the group is ready to visit another church. Angela told you she was coming but she is already thirty minutes late. What should the body of Christ do?

Gary is a member of the youth group who recently lost one of his parents. At a youth meeting Gary suddenly begins to cry and walks out of the meeting. What should the body of Christ do?

Spend some time discussing the various responses to these situations. Have the group name the ideas or principles from the Bible, the Statement of Faith, or some other sources that guided them in their responses.

AFFIRM THE GIFTS OF THE BODY OF CHRIST (10 MINUTES)

Have the confirmands turn to the "Gifts Bingo" game in the *Confirmand's Journal* on page 147. The object of this game is to have each player approach others in the group and ask them to write their initials in the square that names a gift or quality the player sees in the other person. The first person to get the initials of everyone in the group (including leaders) *and* make "bingo"—completing a vertical, horizonal, or diagonal line— becomes "it" and begins to hum "We Are One in the Spirit." If the group is smaller than the number of squares needed, individuals may sign more than one square. When other players have all the initials, they attach themselves to "it" by locking arms, parading around the room, and humming until everyone is joined to "it." Complete the game by singing "We Are One in the Spirit," if desired.

Going

WORSHIP TOGETHER (5 MINUTES)

Use this litany from the journal to complete the session:

One: *For the talents and abilities that we have,*
All: *We thank you God.*
One: *For the faith that stirs and grows in our hearts,*
All: *We thank you God.*

One: *When we doubt your presence during difficult days,*

All: *Help us to trust in you.*

One: *When we are afraid to be who we really are,*

All: *Help us to trust in you.*

One: *As we risk sharing ourselves with others,*

All: *Be with us, O God.*

One: *As we receive what others have to give us,*

All: *Be with us, O God.*

As you say goodbye, ask the confirmands to complete the discipleship survey on page 154 of the *Confirmand's Journal* in Session 17.

Connecting with the Congregation

Have a panel discussion with church leaders. Invite the leaders of the church (e.g., chairpersons of councils, boards, or committees; music leaders; Christian educators) to attend this session and use the following questions for discussion:

- Tell about an experience in worship that was meaningful for you. How did it bring you closer to God?
- What do you learn at church? Do you think you have taught anything?
- What talents or abilities did you share in some way this past week because you are a follower of Christ?

Thinking About This Session

Did the confirmands understand the idea that the church is not simply a place, but a people striving to be faithful to God in all the settings of life? What example for your church's life will help to reinforce this concept?

Planning Ahead

Read the next session and gather needed supplies. Complete the discipleship survey in the journal (page 154) for yourself.

FOLLOWERS OF CHRIST

YOU CALL US INTO YOUR CHURCH . . . TO ACCEPT THE COST AND JOY OF DISCIPLESHIP.

—STATEMENT OF FAITH

Themes

@ Following Christ is a lifelong commitment.

@ Following Christ has a cost.

@ Following Christ brings great joy.

Scriptures

JOHN 21:15–17—The risen Christ commands Peter to care for God's people.

MATTHEW 4:18–22—Jesus meets two fishers and challenges them to follow.

MARK 8:34–35—Jesus gives the ultimate challenge of discipleship: take up the cross.

LUKE 8:1–3—Mary Magdalene, Joanna, and Susanna follow Jesus as he proclaims the good news of God's reign.

Objectives for This Session

@ Explore the meaning of discipleship.

@ Hear the stories of the cost and joy of discipleship.

@ Consider the promises made in the rite of confirmation.

Session at a Glance

GATHERING

Make a graffiti wall (15 minutes)

EXPLORING

Dramatize the cost and joy of discipleship (30 minutes)

Discover a modern-day disciple's definition of discipleship

(15 minutes)

CONNECTING

Take a discipleship survey (15 minutes)

Consider the questions for the confirmands (10 minutes)

GOING

Worship together (5 minutes)

Biblical and Theological Background

For the first disciples, the rigors and sacrifices of following Christ were real. Jesus asked them to do no less than leave their life's work and familiar surroundings to become part of a ministry that changed the world. In John 21:15–17, the risen Christ confronts Simon Peter by three times asking him the question: "Simon, son of John, do you love me?" When Peter replies, "Yes!" all three times, Jesus tells him to "feed my lambs," "tend my sheep," and "feed my sheep." What do you suppose Jesus meant by these requests?

In simple terms, it means caring for and loving others. It means reaching out with the same quality of love to all people, even those different from ourselves. This kind of love, described in 1 John 4:7–12, is love incarnate through caring action. It is love demonstrated in various ways. It shows itself in those who volunteer in hospitals and clinics, those who help victims of natural disasters, and those who participate in programs to house, clothe, and feed the hungry. Often for youth, incarnate love is demonstrated to their friends in day-to-day relationships of care and affirmation. Young people whose gifts are recognized and affirmed are more likely to be motivated to use their gifts, abilities, and talents to serve others.

But there are challenges when one expresses discipleship through caring action. In the story from John 21, Peter felt hurt when Christ questioned him repeatedly. But Christ's persistent questioning underscores the seriousness of discipleship. Following Christ is a way of life, an ongoing commitment to faithfulness as disciples. The Statement of Faith makes this clear when it proclaims there is a cost to discipleship.

But the Statement of Faith gives equal emphasis to the joy of following Christ. The realities of life today may be so overwhelming to youth that it becomes imperative for churches to help them know the joys as well as the costs of serving others. They will understand Christ's demand of Peter to "tend my sheep," even if it is just a simple act of visiting an elderly, homebound friend or offering to help a family member with a project. Youth who have experienced the joy of serving others often find strength in that joy to live with grace in the struggles and difficulties of life.

The cost of discipleship is summed up in Jesus' words: "If any want to become my followers, let them deny themselves and take up their cross and follow me. For those who want to save their life will lose it, and those who lose their life for my sake and for the sake of the gospel, will save it" (Mark 8:34–35). This statement embodies the unconditional, sacrificial love that God demonstrates through Christ. It means living fully with love for ourselves and others. It means seeking ways to serve with integrity. In simple terms, it means caring for and loving others. It means reaching out with love to all people, of different races, cultures, and life experiences.

Is there anything happy, cheerful, fun about being followers of Christ? The Beatitudes tell us of "blessedness," the happiness felt upon receiving the favor of God's blessings. The follower of Christ who is committed to living the lifestyle of a disciple will enjoy the fruits of the Spirit outlined in Galatians: love, joy, peace, patience, kindness, goodness, faithfulness, gentleness, and self-control (Galatians 5:22–23).

There is also joy and peace when followers of Jesus look to the fulfillment of God's promise. The prophet Isaiah spoke of such a time of joy, when "the wolf shall dwell with the lamb" and "the earth shall be full of the knowledge of God" (Isaiah 11:6–9). In these days of chaos, violence, wars, famine, disasters, the hope that a day is coming when God shall "wipe away every tear" brings joy (Revelation 7:16–17).

Materials Needed

- Bible for each participant
- *Confirmand's Journal* for each participant
- Paper, pencils
- Newsprint, markers, tape
- Dictionary

Preparing for This Session

Read the background portion of this session and reflect on the struggles, pain, or difficulty, as well as the joys, you encountered in your journey as a disciple. Then consider some of the struggles and difficulties of the youth in your group.

You might consider having a meeting with the mentors to explore various issues of discipleship and consider the faith growth experiences that are available to those in your faith formation group.

Prepare a "Graffiti Wall" by taping three or four newsprint sheets together to cover a large portion of the wall in your meeting space. In the center write "Discipleship" in big letters. Under that, write the words from Mark 8:34–35. Underline "deny themselves," "take up the cross," and "follow me."

Gathering

MAKE A GRAFFITI WALL (15 MINUTES)

As the confirmands come into the room, direct their attention to the "Graffiti Wall." With marking pens, invite them to draw symbols, pictures, or words to illustrate what following Christ means to them.

After everyone finishes some work on the wall, call the group together. Talk about the pictures, words, or symbols that were added to the newsprint. Point out that *discipleship* comes from the word *disciple*. Have group members look up the meaning of *disciple* in the glossary at the back of their journals.

Exploring

DRAMATIZE THE COST AND JOY OF DISCIPLESHIP (30 MINUTES)

Ask group members to find John 21:15–17, Matthew 4:18–22, and Luke 8:1–3 in their Bibles. Ask them to read these three passages aloud, one at a time, in unison.

Ask confirmands to work together to dramatize each passage using the guidelines provided below. (For large groups, divide the confirmands into three smaller groups. Each group would take one scripture reading to study.)

John 21:15–17: Act out this reading with someone playing Jesus, someone playing Peter, and others playing the part of the witnesses. Have the players consider these questions as they act out the story:

- At what time of day did this conversation between Jesus and Peter happen?
- What was Jesus' question?
- How many times did he ask this question?
- How did Peter feel about being asked this question? Why?
- What do you think Jesus means by "feed my lambs" or "tend my sheep"?

Matthew 4:18–20: Act out this story with Jesus, Simon Peter, Andrew, James, John, and Zebedee. If your group has fewer than six members, have some take more than one part. Consider:

- What is the setting of this story?
- What type of work or vocation is described here?
- What is the relationship between the people involved in this story?
- What do you think Jesus meant when he said, "I will make you fish for people"?

Luke 8:1–3: Dramatize this reading as if it were an "On the Scene" report being produced by an investigative news reporter. The reporter could be interviewing Mary Magdalene, Joanna, Susanna, and other people from the cities and villages where Jesus preached and healed. You will need a news reporter, camera operator, the women, and other witnesses. Consider:

- What type of places did Jesus go?
- What was he doing there?
- Who were his companions?
- Why were they following Jesus?

DISCOVER A MODERN-DAY DISCIPLE'S DEFINITION OF DISCIPLESHIP (15 MINUTES)

Provide some background about Dietrich Bonhoeffer, a modern-day disciple. Bonhoeffer was a Lutheran pastor and leader in the Confessing Church in Germany at the time of Hitler's Third Reich. This church group spoke out against the injustice and terror instituted by the Nazis before and during World War II. In 1943 Bonhoeffer and several others were arrested for plotting to kill Hitler. While Bonhoeffer was in prison, he wrote many letters and articles that people today still read. In 1945 he was hanged in a concentration camp. Refer the confirmands to their journals for his description of the qualities of a disciple; he used Jesus' words from Matthew 5:3–12, called the Beatitudes, as a guide.

TAKE A DISCIPLESHIP SURVEY (15 MINUTES)

This activity may help confirmands connect discipleship with their lives. Have them find the survey in their journals on page 154. They were to log their activities of the past week and wait to complete the cost/joy column at this session. If they did not complete the situation column, allow some time for that to happen. Then discuss each situation and ask the group to talk about the costs and joys in dealing with each.

CONSIDER THE QUESTIONS FOR THE CONFIRMANDS (10 MINUTES)

In the rite of confirmation the question is asked, "Do you promise, by the grace of God, to be Christ's disciple, to follow in the way of our Savior, to resist oppression and evil, to show love and justice, and to witness to the work and word of Jesus Christ as best you are able?" Ask group members to discuss how they think their experiences of the cost and joy of discipleship will influence their answer to that question?

Going

WORSHIP TOGETHER (5 MINUTES)

Ask the group to sit in a circle and join in prayer. Invite group members to offer words of hope to express what they wish for themselves, for others in the group, and for the world. As a leader, you may wish to start the prayer. Invite the youth to speak spontaneously, whenever they wish, not in any particular order. Remind them that as they struggle to be faithful followers of Christ, they may experience the joys of discipleship when they work along with others in the church.

When everyone who wished to do so has prayed, pass the peace by saying, "The peace of Christ be with you," "Peace be with you," or "Peace" and shaking hands, hugging, or whatever is comfortable.

Additional Activity

VIEW VIDEOS

There are many good video resources telling stories of persons involved in both the cost and joy of discipleship. Arrange to borrow or rent one of these resources and plan an additional session around it. Some possibilities include:

- "How to Get Blessed without Sneezing" (30 minutes)—Ecufilm, 810 Twelfth Ave. S., Nashville TN 37203, 800-251-4091

    Description: Several 4–5 minute stories of a person facing trials of daily life and characters he meets who are caught up in our culture's way of seeing things.

- "Hawaii Street People" (1 of 3 parts, 30 minutes)—Available for rent from United Methodist Church, Hawaii District Resource Center, 20 S. Vineyard Blvd., Honolulu HI 96813, 808-536-1865

    Description: Rev. Claude DuTeil, who established the Hawaii Institute of Human Services, comments on the plight of Honolulu's street people. This video shows personal interviews with the homeless and the work of HIHS, where food, health care, and lodging are provided.

- "Bridging the Divides, Seeking Transformation" (approximately 40 minutes)—Available free from United Church of Christ Resources, 700 Prospect Avenue, Cleveland OH 44115-1100, 1-800-325-7061 or 1-800-537-3394

    Description: This video tells the story of the founding of the American Missionary Association (a vital part of the United Church of Christ) in 1846. It contains four segments: the Amistad Event, Ministries of Justice, Today in the United Church of Christ, and Facing the 21st Century.

Connecting with the Congregation

INVITE A VISITOR

Invite a person from your community to attend this session and share a story that illustrates the consequences of following Christ. It may be a grandparent or relative of a confirmand, a longtime church member, or someone who is a respected member of your community. Ask this person to describe both the cost and the joy of discipleship.

Thinking About This Session

What did the discipleship survey activity reveal to you about the experiences of your group? What evidence do you have that indicates that the group is discovering the meaning of discipleship?

Planning Ahead

Read the next session design and gather the needed materials, including current copies of *In Mission: A Calendar of Prayer for the United Church of Christ*, if possible.

WITNESS AND SERVICE

YOU CALL US INTO YOUR CHURCH . . . TO BE YOUR SERVANTS IN THE SERVICE OF OTHERS, TO PROCLAIM THE GOSPEL TO ALL THE WORLD, AND RESIST THE POWERS OF EVIL.

—STATEMENT OF FAITH

Themes

- A disciple of Jesus Christ is an active servant in the world.
- Faith is made real through one's choices and actions.
- Choosing life and resisting evil are part of discipleship.

Scriptures

JAMES 2:14–17—Faith and works together bring life.

JOHN 13:3–15—Jesus washes the disciples' feet.

MATTHEW 28:16–20—Jesus sends the disciples out to the nations.

1 JOHN 3:17–18—God's love calls for words and action.

Objectives for This Session

- Discover the call in Scripture to witness and service.
- Explore stories of modern-day servants of God.
- Participate in a handwashing ritual.

Session at a Glance

GATHERING

Paraphrase scripture readings (15 minutes)

EXPLORING

Discover stories of people in witness and service (20 minutes)

CONNECTING

Consider what it means to serve (20 minutes)

Consider Jesus' actions (15 minutes)

GOING

Worship together (20 minutes)

Biblical and Theological Background

Making faith real through one's actions is the focus of this session. People are influenced by those whom they trust and believe. We come to trust and believe others through relationship and observation. If another person acts on what he or she says, we begin to place trust in that person. On the other hand, if a person says one thing but does something completely different, then believing and trusting that person are difficult, if not impossible.

The disciples observed Jesus' ministry. They were firsthand witnesses to Jesus' actions as he preached, taught, and healed. As the disciples traveled with him, they began to trust and believe in him because he lived and practiced what he taught. Through his words and actions the disciples began to understand the new covenant that Jesus came to establish. As they observed Jesus' life, the disciples began to understand that they too should be true to themselves and to God.

Jesus expected the disciples to be witnesses to God's love to the world, and encouraged them to live as faithful people acting on their own understanding of God's love. In Matthew 26:16–20, Jesus commissions (sends) the disciples to "go and make disciples of all nations, baptizing . . . and teaching them to obey everything that I have commanded you." The disciples were sent to be witnesses of Jesus Christ through their words and actions so that others might also become believers.

The disciples' lives were changed because of what they saw in the person of Jesus. Today lives are changed because persons see the love of God made real in another person. The influence of other people in our lives is important. Perhaps you can think of a way in which your life is different because of another person. Family members, friends, teachers, peers, and sometimes even strangers all help shape us and influence how we live our lives. The Christian faith grows and flourishes because people are willing to witness in word and deed to God's amazing love in Christ.

Actions that make one's devotion to Christ real lie at the center of faith formation. Christianity's power emerges in the world when followers not only "talk the talk, but also walk the walk."

The letter to James is an important testimony in helping Christians understand the connection between faith and works, between witness and service. James is writing to those who have heard about Jesus and have already received the gift of faith through grace. He writes to encourage them to live a life of active service. The letter makes clear the fact that inward, private faith that has no expression in outward action toward others is, at best, empty faith. James 2:14–17 describes the situation where someone without two of the most basic necessities of life, clothing and food, is encountered by a "faithful" person who offers only words of encouragement rather than clothing and food. This leads the writer to conclude that "faith by itself, if it has no works, is dead."

In the church, one of the main tasks of the community is to enable people to distinguish good from evil, death from life. This process is of critical importance to the mission of the church. Young people may be strengthened, nurtured, and challenged by becoming involved in the struggle to discern how one's actions address the power and presence of evil in their own lives and in the life of the community. As servants, our lives and our own ministries bear witness to God's love and life-giving nature. It is through our lives, through our love in action, that evil meets its strongest resistance. Jesus overcame evil and temptation in his own life through his words, but even more powerfully through his actions. This love in action is made concrete through the exploration of the account of the footwashing.

Jesus offers an example of love in action by washing the disciples' feet (John 13:3–15). The roads of Jesus' day were not paved. In dry weather they were dusty, and in wet weather they were muddy. The footgear worn in those days (if any) was sandals, which were mainly soles held on the foot by a few straps. Because of this there was always a basin or jar of water near the entrance to a house for washing one's feet prior to entering the household. To offer this to a guest was an expression of hospitality. The job of footwashing was dirty work and was most often performed by one of the servants.

When Jesus began to wash his disciples' feet, they were confused, amazed, and startled. This humble demonstration of self-giving love was a simple act that the disciples remembered long after Jesus' death and resurrection. Jesus showed them a new way to view their relationship to the world by taking on the role of a servant.

Not many of us would choose to be a servant—the job description is not appealing. In today's world many people live expecting to get something out of life. The Christian faith is built on the understanding that it is what we give, not what we get, that is important. The church community encourages its members to use their gifts in the service of others.

This is not to say that there aren't any rewards in serving. An active disciple is engaged in bringing God's hope and love to a hurting world. There is reward in knowing that we are doing what we believe God wants us to do. When we engage in acts of kindness and love in partnership with others (mission), a sense of community and togetherness often develops among the participants. When the church works as a community for good in the world, its members often grow closer to one another and those whom they serve.

In this session the participants will have an opportunity to explore together the nature of witness and service as it appears in the scripture texts and as it relates to their own lives. They will have opportunities to witness other servants in action, to share ways in which they are already engaged in service, and to provide new ways in which they may serve.

Materials Needed

- Bible for each participant
- *Confirmand's Journal* for each participant
- Cassette tape or CD of quiet music
- Cassette or CD player
- Basins for water, towels
- Newsprint or posterboard, markers
- Current copies of *In Mission: A Calendar of Prayer for the United Church of Christ*, if possible

Preparing for This Session

Read the scriptures for this session: James 2:14–17, John 13:3–15, Matthew 28:16–20, and 1 John 3:17–18. Reflect upon your own sense of servanthood and witness to Jesus Christ. How does your own life bear witness to your faith? Are there people in your life who you look to (or have looked to) as examples of faithful witness? How does our culture inhibit and promote servanthood? How do you understand the presence of evil in the world? In what ways are you called upon in your daily life to resist evil?

Note: Be sensitive to the issues that may surface in the exploration. There may be members of the group who have experienced (or are experiencing) serious evil in their lives, such as sexual or physical abuse. Be prepared to refer such persons to help in dealing with issues. Some good referral sources may include pastors, therapists, social workers, and children and youth services.

Set up for the handwashing ritual that will be a part of the closing worship (see "Going," page 166). Ideally, set up the basins and towels in a nearby room separate from your meeting space. Choose a room for the handwashing that is comfortable and can tolerate a little spilled water. Make a sign that says, "Faith without works is dead," and display the sign in your meeting space so all can see it.

Gathering

PARAPHRASE SCRIPTURE READINGS (15 MINUTES)

Welcome the group. Ask the youth to take turns reading aloud the following scriptures: James 2:14–17, Matthew 28:16–20, 1 John 3:1–18. Then work as a group or divide the group into three to retell each scripture in their own words and write it on newsprint. Then consider the question for each text: What does this scripture say about witness and service? Make a list for each on the newsprint.

Exploring

DISCOVER STORIES OF PEOPLE INVOLVED IN WITNESS AND SERVICE (20 MINUTES)

Have the youth turn to page 160 in the *Confirmand's Journal* to review the stories of persons involved in witness and service and resisting the powers of evil. In the space provided in the journal, have them respond by writing an imaginary letter to one of the persons featured in the stories.

If possible, have current copies of *In Mission: A Calendar of Prayer for the United Church of Christ* for the confirmands to read about more witness and service stories in the United Church of Christ.

Next ask the confirmands to look at the log of activities they kept for Session 17, "Followers of Christ." Look at each one and take a moment to remember doing it. Read your comments on how you felt at the time. Make a checkmark next to all the ones you did to help others. If some did not keep a log, ask them to think about their activities in the last couple of days and make a quick list of what they did, then circle the items that helped others.

Ask the confirmands to think about why they did each activity. Was it something someone expected of them? Did they want to do it? How did they know it was the right thing to do? Pose the question to them:

@ If someone you helped asked you, "Why did you do this?" what would you say?

Connecting

CONSIDER WHAT IT MEANS TO SERVE (20 MINUTES)

Introduce this experience by describing what confirmands are asked to promise in the rite of confirmation:

Do you promise, by the grace of God, to be Christ's disciple, to follow in the way of our Savior, to resist oppression and evil, to show love and justice, and to witness to the work and word of Jesus Christ as best as you are able?

Then lead a discussion about this using the questions listed here and in the journal (page 163):

@ Who are some of the people you turn to as examples of servants or disciples of Christ?

@ What is it about this person(s) that encourages you to be a servant?

@ What value does our culture put on service?

@ How does our culture encourage service? discourage service?

@ How are witness and service connected to the practice of resisting evil?

@ In your own congregation, what ways are persons your age encouraged to serve?

@ What do you wish you could do?

@ Where do you hear the call to serve in your church?

@ Where do you hear the call to serve in the world?

@ How has your own servanthood deepened your faith?

CONSIDER JESUS' ACTIONS (15 MINUTES)

Have the group read the passage on footwashing found in John 13:3–15. Use the information in the background section to talk with the group about ways this act of Jesus was so significant.

Going

WORSHIP TOGETHER (20 MINUTES)

Plan to do this exercise in the sanctuary or in a worshipful setting. Have the youth sit in a circle around the basin of water and towel. You may wish to start in order to set an example for the others to follow. Quiet music played in the background may help contribute to a prayerful atmosphere. Turn to the person on your right and hold his or her hands over the basin. With your hands, scoop up some water and pour it over the hands of your partner. Then, taking the towel, gently dry your partner's hands. That person then turns to the person on his or her right and repeats the washing ritual until all have participated.

Close by singing or saying together "Called as Partners in Christ's Service," found on page 230 of the journal and page 236 of this guide.

Additional Activities

HEAR STORIES OF WITNESS AND SERVICE

Invite to your meeting a person who works or volunteers in the community in a servant role: a hospice worker, a family counselor, an HIV/AIDS support worker, a physical therapist in a rehabilitation center, and so on. Have the visitor tell not only what he or she does, but why he or she is engaged in this ministry. Have that person talk about the joys and the challenges of the work.

WRITE LETTERS TO PEOPLE IN MISSION

After reviewing the stories of mission and service in the current copy of *In Mission*, have the confirmands write a letter to a person, church, or agency whose ministry is profiled. Some people may be contacted via electronic mail as well.

CONDUCT A SERVICE OF FOOTWASHING

If desired, your group could have a footwashing service for the "Going" activity. The preparation is similar to the handwashing service. The *United Church of Christ Book of Worship* has an order for footwashing that you could use and adapt for this experience.

Connecting with the Congregation

WRITE THANK-YOU NOTES

Have the confirmands write thank-you notes to those people in your church and/or community who are engaged in servantlike activities, such as church volunteers, food servers, people who are engaged in volunteer work in the community, emergency medical technicians, police, firefighters, doctors, nurses, and so on.

Thinking About This Session

In what ways have the confirmands shown that they understand the role of a disciple? In what ways are they showing their faith through their actions? How can you encourage them to be "God's servants in the service of others" as the Statement of Faith instructs? How do you live out this call in your life?

Planning Ahead

Read the next session and gather needed materials, including a videotape of a baptism, if possible, and copies of the baptism and communion liturgies used by your congregation. Make arrangements to meet in the worship space for part of the session. Invite the leaders who will be helping with the session. Let the confirmands know if visitors will be present.

THE SACRAMENTS

You call us into your church . . . to share in Christ's baptism and eat at his table, to join him in his passion and victory.

—Statement of Faith

Themes

- Our covenant with God is established in baptism.
- Our covenant with God is remembered and renewed in Holy Communion.
- The sacraments of baptism and Holy Communion signify God's grace and identify God's people.
- The sacraments of baptism and Holy Communion unite us with Christians in all times and places.

Scriptures

Matthew 3:1–17—The account of the baptism of Jesus by John is told.

Luke 22:1–20—Jesus eats the Last Supper with his disciples.

Matthew 28:16–20—Jesus commissions the disciples to baptize and teach.

1 Corinthians 11:23–26—Paul writes about Jesus' meal with the disciples.

Objectives for This Session

- Discover the meanings of the sacraments.
- Review your church's practices of the sacraments.

Session at a Glance

GATHERING

Consider baptism practices in your congregation (15 minutes)

EXPLORING

Consider the meanings of baptism (30 minutes)

Consider the meanings of Holy Communion (30 minutes)

CONNECTING

Write in the journals (10 minutes)

GOING

Worship together (5 minutes)

Biblical and Theological Background

The Statement of Faith affirms that God calls us into the church "to share in Christ's baptism and eat at his table." Both baptism and Holy Communion are central in the lives of Christians, since they express and nurture the covenantal relationship we have with God through Jesus Christ.

In the United Church of Christ, as in other Protestant churches, we celebrate baptism and Holy Communion as sacraments. "In accordance with the teaching of our Lord and the practice prevailing among evangelical Christians, [the United Church of Christ] recognizes two sacraments: Baptism and the Lord's Supper or Holy Communion."[1] Their importance derives, in part, from the fact that they were commissioned by Jesus (Matthew 28:19 and 1 Corinthians 11:23–26). The two sacraments are outward and visible signs of God's grace. They affirm the continuing acts of God out of which the identity and vocation of God's people are shaped into "the mind of Christ" (1 Corinthians 2:16).

The sacrament of baptism celebrates new life in Jesus Christ. "In the United Church of Christ, baptism is the rite of initiation into Christ's church."[2] It is the moment when one comes or is brought forward and, with the help and support of the faith community, affirms a covenant with God through Jesus Christ and the Holy Spirit. Vows are taken and the service of baptism is performed.

Traditionally, baptism is administered with water "in the name of the Father, the Son, and the Holy Spirit," although the earliest baptismal formula said simply, "in the name of Jesus." Within the United Church of Christ there has been interest in expressing the baptismal formula in inclusive language. Some local churches use the form: "I baptize you in the name of the Father and of the Son and of the Holy Spirit, one God, Mother of us all."[3] "The water used is the symbol of washing, and washing means renewal, so that the total rite comes to mean that the person baptized is thereby adopted into the new life which is hid with Christ, and Christ's people, in God."[4]

Persons of any age may be baptized. When infants and very young children are brought forward for baptism, their parents or guardians and sponsors take vows on their behalf. When older children or adults are baptized, they may answer for themselves. Those in the congregation also vow to support and nurture the newly baptized Christians.

Through the sacrament of Holy Communion we renew our covenant with God. "[It] is regarded in the United Church of Christ, as generally throughout Christendom, as the central act of Christian worship. . . . Its form is that of the high moment of any family in any age in any place—the gathering together for a common meal."[5]

As in baptism, Holy Communion uses outward and visible symbols as a sign of God's grace. It recalls the entire history and hope of God's people who are fed and celebrate God's liberating activity. Here bread and cup symbolize Christ's body and blood. During Holy Communion we are reminded that Jesus came for us and our salvation. We remember his life, death, resurrection, and the promise to us of eternal life. Holy Communion celebrates the gift God gives us in Jesus and celebrates the new covenant we have together in Christ Jesus. When the sacraments are celebrated in worship, they bind us together with Christians in all times and places and remind us of the coming of the reign of God.

Christians can be baptized by a variety of methods. Some baptize by immersion (complete submersion in water), some by affusion (pouring water), some by sprinkling (touching with water). Some congregations believe baptism is appropriate only at certain ages (i.e., infants, youth) while others baptize persons of any age. In any case, we affirm that there is "one Lord, one faith, one baptism" (Ephesians 4:5). When one is baptized, he or she does not become a United Methodist, an Episcopalian, a Roman Catholic, or even a United Church of Christ member. One becomes a Christian.

Similarly, all Christians celebrate Holy Communion, though the manner and understanding of the celebration may vary. Some see the meal as a memorial, reminding them of the Last Supper Jesus celebrated with the disciples. Others see it as a sign of Christ's presence now in the bread and cup and in the congregation. In the meal itself, some churches use individual cups; some use a common cup. Some use small cubes of bread; some use unleavened bread or wafers; some use a whole loaf of bread. Some congregations serve Holy Communion in the pews; others invite worshipers forward to receive at a rail or at stations. In the United Church of Christ there is a wide range of practices.

It is important for confirmands to learn about the variety of ways in which congregations celebrate the sacraments. Some denominations offer Holy Communion to baptized or confirmed members only; others invite anyone who desires Christ's presence; still others see confirmation as a prerequisite for receiving Holy Communion. What is the practice in your congregation? Is special preparation necessary before one may receive this sacrament?

The sacraments are central to our Christian identity. They are particular expressions of God's covenant promises to us. They come from Jesus' life, teaching, and ministry, ordained by him as a means of spiritual rebirth and new life. They have been celebrated, in various forms, since the beginning of Christianity.

The sacraments help us remember what binds us together as Christians, not what separates us into denominations. Long after each of us is gone, Christians all over the world will be establishing their covenant with God through baptism and remembering and renewing it through Holy Communion.

Materials Needed

- Bible for each participant
- *Confirmand's Journal* for each participant
- Copies of the baptismal and communion liturgies used by your congregation
- *United Church of Christ Book of Worship*
- The communion ware used by your congregation
- The baptistery or baptismal font or bowl
- Writing materials
- Video player and videotape of a baptism, if possible

Preparing for This Session

Read Matthew 3:1–17 and Luke 22:1–20. Reflect on your own experience with baptism and Holy Communion. In what ways do you find the sacraments meaningful? What does it mean to you to think of baptism and communion as ways to connect to Christians in all times and places? How has the communion service ministered to you?

If there are aspects of the sacraments that you would like to know more about, consult other church leaders before the session.

It is possible that not all the confirmands have been baptized. Some may not know whether or not they have been baptized. If you do not already know which have and which have not, take time to find out. Inquire with sensitivity. Make sure the pastor and other leaders know who will be baptized prior to the rite of confirmation.

If possible, have a videotape of a baptismal service to show to the confirmands during this session. Write the meanings of communion on newsprint and have them ready to display later in the session.

Arrange for the pastor(s), deacons, and others who assist with baptism and Holy Communion to be present for the session. Let the confirmands know ahead of time that they will be there.

Arrange to meet in the worship space of your congregation for part of the session. Make sure the communion table is in place and the baptistery or baptismal font or bowl is visible.

Gathering

CONSIDER BAPTISM PRACTICES IN YOUR CONGREGATION (15 MINUTES)

Introduce the pastor(s), deacons, and other lay leaders to the confirmands.

Read or have a volunteer read aloud Matthew 3:1–17, the baptism of Jesus by John. View a videotape of a baptismal service in your congregation, if available. If you do not have a videotape available, ask the confirmands to describe what happens during a baptism in your church. Involve all in relating their own experiences of watching and/or participating in services of baptism. Ask confirmands and leaders to tell stories of their own baptisms that they may remember or have heard from others.

Exploring

CONSIDER THE MEANINGS OF BAPTISM (30 MINUTES)

Go to your congregation's worship space to examine the baptistery, baptismal font, or bowl. Fill the font with water. Invite the confirmands to touch it. Have available copies of the baptismal liturgy used by your congregation. Refer to the section called "Baptism is . . ." on page 168 in the *Confirmand's Journal*. Review the prayer with the group. Then look at the questions asked of the candidates or their parents or guardians and the promises made by the congregation. Ask the group to discuss these questions:

@ Which promises asked of the candidates, parents or guardians, sponsors, and congregation at baptism do you think are the easiest to keep? Why?

@ Which promises asked of the candidates, parents or guardians, sponsors, and congregation at baptism are the most difficult to keep? Why?

CONSIDER THE MEANINGS OF HOLY COMMUNION (30 MINUTES)

Move now to the communion table. Have someone read the account of the Last Supper from Luke 22:1–20. With the help of the pastor(s), deacons, and lay leaders, prepare the table as it would be for a communion service.

If there is a special room or area used to prepare communion, take the confirmands there and show them where the communion ware is kept. Take the communion ware to the communion table. Point out the items that are used. If the items were given as memorials, or have any particular history, research this and share the information with the group. Invite the confirmands to touch and handle the items, as appropriate. Work together as a group and set the table up the way it would be for Holy Communion.

Who usually does this? Where does the bread go? Where is the cup? What else goes on the table? Where do people stand?

Distribute copies of the communion liturgy used by your congregation. Refer to the section called "Holy Communion is . . ." on page 172 of the *Confirmand's Journal*. Read 1 Corinthians 11:16–20. Look at the portions of the communion liturgy included in the journal, pointing out the communion prayer, including the consecration of the bread and cup, breaking the bread and pouring the cup (also known as the words of institution), sharing the elements, and the prayer of thanksgiving. Compare the liturgy to the words of 1 Corinthians 11:16–20. Then consider these questions about communion:

- How often does your congregation celebrate Holy Communion? (Practices vary throughout the United Church of Christ from weekly to monthly to every three months or on special holidays.)
- Where does the communion happen in the order of worship?
- Who is included? Why?
- How are the bread and cup served? (In the pews or by coming forward; using a common cup or individual cups; by intinction, where the bread is dipped in the juice and eaten individually.)
- Is grape juice or wine or both used?
- What kind of bread is used? Why?
- What is the mood in church when you celebrate Holy Communion? Why do you suppose this is? How is the mood conveyed?

Ask all those present who have participated in or observed the sacrament of Holy Communion to think of some of the meanings they find in the sacrament. Display the newsprint on which the possible meanings of communion are printed. Have extra newsprint available to add other meanings if necessary:

- Remembering Jesus and his words: "Do this in remembrance of me."
- Experiencing the presence of Christ.
- Receiving the assurance of forgiveness for sins and grace to live into the future.
- Being a part of the "body of Christ," the church.
- Giving thanks for the presence of Christ. ("Eucharist," another word for communion, is the Greek word for giving thanks.)
- Making a commitment to be a Christian and participate in the mission of the church.
- Uniting with Christians in all times and places.

Ask if there are any more they would like to add. Then ask the group to review the meanings that are listed by taking turns reading them aloud. Discuss with the group which of the meanings of communion are most significant for them now and why. Then explore which meanings they hope will become important to them in the future and why.

Connecting

WRITE IN THE JOURNALS (10 MINUTES)

Ask the confirmands to spread out in the worship area with their journals and find a private space. Tell them the next ten minutes are for prayer, meditation, or journaling. Ask them to think about baptism and Holy Communion and about the covenantal relationship with God that the sacraments make known. Ask them to think about their own faith and relationship to God. Invite them to reflect, pray, meditate, write, draw, or doodle anywhere on the journal pages for this session, paying attention to words or ideas that stir their thoughts and imagination.

Going

WORSHIP TOGETHER (5 MINUTES)

Conclude by offering a prayer in your own words. Then sing or say together the words of the communion hymn "Let Us Break Bread Together" found on page 220 in the *Confirmand's Journal* and on page 226 in this guide.

Additional Activities

VISIT OTHER CHURCHES

You may wish to visit other churches that are different from your own and learn about their traditions and ways of celebrating the sacraments. You could attend worship or speak with the worship leaders, noting the similarities and the differences in practices.

CONDUCT INTERVIEWS

Find a time to interview your pastor, a deacon, an older youth, or any other member of the congregation to ask about baptism and Holy Communion. Begin by asking the interviewee what he or she remembers (or has heard) about his or her own baptism and what participating in Holy Communion means to him or her.

Connecting with the Congregation

PREPARE THE COMMUNION ELEMENTS

If it is possible, your group could offer to prepare the communion elements for your congregation or help to serve them. Baking bread can be a group activity. So can filling (and washing) cups, if your congregation uses these.

Thinking About This Session

Striving to understand the nature and grace of the sacraments can be a lifelong endeavor. What signs do you see that show that the confirmands are on their way to greater depths of understanding of baptism and Holy Communion? What meanings seemed to be most important to them? Look for ways to encourage their participation in worship and celebrating the sacraments.

Planning Ahead

Read the next session and gather needed materials, including a candy bar or dollar bill for each person.

What's best in life comes to us from God, not as a result of our efforts or talents, but by sheer gift.

Our Response

AFFIRMING faith

Our

GOD'S GIFTS AND OUR RESPONSE

FORGIVENESS AND GRACE

YOU PROMISE TO ALL WHO TRUST YOU FORGIVENESS OF SINS AND FULLNESS OF GRACE.

—STATEMENT OF FAITH

Themes

- Grace abounds and we have much for which to be grateful.
- God's grace is sufficient; God's forgiveness is always available.
- God's grace doesn't prevent suffering; it accompanies the one who suffers.

Scriptures

MATTHEW 20:1–16—Jesus tells the parable of the laborers in the vineyard.

COLOSSIANS 3:12–17—God's chosen ones are to clothe themselves with love, forgive one another, and let Christ's peace rule in their hearts.

Objectives for This Session

- Explore the meaning of God's grace.
- Create a visual expression of how God's chosen ones are called to live.
- Give thanks to God for the gift of grace.

Session at a Glance

GATHERING

Give thanks together (15 minutes)

EXPLORING

Hear a modern parable (20 minutes)

Learn a parable from the Bible (20 minutes)

CONNECTING

Make a mural (30 minutes)

Suggest a journaling activity (2 minutes)

GOING

Worship together (3 minutes)

Biblical and Theological Background

When we read the parable of the laborers in the vineyard (Matthew 20:1–16), who among us doesn't immediately identify with the workers who began at break of day? Does it seem somehow wrong that those who showed up at the end of the day were paid the same as those who worked hard all day long? Does it make you angry that some people seem to have gotten something for nothing?

This, of course, was probably what Jesus intended in telling the story. It doesn't seem right when some people are rewarded in a way that they don't appear to deserve. Imagine a student in school who gets an A without doing the work, or a part-time worker who makes exactly what a full-time worker makes.

It's natural for us to identify with those who worked all day but are not given anything extra for their additional labor. But this parable puts before us a different question: "Are you the ones who have worked all day, or are you really the ones who began about five o'clock?"

This story is about a landowner who just happens to be extraordinarily generous with those who do the work—even if they've done very little. The sense we get, as we read it, is that this is the way God is as well. God gives to us, not on the basis of what we've earned, but simply by a standard of divine generosity—a generosity that gives without regard to what is actually earned.

For most of us, the unspoken assumption is that good things happen as you work for them. You get good grades if you study diligently. You make a lot of money if you apply yourself. You're respected if you act nice and do things for others. What's good comes to us, we assume, only if we earn it.

This parable turns that assumption on its head. What's best in life comes to us from God, it says, not as a result of our efforts or talents, but by sheer gift. Grace makes itself known in many ways. Sometimes it's a healing we've experienced, or being forgiven some terrible wrong; sometimes it's a vision that comes seemingly out of nowhere to remind us that we're loved; sometimes it is an overwhelming sense of peace or joy that we cannot explain. These things do not happen because we cause them to. They are gifts that come to us whether we merit them, whether we deserve them. They are gifts of God.

We can help confirmands in the group identify moments in their lives when they have experienced grace. The concept of grace is difficult for many to understand. Not until we become aware of it in our own lives does it begin to make sense. In a world in which "there's no such thing as a free lunch"—a world in which nearly everything desirable must either be earned or paid for—the concept of grace may seem utterly foreign to the youth.

The task of this session is to help confirmands identify grace in their lives—grace that comes to us as a gift from God—like the workers in the vineyard who received the wages they needed to live, no matter how long they worked. All of us have had experiences of grace. The challenge is to identify these experiences as such. Naming and celebrating graces, in what is often an ungracious world, may prove to be transforming.

However, the presence of grace (and of God) does *not* mean the absence of suffering. Recognizing the grace that has been given to us does not mean that we will be spared all pain. Being human means that trauma, despair, grief, and failure cannot be evaded. What can be affirmed is that grace is often known most profoundly in the midst of pain or despair.

It is through grace that we receive God's forgiveness. The Bible's major themes are that God forgives our sin and gives us a way to live despite our being separated from each other, from what is best in ourselves, and from God. As we discovered earlier, sin can be defined as *separation*. The many things we as human beings do that we consider wrong are a result of this fundamental separation. It is God's grace that frees us to live. This is not to say that anything goes, that whatever we do—no matter how mean or insensitive—is acceptable in God's sight. It is not. But as we confess our sin, as we acknowledge the separations that are part of our lives, God gives us a new beginning. When we confess our sins, forgiveness, through grace, is offered whether we "deserve" it or not.

Finally, what makes an act gracious or forgiving in our interactions with others? If it is done freely and generously, without regard to whether someone has earned it or deserved it, it is an act of grace and forgiveness. It might be worthwhile to ponder how each of us may live as givers of grace and forgiveness in our lives, offering to others without demanding anything in return.

Materials Needed

- ℮ Bible for each participant
- ℮ *Confirmand's Journal* for each participant
- ℮ Dollar bills or candy bars

Preparing for This Session

Before leading this session, take some time to identify experiences of grace in your own life. Reflect on the ways you have been blessed. Bring to mind occasions when you've been forgiven. Recall and give thanks for special insights you may have gleaned, a vocation that you have discerned, a healing you've experienced, love that has sustained or transformed you.

It is also important to listen intently to the parable of the laborers in the vineyard (Matthew 20:1–16) and to try to hear what it is saying to your own life and community.

During this session the group will role-play the parable of the workers in the vineyard. Read through the introductory script for the role play so that you are familiar with the modern situation in which it is set.

Gathering

GIVE THANKS TOGETHER (15 MINUTES)

Welcome each person. Gather in a circle. Invite persons to name something in their lives for which they are
grateful. Leaders might begin this. Try to have participants talk of recent events or current conditions
rather than long-ago events or conditions. Also encourage responses that are specific.

Offer a prayer in which God is thanked for those specific blessings (or as many as may be remembered).

Sing or say the words to a hymn about God's grace called "Spirit of the Living God." It is found on page 222
in the *Confirmand's Journal* and page 228 of this guide.

Exploring

HEAR A MODERN PARABLE (20 MINUTES)

Ask confirmands and leaders to act out the following parable that is found in the journal on page 182. Have
someone in the group read the parable. Tell the group that they are going to dramatize it themselves.

*God's special world is like this. The owner of a video store had a number of full-time workers whom she paid
pretty well. One year, because the Christmas rush was coming, early in December she hired extra workers for
the season. She promised to pay them what was right. A week later, and again two weeks later, she did the
same thing. Finally, on the morning of Christmas Eve, anticipating a frenetic day, she did the same thing. "I
need you to work in the store too" she said.*

*When that last day before Christmas had finally ended, she called all her workers to her to pay them. First
she paid those she had hired that day. She paid them as if they had been there for the entire month. Then she paid
those who had come two weeks ago, then those who had started three weeks ago. Each of them also got a full
month's wage.*

*When the full-time workers came, they expected they would receive more. But each of them received what
the others had been given. And when they looked at their paychecks, they bad-mouthed their boss, saying,
"The last people you hired worked only a day, and you have made them equal to those of us who worked so
hard for the whole month."*

*But the owner said to them, "I'm not doing anything wrong to you. Didn't we agree on your pay? Take
what belongs to you and go. I choose to give to the ones I hired today the same as I give to you. Am I not
allowed to do what I choose with what belongs to me? Or are you envious because I am generous? So the last
will be first, and the first will be last."*

Have confirmands and leaders role-play the various parts. Have someone play the store owner, a few play the full-time employees, one or two play those hired later, another one or two play those hired still later, and the remainder play those hired at the end. This could be acted out with as few as three people in a small group: a store owner, someone hired early, and someone hired late. Act out the way each hiring might have happened. What do the employees ask for in terms of pay? What does the employer promise?

At pay time, let the owner have enough dollar bills or candy bars so that each worker will get one. (Be sure to have enough "extra" so that those not playing workers in the role play may have one at the end of the experience.) What kind of grumbling goes on? What do the various employees feel? Encourage imaginative, honest dialogue and action.

After the role play, have a discussion about what was going on. Let each character express her or his perspective on the situation. List on newsprint the feelings of each character. What was it like for the employer to hear all this resentment? What was it like to receive thanks, if any was expressed? Then have everyone, including the audience if there is any, reflect on the scene.

@ What was it like to be one of the workers who was there from the beginning who didn't receive any more than a worker who arrived on the last day?

@ What was it like to work for one day and be paid so extravagantly?

@ What was it like to be an employer who rewards so generously?

LEARN A PARABLE FROM THE BIBLE (20 MINUTES)

Now read the parable from Matthew 20:1–16. How is this parable similar to the modern-day story? How is it different? What feelings are the same among the characters? What feelings are different?

Connecting

MAKE A MURAL (30 MINUTES)

Now read Colossians 3:12–17 by taking turns and having each person in the group read a verse. If not everyone has a turn, go to the beginning and repeat the passage.

Now ask the group to make a mural that shows their church or community living as the scripture reading describes. They may draw scenes that are already happening around them as well as those they wish could happen.

When the mural is completed, have the group decide how they will share it with the rest of the church, such as at a worship service, during a fellowship time, or at a committee meeting.

SUGGEST A JOURNALING ACTIVITY (2 MINUTES)

Point out the "Questions to Consider" in the journal (page 183) and suggest that the confirmands spend some time with this activity following the session.

Going

WORSHIP TOGETHER (3 MINUTES)

End the session by joining in the following litany found in the *Confirmand's Journal* (page 186):

One: *Let us pray. O God, we give thanks today for your incredible blessings,*

All: *For the bounties of earth and sky,*

One: *For the great generosity of family, friends, teachers, and church members,*

All: *For the privileges that we enjoy.*

One: *We give thanks, as well, for the power of forgiveness.*

All: *Open our eyes and hearts, so that we may see how much comes to us by sheer gift.*

One: *And help us to live always as grateful people. Amen.*

All: *Amen.*

Connecting with the Congregation

CREATE A PERMANENT MURAL

Seek permission from the appropriate church committee to re-create the mural as a permanent display on a wall in the church. Involve others who have artistic abilities to help with the project.

Thinking About This Session

How well did the group embrace the concept of God's grace? What have you observed that helps you to know that the members of the group are learning to trust God?

Planning Ahead

Read the next session and gather the needed supplies, including a globe or world map. If you choose to do the additional activity or make a peace pole, you will need a chocolate candy bar for each person, a world almanac or encyclopedia, a wooden pole or stick, and a ribbon (2" wide).

JUSTICE AND PEACE

YOU PROMISE TO ALL WHO TRUST YOU . . . COURAGE IN THE STRUGGLE FOR JUSTICE AND PEACE, YOUR PRESENCE IN TRIAL AND REJOICING.

—STATEMENT OF FAITH

Themes

- God is a God of justice and peace.
- God has a special regard for the poor and the oppressed and requires that we show this same regard for them.
- God is present in times of trial and times of joy.

Scriptures

ISAIAH 58:6–12—God opposes injustice and cares for those in need.

PHILIPPIANS 4:4–7—The faithful are called to rejoice in God.

Objectives for This Session

- Consider actions that promote justice and peace.
- Learn about justice through hunger issues.
- Write a psalm about God's promises and presence.

Session at a Glance

GATHERING

Create symbols of justice, peace, trial, and rejoicing (10 minutes)

Read together "Liz's Story" (5 minutes)

EXPLORING

Learn about the distribution of people and food resources in the

world (30 minutes)

Read words from Isaiah (10 minutes)

CONNECTING

Find phrases in the Psalms (30 minutes)

GOING

Worship together (5 minutes)

Biblical and Theological Background

God is a god of justice and peace. These attributes of God are interconnected and interrelated. The justice and peace of God are characterized by a special regard for the wholeness or well-being of those in need, particularly the poor, the disenfranchised, the disempowered, and those with physical challenges (Job 29:12–17, Psalm 146:7–9, Malachi 3:5).

Isaiah 58:6–12 is from the portion of Isaiah known as Third Isaiah (chapters 56–66). Third Isaiah was most likely a disciple of Second Isaiah who lived and worked in Jerusalem following the return from the exile in Babylon. The focus of the writing was to emphasize the message of Second Isaiah (chapters 40–55): imaging a restored Jerusalem—a place of justice, righteousness, peace, and rejoicing .Jerusalem could be restored because the people had been returned to their homeland. In Isaiah 58:6–13 we learn that ritual fasts (going without food for a period of time) and other acts intended to win God's favor count for nothing unless people act justly by caring for the poor. By providing such care, Third Isaiah makes clear that obedience is based on faith in God, not on social justice alone (Isaiah 58:1).

Not unlike today, Isaiah's society didn't always know what to do. Some people even took advantage of the situation. Others sought to focus on God through particular practices such as religious fasts.

In Philippians 4:4–7, we hear the call to rejoice, to be gentle and forthright, even in the midst of situations that would cause us to be anxious, and to disclose all of our hopes and concerns to God. We are assured of God's abiding peace and presence when we live into the future in this way.

God requires that we show regard for the poor and the oppressed. God's demand is so significant that other responses we may have are of little or no value without it (Matthew 23:23, 2 Corinthians 9:8–10).

Therefore, God's justice is about the rights of individuals or communities in need and God's peace is about the wholeness or well-being of such persons or groups. The struggle for justice and peace requires us to anchor our trust and courage on God, who promises to be with us.

Materials Needed

- Bible for each participant
- *Confirmand's Journal* for each participant
- Construction paper, scissors, markers
- Newsprint
- Globe or world map
- Loaf of bread (uncut)

- @ Box of toothpicks
- @ Transparent tape
- @ **For global interdependence activity (optional):** a chocolate candy bar for each person, a world almanac or encyclopedia, newsprint, marker
- @ **For "peace pole" activity (optional):** "Peace" words list, wooden pole or stick, tacks or tape, ribbon (2" wide), markers

Preparing for This Session

Review the scriptures for this session and set aside time for prayer and reflection.

The "Exploring" activity in this session highlights the focus themes within a global context. In advance, make large paper cutouts in the shape of each of the continents to post on a wall or lay on the floor or a large table.

Set up the meeting room with chairs in a circle. Have the materials ready for the "Gathering" activity. Have a table or area of the room set up ahead of time for the "Going" experience.

Gathering

CREATE SYMBOLS OF JUSTICE, PEACE, TRIAL, AND REJOICING (10 MINUTES)

As confirmands arrive, have them choose a piece of construction paper. Ask each person to cut a symbol out of the paper or draw a symbol on it that will convey one of the following: justice, peace, trial, rejoicing.

When the symbol is completed, ask each confirmand to write his or her name on the back and post it on the wall. The leaders may do the same.

Begin the session by going around the entire group and asking each person to share a few sentences about the meaning of his or her symbol.

READ TOGETHER "LIZ'S STORY" (5 MINUTES)

Ask a volunteer to read aloud "Liz's Story" found on page 192 in the journal. Take a moment to hear reactions of the group before moving to the next activity. Ask:

- @ Has anything like this ever happened to you?
- @ If you were Liz or one of her friends, what would you have done?

Exploring

LEARN ABOUT THE DISTRIBUTION OF PEOPLE AND FOOD RESOURCES IN THE WORLD (30 MINUTES)

Ask the confirmands to look at the world map in their journals (page 193). Point out the five most populated continents and islands: Africa, Asia (including the islands), Europe, North America, and South America. Ask them to think about what percentage of the population of the world lives on each of the five continents. Have them write their estimates in the space provided in the journal. Then give them the figures:

- ℮   Africa 12%
- ℮   Asia...58%
- ℮   Europe.....................................16%
- ℮   North America 6%
- ℮   South America..........................8%

Were they surprised at these figures? Next make a visual display of the distribution of the world's population by posting the shapes of the continents on the wall or laying them on the floor or a large table. Have the group count out toothpicks to represent the population by area and place them on the appropriate continents. For example, Africa would have 12 toothpicks to represent 12%, Asia, 58 toothpicks, and so on.

Then, to visualize the distribution of food resources in the world, hold up an uncut loaf of bread. Explain that it represents all the food that will be eaten in the world today. Then divide the loaf according to the percentages eaten on the five continents:

- ℮   Africa...8%
- ℮   Asia...23%
- ℮   Europe 36%
- ℮   North America......................22%
- ℮   South America 11%

Place the pieces of the loaf on the appropriate continents. Have the group help you poke the toothpicks into the bread to show how much food would be available for the number of people.

Ask the group to look at the people/food ratio for each continent. What do they notice? Have them imagine how they would feel if they lived in Africa, Asia, Europe, South America, or North America. Give them time to journal their thoughts and feelings before you invite them to discuss as a group. What would they want to be different, if anything, about the people/food ratio in the world? What could they do about it?

READ WORDS FROM ISAIAH (10 MINUTES)

Invite confirmands to take turns reading a verse at a time from Isaiah 58:6–12. Consider these questions:

- What is the good news that the prophet Isaiah announces when justice and peace are present in relationships with others?
- Compare the words from Isaiah 58 with your learning about the people/food ratio in the world. What are the common themes? What part do we play in the modern-day situation?

Connecting

FIND PHRASES IN THE PSALMS (30 MINUTES)

Have the youth work in pairs. Each pair will need a Bible and their journals. Give them time to look through the book of Psalms to find words or phrases that match the idea of the Statement of Faith portion for this session: [God] promises to all who trust [God] . . . courage in the struggle for justice and peace, [God's] presence in trial and rejoicing. They may write the phrases in their journals. Then, in the space provided in the journal (page 195), have them write or draw their own psalm on the theme of God's promise to support those who work for justice and peace. When everyone has had an opportunity to finish, invite those who wish to share their work with the rest of the group.

Going

WORSHIP TOGETHER (5 MINUTES)

Invite confirmands and leaders to remove the symbols they made earlier and lay them on the worship table. Read aloud Philippians 4:4–7. Then invite the confirmands to sing or say "Nada te Turbe" on page 223 of the journal and page 229 of this guide.

Additional Activity

DISCOVER OUR GLOBAL INTERDEPENDENCE[1]

Form groups of four or less. Distribute a chocolate candy bar to each person. Place a sheet of newsprint on a wall or bulletin board. Using a marker, have a volunteer make nine columns on the newsprint. In the first column write the heading "Ingredients." In the remaining columns write the names of the following continents and islands: Africa, Antarctica, Asia, Australia, Europe, North America, South America, and the Islands.

Identify several basic ingredients in the candy bar, such as sugar, milk, cocoa butter, and chocolate. (Note: If you are working with a large group, you could expand this activity to include other ingredients in various candy bars, such as nuts, coconut, and fruit.) Place the names of the ingredients in the ingredients column. For each ingredient, use the information found in the encyclopedia or world almanac to indicate where the ingredient is found by writing the name of the countries in the proper continent column(s).

Note how the candy bars we eat are made from ingredients that come to us from many parts of the world. Ask confirmands to reflect on their research findings as they answer the following questions:

- What would happen to your candy bars if political unrest prevented the export of the ingredients?
- What would happen to the people in the country?
- What would happen if our demand for candy bars went down?
- What would happen to candy bars if war, famine, or bad weather prevented the export of one of the ingredients?
- If the size, ingredients, and cost of a candy bar could be affected so dramatically, what would be the impact on other material needs such as land, food, clothing, and shelter?

Consult the encyclopedia or world almanac to determine the living standards and conditions of the countries from which the ingredients for the candy bars come. What are the wages for workers? Do people have enough to eat? Do they have adequate shelter? Are any of the countries experiencing civil war or war with neighboring countries? If so, what are the reasons for the conflict?

Connecting with the Congregation

MAKE A "PEACE POLE"

World peace is the hope of many throughout the world. Use the following "Peace" words list to make a "Peace Pole" to remind the congregation of God's call to work for justice and peace. This activity could be done before or after a worship service.

Have the confirmands use the permanent markers to write (or show other members of the congregation how to write) the words for "peace" from the list onto strips of ribbon that have been precut. Tack or tape the ribbon to the wooden pole or dowel. Display the pole in a prominent location.

PEACE WORDS[2]

PAZ SPANISH PORTUGUESE   **МИР** RUSSIAN

शांति HINDI   **AMANI** SWAHILI

FRIEDE GERMAN   **PAIX** FRENCH

平和 CHINESE JAPANESE   שלום HEBREW

EIPHNH GREEK   **PACE** ITALIAN

Thinking About This Session

What new insights about justice and peace did the confirmands exhibit after this session? How might this affect the witness and service projects you are working on? How could they share these insights with others in the congregation?

Planning Ahead

Gather a variety of art supplies for the next session. If possible, locate a cassette tape or CD with the song "Tears in Heaven" by Eric Clapton. If you are able, read chapter 14, "Resurrection to Eternal Life," in *To Begin at the Beginning* by Martin Copenhaver (United Church Press, 1994).

ETERNAL LIFE

YOU PROMISE TO ALL WHO TRUST YOU . . . ETERNAL LIFE IN YOUR REALM WHICH HAS NO END.

—STATEMENT OF FAITH

Themes

◉ Eternal life is a gift from God.

◉ Eternal life is given to believers now, but its fullness is known after we die.

Scriptures

JOHN 17:1–3—Eternal life is knowing God.

JOHN 5:24–29—Through Christ the coming age of God's reign is now here.

REVELATION 4:1–6—A vision of heaven is described.

ROMANS 8:31–39—Nothing can separate us from the love of God.

Objectives for This Session

◉ Explore the meaning of eternal life.

◉ Honor the lives of God's saints.

◉ Convey God's eternal care through artistic expression.

Session at a Glance

GATHERING

Write thoughts about heaven (15 minutes)

EXPLORING

Imagine eternal life (15 minutes)

Consider the meaning of eternal life (15 minutes)

CONNECTING

Fashion a picture or symbol of God's eternal love and care

(30 minutes)

Remember God's saints (10 minutes)

GOING

Worship together (5 minutes)

Biblical and Theological Background

As the last affirmation of the Statement of Faith, the promise of eternal life reminds us that the assurances of God are not just for the earthly life we now lead, but also are intended for life after death. No Christian statement of faith would be complete without some declaration that resurrection overcomes the power of death. "Death has been swallowed up in victory," wrote the apostle Paul (1 Corinthians 15:54), reminding us that earthly death is not the end of our relationship with God. Or, as Paul wrote in another letter, "Neither death nor life . . . will be able to separate us from the love of God" (Romans 8:38–39). The overwhelming Christian witness is that even after physical death we are still in the care of God. When the Statement of Faith declares that eternal life is offered to those who trust God, this is at least part of what is being affirmed: that death is not a barrier to the love of God.

There are many facets of eternal life that we could explore in a session with confirmands, but there are three that are especially fruitful. The first is that eternal life is fundamentally a gift from God. The Gospel of John gives us the fullest treatment of the phrase *eternal life*. One of that gospel's central convictions is that eternal life is not something that we can manufacture or earn. It can only be received as a gift. Eternal life cannot be managed or controlled. It cannot be induced with the correct formula. It cannot be guaranteed with the right sort of behavior. It is the result of God's grace rather than our abilities. It is granted by God alone (see John 17:2). It is a gift.

Another characteristic of eternal life taught by Jesus in John 5:24–29 is that this gift is offered in both the future and the present. Eternal life is not just something given to us once our bodies have given out. It is also something available to us now. In fact, it would not be overstating it to say that, for John, the present meaning of eternal life is of even greater significance than its future meaning. What the evangelist wants the reader to know is that eternal life is available, not just in some distant future, but now; that it is a gift of God; and that it can be received, right now, by faith in Jesus Christ.

"And this is eternal life," goes John 17:3, "that they may know you, the only true God, and Jesus Christ whom you have sent." In John's eyes, eternal life is received by knowing God in Jesus Christ. The questions for the seeker then are: what does it mean to have faith in Christ; what does it mean to "know" the one true God?

Materials Needed

- ℮ Bible for each participant
- ℮ *Confirmand's Journal* for each participant
- ℮ Pens, paper

@ Newsprint, markers

@ Clay, chalk, paints, paintbrushes, wire, fabric

@ Cassette tape or CD with the song "Tears in Heaven" by Eric Clapton, if possible

@ Cassette or CD player

Preparing for the Session

Reflect on images of eternal life. What comes to mind as you consider the phrase? What do you imagine its nature to be? What do you believe happens at death? What do you suppose "heaven" would be like? Given your images of heaven, what might "heaven on earth" look like? Is there a connection between "heaven" and "heavenly" experiences in your present life?

Read John 17:1–3, John 5:24–29, Revelation 4:1–6, and Romans 8:31–39. Identify the qualities you associate with eternal life. Are they individual? Are others included in the picture? How? What part does God play?

The emphasis of this session is on eternal life. However, during the session someone may raise a question about hell or eternal punishment. You might want to think about how you would respond if such issues emerge. Martin Copenhaver, in the chapter "Resurrection to Eternal Life" in his book *To Begin at the Beginning*, provides some helpful insights about this question:

Heaven and hell, then, are not two different places. Rather, when we die, we all die into the eternal presence of God. Some will experience that as heaven and others as hell. If we have spent our lives serving, obeying, and praising God, when we die into the eternal presence of God, it will be the fulfillment of our desire. . . . But if, instead, we have spent our lives scoffing, disobeying, and denying God, when we die into the eternal presence of God, it will be a very different experience. To face the God whom we have disobeyed and denied, and to face in God's presence the truth about our own lives, is to know some of the torment and remorse we associate with hell.[1]

It is also worth considering how to respond if the subject of death is a difficult one in the group. Someone in the group may have experienced a recent or past loss that still affects him or her strongly. Be prepared to respond with care if anyone is troubled or disturbed by this. These are issues for which your pastor or your conference or association resources may be helpful.

Arrange for a meeting room that will give confirmands space to spread out during the times for reflection. The room will also need work space for drawing, painting, or sculpting. Prepare a sheet of newsprint with the following words adapted from Romans 8:39 printed in the center: . . . will not separate me from the love of God in Christ Jesus.

Gathering

WRITE THOUGHTS ABOUT HEAVEN (15 MINUTES)

Welcome the youth. As they gather, invite them to open their journals to page 198 and, in the space provided, reflect on the story there and write words, phrases, feelings or draw images that they associate with the idea of heaven. Then have them reflect on the lyrics on page 200 in the space provided. When all have had an opportunity to add something to their journals, have the group form a discussion circle to share what they discovered.

Exploring

IMAGINE ETERNAL LIFE (15 MINUTES)

Have a volunteer read aloud Revelation 4:1–6. Explain that the vision described is one person's view of what heaven is like. Ask the youth to imagine for themselves what heaven might be like. They can refer to their journals, to the scripture from Revelation, or to other scriptures to start the discussion, but encourage them to expand upon these ideas. When all who wish to have shared, explain that one of Christianity's fundamental convictions is that God cares for us after we die—that death is in no way the end of our connection to God. God gives us eternal life, and that gift does not stop with physical death. If that is true, then divine care continues after our earthly lives. Ask:

- What do you imagine that kind of care from God is like?
- How is that kind of care expressed by God to us here and now?
- How would you describe "heaven on earth"?

CONSIDER THE MEANING OF ETERNAL LIFE (15 MINUTES)

This is the time for leaders and confirmands to think about the meaning of eternal life for them now. Several questions could be considered. In light of what's been done and discussed, how do participants conceive of what happens at death? Do they imagine that God continues to care for all of us, and, if so, how? What might it mean for each one to know that eternal life can be received by knowing God? In a culture that often seems to discourage faith or trust in a divine power that can't be seen or proved, ask the group what is desirable about putting their trust in God? What does it mean, in each life, to do so? Give particular examples. Ask a volunteer to read Romans 8:31–39. Display the newsprint or poster that has written in the center the words adapted from Romans 8:39. Invite the youth to think about how they would begin that sentence. What can they name in their life that challenges them so that, in spite of its challenge, it will not be enough to separate them from God's love? Provide markers for them to write their responses on the newsprint or poster.

Use this discussion to point out that eternal life really begins in the present for believers and that through Christ the coming age of God's reign is now here. It is comforting to know that no matter what challenges we face, God's love and care can sustain us.

Connecting

FASHION A PICTURE OR SYMBOL OF GOD'S ETERNAL LOVE AND CARE (30 MINUTES)

Have a variety of art supplies, such as clay, chalk, paint, fabric, and wire, available for the confirmands to use to create a symbol that expresses to them God's eternal love and care. Encourage them to recall their journaling time as well as the discussion on eternal life to spark their creativity. Play quiet music in the background. You may want to play "Tears in Heaven" by Eric Clapton.

When all have had time to create, ask those who wish to describe their symbol or picture to rest of the group.

REMEMBER GOD'S SAINTS (10 MINUTES)

Distribute a list of names of the persons from your congregation who have died in the last year. Ask them if they have names of other persons who have died whom they wish to remember. Then have the group look at the hymn "For All the Saints" on page 217 of the journal and page of 225 of this guide. Read aloud together verses 1 through 4. Then ask each one in the group to say "For [name of person]," substituting the name of a person on the list in place of the words "all the saints"; go around the group until all the names are spoken, then have all the group complete the rest of the verse aloud, continuing with the words "who from their labors rest . . . ," and finishing the verse.

Going

WORSHIP TOGETHER (5 MINUTES)

To close, gather people together and call them to prayer. Call on participants to remember silently the promises of God to care for us in death and in life. Invite them to give themselves into God's care in that moment, to trust that they are in God's hands.

Then finish by saying together the Statement of Faith in the form of a doxology found on page 234 of the journal and page 239 of this guide.

Connecting with the Congregation

DISPLAY PICTURES AND SYMBOLS OF GOD'S ETERNAL LOVE AND CARE

Gather together the creative work of the group and arrange to display it in a prominent place in the church. If the confirmands wish, they can write a brief description of the meaning of the picture or symbol and include it with the display.

Thinking About This Session

What activities or discussion questions seemed to help open the confirmands to the concept of eternal life?

Planning Ahead

Complete plans for the closing retreat.

THE FAITH JOURNEY CONTINUES

The theme of this final retreat is "The Faith Journey Continues."

Throughout *Affirming Faith*, the confirmands were invited listen for God's call to take the next steps on their own journey of faith.

Growing in faith is a process, not an accomplishment. Because of this, no two people are likely to find themselves at exactly the same place on a faith journey. Some confirmands may be eager to affirm their baptism in the rite of confirmation. Others may have reservations about such an affirmation. Some may decide not to participate in the rite of confirmation at this time. Be aware, too, that some may be anticipating baptism itself, if they were not baptized earlier.

Because the confirmands may be at different places on their faith journeys, they may feel some anxiety. That often happens when people find that others' experiences do not match their own. Throughout this retreat, therefore, the leaders need to be sensitive to potential differences and honor them. Participants should go home from the weekend having received at least this message: each person makes the journey of faith at his or her own pace.

The activities during the retreat will invite participants to look at the journey from various angles: backward, forward, and inside-out. Among the exercises is a skit, "The Call of Jeremiah," which focuses on God's call to the youth, Jeremiah, and Jeremiah's questions about his ability to live up to the responsibility of the call. A commissioning service follows the skit. At mid-retreat, confirmands will be asked to devote time to individual reflection on the question: "Where am I on my faith journey?" They will be given the "Time Capsules" they made at the beginning of the *Affirming Faith* journey to help them remember the places from which they have come. They will also be invited to consider if they feel moved to affirm their baptism (or be baptized) and participate in the rite of confirmation. There will be opportunities for them to share their reflections with their mentors, other adult leaders, and the group, if they wish.

The confirmands have been on their own individual faith journeys, but they have also shared a collective journey. An activity on the second evening will give them time to celebrate this collective journey. The worship times on the second and third days are designed to prepare them for faith journeys to come. Eveniung worship on day two will invite them to think about the things that may hinder their faith commitment, while morning worship on day three will celebrate the growth they can anticipate as their faith continues to grow beyond confirmation.

Wherever a confirmand is on his or her journey—confident or questioning, assured or doubting—it is his or her own authentic place on the journey that needs to be affirmed.

Retreat Schedule

This retreat is designed for a forty-hour experience, starting on the evening of the first day and going to noon on the third day. Plan to have the retreat at a location where participants will be comfortable, will have access to recreational activities during free time, and where meal times can be easily arranged.

DAY ONE

Arrive and check in

Serve dinner (optional)

Introduce the purpose of the retreat (10 minutes)

Worship together (10 minutes)

Mark our journeys (Part 1) (30 minutes)

Break (15 minutes)

Have a "Testimonial Banquet" (30 minutes)

Worship together (30 minutes)

Have leisure time, if desired

DAY TWO

Watch a skit, "The Call of Jeremiah" (30 minutes)

Consider "What is my call?" (30 minutes)

Break (15 minutes)

Think about commitment (30 minutes)

Explore the responsibilities of church membership (30 minutes)

Serve lunch (45 minutes)

Open "Time Capsules" and write a prayer (1 hour)

Meet with mentors or other adult leaders (30 minutes)

Have free time

Serve dinner (1 hour)

Mark our journeys (Part 2) (30 minutes)

Share prayers (30 minutes)

Worship together (30 minutes)

Have leisure activities and snacks

DAY THREE

Worship together (1 hour)

Pack up, clean up, and depart (30 minutes)

Objectives for the Retreat

- Create a faith journey symbol with the group.
- Write a life journey testimonial.
- Experience the call of Jeremiah and consider individual call.
- Explore the responsibilities of church membership.
- Review "Time Capsules" from the opening retreat.
- Worship together.

Materials Needed

- Bible for each participant
- *Confirmand's Journal* for each participant
- Traffic signs made of construction paper
- Road maps for display
- Road maps cut into puzzle pieces
- Snacks and beverages
- Paper, pencils, crayons, markers
- Roll of butcher paper or newsprint
- Tempera (poster) paints and flat pans
- Old towels, soap, basin and water
- Candle, matches
- Communion elements of bread and grape juice
- Flower seeds, tongue depressors, and a bowl of potting soil
- Centerpiece composed of grapes and several wheat stalks (optional)
- Small vial of oil
- Handouts ("A Testimonial Banquet," pages 217–18, and "Mentor's or Leader's Guidelines," page 219)

Prepare for the Retreat

This retreat is for confirmands, leaders, and mentors, if mentors are part of your program. Schedule the retreat well in advance, and ask confirmands to invite their mentors to attend. Send a letter of invitation to the mentors from the leaders, as well, providing the schedule and other details.

Review the design of the entire retreat and meet with other leaders to plan the event. On Saturday morning, a presentation on the "responsibilities of ministry in the church" is scheduled. This will require two things:

1. Have your local church council or board responsible for the church's ongoing ministry prepare a short statement by that answers the question: "How do members of this church express their faith and call from God to love and serve?"

Ask the board to be as specific as possible, naming the various ministries of the church, expressed locally and beyond. One local church included the following: serving on committees, giving to the church, voting at congregational meetings, worshiping and praying regularly, participating in mission and service projects, and committing to lifelong learning. Another church reviewed the "Time and Talent" inventory checklist it gives to members each year to enlist their help and used it to form its statement.

2. Recruit two or three adults (mentors, leaders, or other appropriate adults) well in advance to share with the whole group their stories about what faith and church involvement has meant to them.

Prepare the main gathering room of the retreat by decorating it with road maps and traffic signs made from construction paper. Have signs such as "Stop," "Yield," "Bump," "Rest Area," "No Turn," "Dangerous Intersection," "Proceed with Caution," "All Services This Exit," "Steep Grade," "Dead End," "Crosswalk," "Slow," "Detour," "Walk," "Don't Walk," "Construction Zone," "Road Closed," "Welcome to Our Community," various curve and intersection signs, and a traffic light flashing green, if possible.

Recruit several adults to perform the skit "The Call of Jeremiah" (page 207). Encourage them to memorize the parts and use costumes and props. If possible, find a youth who has already been confirmed to play the part of Jeremiah.

Day One

ARRIVE AND CHECK IN

Have participants make name tags, if desired. When all are present, welcome the group.

SERVE DINNER (OPTIONAL)

INTRODUCE THE PURPOSE OF THE RETREAT (10 MINUTES)

Introduce the participants if not everyone knows all those present. Talk about the theme of this retreat: "The Faith Journey Continues." Describe the Christian life as a journey, a journey of lifelong learning, loving, and serving God. Point out that throughout the faith formation process with *Affirming Faith*, the confirmands have been on a journey. They have been learning about themselves and the Christian life, discovering what it is that Christians believe, and what it is that God calls them to do to live out their faith. Now, with this weekend, they have come to a "crossroad" on the way, as they consider how they want to continue this journey. The rite of confirmation is one of many times and possibilities in life when your baptism is affirmed. This retreat is designed to help you—confirmands, mentors, and leaders alike—discern what this rite will mean for you on the day that it is celebrated.

Give a brief summary of the schedule for the retreat and post the schedule in a prominent place for the group to see. Clarify any "housekeeping" details or other expectations for the weekend.

WORSHIP TOGETHER (10 MINUTES)

Gather in a circle. The leader will lead everyone in the dialogue prayer (the *Sursum Corda*), as described below. Each pair of phrases is accompanied by movements; the group will mirror the leader's gestures in each successive response it makes:

Leader: *God be with you. (Extend arms toward the group, palms upward.)*

Group: *And also with you. (Extend arms toward the leader.)*

Leader: *Lift up your hearts. (Lift arms above the head.)*

Group: *We lift them to God. (Lift arms above head.)*

Leader: *Let us give thanks to God. (Bring hands down and together to clasp them in a gesture of prayer before the heart.)*

Group: *It is right to give God thanks and praise. (Repeat the gesture.)*

Sing together or recite the words to one or more of the following songs: "Gathered Here in the Mystery of the Hour," "We Are Your People," or "Be Still and Know That I am God" (pages 211–32 in the journal; pages 221–37 in this guide).

MARK OUR JOURNEYS (PART 1) (30 MINUTES)

Pour the tempera paints into separate pans and roll out the length of butcher paper with the waxed side down. Invite confirmands to take their off shoes and socks, dip their feet in the paint, and walk the length of paper. (Ideally, each confirmand will use a different color paint.) The pans should only hold enough paint to mark the soles of the feet. More paint may be added to the pans as needed. Place a basin of soapy water and old towels at the end of the roll of paper for them to use to wash their feet.

This is the first stage in creating a group poster that will symbolize the faith journeys the confirmands have taken. Work will be completed on the poster on the second evening, and the poster may be hung in the church on the day the rite of confirmation is celebrated.

BREAK (15 MINUTES)

During the break set the room for a "banquet." Put out snacks and beverages.

HAVE A "TESTIMONIAL BANQUET" (30 MINUTES)

People nearing the end of their lives often have little difficulty seeing their lives as a journey. The following exercise encourages the group members to use their imagination to jump years ahead in their own lives to develop some sense of their own life journeys.

The leader may introduce the activity by saying:

When a person retires, friends, co-workers, or family often have a party or banquet to honor the person and his or her accomplishments. Many times the party includes a time where others give a testimonial, a short speech that highlights the events in the person's life. Most testimonials are written by others about the person to be honored. But right now, you're going to have the opportunity to write a testimonial for yourself. Imagine it is fifty years or so from now. Imagine that you are looking back on the events of your life. What has happened? What events do you wish to highlight? How would you like to be remembered? What would you say about the life you have led?

Distribute the "Testimonial" handout from page 217. Give everyone ten minutes to fill it out. When time is up, collect the handouts, shuffle them, and redistribute them so that no one has his or her own testimonial to read. In turn, have each person stand, if able, and read aloud a testimonial. At the conclusion of each testimonial, invite everyone to applaud in celebration of the person's "life."

When all the testimonials have been read, share the snacks you have prepared.

WORSHIP TOGETHER (30 MINUTES)

In preparation for worship ask confirmands to spend ten minutes writing in their journals, reflecting on these questions:

- @ In what ways does my faith in Jesus Christ influence and shape my life?
- @ How will my faith shape my future?

Suggest that tomorrow during the time alone they will be referring to what they have written.

Sing together "Nada de Turbe (Nothing Can Trouble)" found on page 223 of the journal (and page 229 in this guide).

Lead a guided meditation as part of the worship experience. Ask the group to find a comfortable place in a chair or on the floor for the guided meditation. Those unfamiliar with guided imagery exercises might need some time to relax enough for this activity to work. Be attentive to how the group is responding. Tell them you are going to lead them on an imaginative journey—a trip in a hot air balloon. You'll say some things to guide them, but they are to allow their imaginations to take them where they will in the imaginary journey.

Invite them to relax, close their eyes if they wish, and take slow, deep breaths, concentrating on the action of their breathing. Pause to allow them to take about three deep breaths. Then say:

It is a warm summer day. It would be a great day for a swim, but the lake is several miles away. Suddenly you see a hot air balloon, inflated and ready to take you on a journey. (Pause.) See its colors; hear the roar of its propane burner. (Pause.) You climb into its basket. The tethers are released, and up, up, up, you go. (Pause.) See the people, the fields, the buildings, and everything below grow smaller as you go up. (Pause.) A wind catches you, and you begin to move along. (Pause.) Feel yourself soar through the air like a bird. (Pause.) Watch the land move under you, the clouds go by around you. (Pause.) After a while, the balloon begins to descend. (Pause.) It descends toward a lush, green field next to the small, peaceful lake where you had hoped to swim. (Pause.) Your balloon gently lands. You climb out of the basket. The day is so nice and warm, the water so inviting, you don't waste a moment. (Pause.) The water feels great! (Pause.) As you come out of the water, you decide to lie down on the soft, green grass. The warmth of the sun dries you quickly. (Pause.) It's such a delightful place, such a wonderful day. You feel God's presence with you as you lie in the sun. (Pause.) You feel God's love in the sun's warmth. (Pause.) You wish you could lie here forever, bathed in God's presence and love.[1]

After a few minutes, gently invite all to open their eyes. Then take a few minutes in the large group to talk about the experience, if they wish.

Bring the group together in a circle and join hands. Invite them to suggest prayers for the evening. They may name something for which they are thankful or a concern they have. A leader or confirmand may offer a closing prayer. Close by singing the song "I Thank You, Jesus" (page 216 of the journal and page 224 in this guide) or another favorite.

HAVE LEISURE TIME, IF DESIRED

The remainder of the evening is free. You may want to offer snacks, play some games, or organize a sing-along.

Day Two

WATCH A SKIT, "THE CALL OF JEREMIAH" (30 MINUTES)

Introduce the skit by saying:

The Bible is full of stories of God calling people—Abraham and Sarah, Moses, Aaron and Miriam, Ruth, Esther, Samuel, Elizabeth, Mary, Paul, Timothy, and many others—to important tasks of love, justice, and mission. But one story can be especially meaningful to youth. It is the story of the call of Jeremiah. When God called Jeremiah to become a prophet, Jeremiah was only fourteen or fifteen years old. The story of the call is found in Jeremiah 1:4–10.

Have the volunteers put on the skit for the group. Following the skit, ask the group to discuss these questions:

- How do you think Jeremiah felt when he was asked to become one of God's prophets?
- How do you think you would feel?
- How do you think God calls people today?
- How do you think one experiences God's call?
- Who are some people today whom God has called?
- What are some ways people show that they have answered God's call?

THE CALL OF JEREMIAH

Cast: Narrator, God, Jeremiah (about 15 years old)

Scene: In Jeremiah's room at home.

Narrator: Jeremiah was only about fifteen years old when the call of God first came to him. It happened when he was home one day.

God (calling from off-stage): Jeremiah!

Jeremiah: Huh? Who's there?

God: It's me—God.

Jeremiah (skeptically): Sure it is.

God: I'm telling you the truth, Jeremiah. It's really God.

Jeremiah: Prove it. Throw a lightning bolt or something.

God: Sorry, that's not my style.

Jeremiah: So how can I know for sure you're really God?

God: Trust me. Are you in the habit of hearing voices?

Jeremiah: Okay, suppose I really believe it *is* you, God. What do want from me?

God: I'm calling you, Jeremiah. I need you. I need you to work for me and speak for me. I need you to remind the people of the promises we have made together. I need you to remind them that I am their God and they are my people.

Jeremiah: Me? Are you sure you have the right person, God?

God: Yes, Jeremiah. I've had you picked out for something special for a long time now. Even before you were born I knew you and wanted you to be my messenger when the proper time came.

Jeremiah: So why are you coming to me now? I'm pretty busy.

God: The leaders and the people of your country have become unbearably selfish in their ways. They are not caring for those who are poor, needy, or oppressed. Have you noticed this, Jeremiah?

Jeremiah: Yeah, it seems like people only look out for themselves.

God: Do you think that's right?

Jeremiah: No. I don't think that's right at all.

God: Well, what I want you to do is go to them and tell them to change their ways.

Jeremiah: Surely, you're joking, God! Me go to the leaders? Me try to tell the rest of the country what to do? Who's going to listen to me? I'm just a kid. What am I even going to say? I don't know how to speak. I am too young!

God: Do not say to me you are too young. I know you and I call you to this important job. Look, you know that what they're doing isn't right. You know it hurts me to see so many in need. How can you not speak up? Tell them what is wrong in my sight, do not be afraid of them, and I'll make you a promise—I will be with you to help you find the words to say. I will be with you always. That's a promise.

—Adapted from Jeremiah 1:4–10

CONSIDER "WHAT IS MY CALL?" (30 MINUTES)

Lead a discussion using the following information:

Baptism marks an important point on a Christian's journey of faith. In baptism we respond to God by taking vows and making promises to seek the ways of God and to follow them. In the case of infants and young children, these promises are made by parents or guardians and the congregation on their behalf. In the case of those who have not been baptized, baptism will take place prior to confirmation.

Confirmation is a rite of the church in which Christians say "yes" to their baptism. Because it is a rite of the church done in public worship, the congregation representing the whole church of Jesus Christ also says "yes" to the faith of those being confirmed. Whenever the rite of confirmation is celebrated, it provides an important opportunity to answer God's call as Jeremiah did.

We are God's children. God declares that to us and it is affirmed at our baptism. In the rite of confirmation, we affirm our faith, dedicating ourselves to God in a special way.

Ask the confirmands to find the "Quetions of the Candidate" from the *Book of Worship* that are printed on page 206 of the *Confirmand's Journal.* Explain that the questions focus on the call of God in our lives. They point to a new and special relationship that is recognized through the rite.

Questions of the Candidates

- Do you desire to affirm your baptism/be baptized into the faith and family of Jesus Christ?
- Do you renounce the power of evil and desire the freedom of new life in Christ?
- Do you profess Jesus Christ as Lord and Savior?
- Do you promise, by the grace of God, to be Christ's disciple, to follow in the way of our Savior, to resist oppression and evil, to show love and justice, and to witness to the work and word of Jesus Christ as best you are able?
- Do you promise, according to the grace given you, to grow in the Christian faith and to be a faithful member of the church of Jesus Christ, celebrating Christ's presence and furthering Christ's mission in all the world?[2]

It is each confirmand's choice, of course, whether she or he will make this affirmation at this time. This commitment requires careful thought.

BREAK (15 MINUTES)

THINK ABOUT COMMITMENT (30 MINUTES)

In the full group, raise the following questions:

- What commitments do you have in life right now? For example, what commitments have you made to parents or guardians, brothers and sisters, sports teams, school, music lessons? What commitments have they made to you?
- Are there any commitments you would like to make, but haven't been able to accomplish?

As group members call out answers, record them on newsprint. Be sensitive to who is answering. If any are being "crowded out" by the more vocal group members, take time to glean any input from the quieter members of the group. Add these to the newsprint list and display it in the room.

On a new sheet of newsprint, write "Commitment" at the top. Draw a line lengthwise down the middle. Label one column "Positive Aspects" and the other "Negative Aspects." Ask each question and record the responses in the appropriate column.

- What are the positive aspects of commitment? (Examples might be: you feel you belong, you have order in your life, you can feel safe, you feel a sense of accomplishment.)
- What are the negative aspects of commitment? (Examples might be: you have to do things you don't always feel like doing, you have to follow someone else's schedule, you may get into conflicts with others about how to accomplish goals.)

Explain that any commitment has its joys and its costs. It is precisely those joys and costs we need to think about as we are called to say "yes" to God. Jeremiah had some concerns about the commitment God was asking him to make. But God promised to be there to help him with his concerns and fears.

Our commitment to God is shown through our commitment to the "people of God," the creation, and the church. We become members of Christ's church when we are baptized. In the rite of confirmation, we affirm our baptism and make our commitment to God and the church stronger.

EXPLORE THE RESPONSIBILITIES OF CHURCH MEMBERSHIP (30 MINUTES)

Hand out the summary from church leaders that answered the question, "How do people in our congregation express their faith?" Lead the group through it, giving a brief outline of the rights, responsibilities, and opportunities of ministry in your local church. Invite questions, so all may understand what ministry in the church implies.

Invite two or more of the mentors or other adult leaders to speak personally about what involvement in the church has meant to them. Encourage them to be specific, direct, and honest, illustrating whatever has been true for them related to the aspects of commitment. Allow the group to ask questions of the adults.

At the conclusion of the presentations, ask each group member to meet with his or her own mentor, if possible, or with another adult leader. Ask them to discuss feelings about three questions:

@ What gifts or talents do you bring to the ministry of this congregation?

@ What gifts or talents do you receive from the ministry of this congregation?

@ What concerns you about being called by God to minister with others in this congregation?

SERVE LUNCH (45 MINUTES)

OPEN "TIME CAPSULES" AND WRITE A PRAYER (30 MINUTES)

Gather as a group. Display the questions that will be used in the rite of confirmation on newsprint. Ask all to reflect on them as they are read through. Then distribute the "Time Capsule" envelopes containing the sheet they completed at the beginning of the *Affirming Faith* journey.

Invite the confirmands to spend the next hour alone in a quiet place reading the responses they made on the "Time Capsule" handout, pondering the affirmations to be made in the service of confirmation. In their time alone, each shall be asked to reflect on these questions:

@ Am I ready to affirm my baptism (or be baptized) by participating in the rite of confirmation at this time?

@ What would it mean in my life right now to continue my faith journey whether or not I participate in the rite of confirmation at this time?

Ask each person to write a short prayer—containing honest wishes, doubts, and fears—during the hour. Call attention to the prayers on page 207 in the journal and below that can be used as models.

Lord God, I have no idea where I am going. / I do not see the road ahead of me, / I cannot know for certain where it will end. / Nor do I really know myself, / and the fact that I think that I am following your will / does not mean that I am actually doing so. / I believe that the desire to please you does in fact please you. / I hope that I have that desire in all that I am doing. / I hope that I will never do anything apart from that desire. / I know that if I do this you will lead me by the right road / though I may know nothing about it. / Therefore will I trust you always / though I may seem lost. . . . / I will not fear, / for you are ever with me, / and will never leave me . . . alone.
                                                                    —*Thomas Merton*[3]

*Speak God, for your servant hears. / Grant us ears to hear, / eyes to see, / wills to obey, / hearts to love; /
then declare what you will, / reveal what you will, command what you will, / demand what you will. Amen.*

—Christina G. Rossetti[4]

God be in my head, and in my understanding;

God be in my eyes, and in my looking;

God be in my mouth, and in my speaking;

God be in my heart, and in my thinking;

God be at my end, and at my departing.

—Old Sarum Primer[5]

The confirmands will be invited to share their prayers with the group if they wish.

While the confirmands are spending time alone, ask the mentors or other adult leaders to review guidelines
for the upcoming talk with their spiritual companion ("Mentor's or Leader's Guidelines" handout, page
219). Alert them that some confirmands may find themselves at a point in their faith journeys that will
cause them to decide *not* to affirm their baptisms or to be baptized. If such should be the case, that decision should be honored, while still striving to be supportive.

When the confirmands' "time alone" is over, provide time for the mentors (or other adult leaders) to meet
with their respective confirmands to talk about participating in the rite of confirmation at this time.

HAVE FREE TIME

SERVE DINNER (1 HOUR)

MARK OUR JOURNEYS (PART 2) (30 MINUTES)

Display the butcher paper with the colorful footprints, and ask everyone to gather around it. Make this a time
for reminiscing. The group has spent some significant time together prior to this final retreat. Encourage
everyone to think of the experiences they've had. Lead a discussion using the following questions:

@ What were some of the most memorable times for you during our group meetings together?

@ What were the most enjoyable? funniest? thought-provoking?

@ What were the most moving? important? difficult or challenging?

Using colored magic markers, ask the group to celebrate the collective journey by making a "communal doodle" on the butcher paper. Invite the group to draw pictures, symbols, or doodles and write key words or phrases

to convey whatever highlights, insights, memories, or learnings they've gained during the time together.

Encourage the group to have fun with this activity. Tell them that the finished banner will be hung in a

prominent place in the church on the day the rite of confirmation is celebrated.

SHARE PRAYERS (30 MINUTES)

Take time to share the prayers everyone has written. Print on newsprint the group response, ". . . every step

of the way." Gather in a circle and ask each person to read his or her prayer. (If there are youth in the

group who did not write a prayer or would rather not share their prayer, they may choose to read one of

the sample prayers in the journal.) At the end of each person's reading, the leader should say: "We

thank you God that you are part of (name)'s journey." The rest of the group should read the response.

If it is appropriate, the prayers written by the confirmands could also be offered during the confirmation service.

Be especially sensitive to any youth who have decided not to participate in the rite of confirmation at this time.

WORSHIP TOGETHER (30 MINUTES)

Arrange chairs or pillows in a circle. On a table in the center of the circle place the communion elements and

a broad pan filled with potting soil. If possible, arrange a simple centerpiece composed of grapes and sev-

eral wheat stalks. Have ready the flower seeds, a bowl of earth, tongue depressors, markers, and crayons.

Call to Worship

One: *Everything as it moves, now and then, here and there, makes pauses.*

All: *The bird as it flies stops on one place to make its nest, and in another to rest in its flight.*

One: *In the same way, God has paused as well.*

All: *The sun, which is so bright and beautiful, is one place where God has paused.*

One: *The moon, the stars, the winds; God has been with them, too.*

All: *The trees, the animals, are all places where God has stopped, leaving the touch of the Holy in all these things.*

One: *We, too, have had God pause in us. We too have the Holy touch in our being.*

All: *Let us now pause ourselves, and listen for the voice of God on our hearts.*

—Teachings of the Lakota[6]

Sing or say together the hymn "Called as Partners in Christ's Service" found on page 230 of the journal (or

page 236 of the leader's guide). Distribute the flower seeds, asking each person to take one and hold it in

the open palm of his or her hand, focusing on it as the scripture is read.

Read aloud Mark 4:26–32. Then give each person a cup and invite him or her to come to the bowl of soil on the table in the center of the circle, scoop some soil into the cup, and plant the seed. When they are finished, they may return to their seats.

Meditation

Have a leader share the following story.

> *Consider the miracle of living things. A mighty tree or a beautiful flower begins as the smallest of seeds or a withered bulb. Yet in that seed or bulb is the plant's potential to grow into something wonderful: a haven for birds to build their nests, or the nectar from which bees make honey.*
>
> *When life begins for humankind we, too, are small and helpless as vulnerable babies. Yet as human beings we carry within us a wealth of potential to grow. Growing comes at different rates to different plants and people. If we are to grow at all, we must be true to ourselves, listening to the pace set by our hearts within.*
>
> *Faith, too, is a living thing. It begins in everyone's life as no more than a seed, and has the potential to grow into something fuller, more fragrant, more wonderful. But growth in faith is not something that can be forced. Each person grows in faith at his or her own pace, according to the movements of the heart.*
>
> *The seed of faith has been planted in you in many ways—for some of you at baptism, for others as you have been nurtured in faith by friends and family. As you near confirmation, you have come to a time to consider the seed that was planted, and to affirm the growth that has taken place in your faith since then. Throughout this time together, we've done several exercises to encourage reflection about your own life of faith—from the personal testimonials you wrote about the lives you'd like to live to the individual time you spent reflecting on your time capsule and writing a prayer. And as we've reflected on these things, part of the message was that the journey of growth in faith is a lifelong one and can have many "speed zones," dips, and turns associated with it. Though we may all be on the same journey, we may be at different places along the way.*
>
> *Where are you on your faith journey? What about your Christian faith, planted as a seed at your baptism, could you affirm right now? What about it could you commit yourself to?*
>
> *Look around the room at the various traffic signs and signals. Which would describe where you are in your faith journey right now? Why? Spend the next couple of minutes thinking about these questions. Then we'll have a time for sharing.*

After two or three minutes, allow the youth to share their answers. To facilitate sharing by the group members, one of the leaders may want to be the first to share, setting the pace.

Distribute the tongue depressors. Ask this question:

@ If you could summarize in one word what your faith means to you at this time, what would that word be? (Some examples might be: peace, hope, love, doubt, uncertainty, challenge.)

Instruct all to use the crayons or markers to spell that word in large letters on their tongue depressors and also decorate it if they wish. When it is completed they may insert it into the soil as a label for the seed they have planted. Then say:

Understanding that faith is a living thing, begun as a seed and then nurtured to grow, I invite you to bring your plant and "faith stake" forward and place it in the pan to form our own "faith garden."

Prayer of Dedication

Ask a volunteer to water the soil. Then offer this or a similar prayer:

We thank you, O God, for your presence in our lives. We thank you for having planted within us the seed of faith. As the waters of baptism rain upon us, encouraging growth, so may your grace shower over [say the names of all present] throughout our journeys; in the name of Christ our Savior. Amen.

Sing or say together the hymn "Great Work God Has Begun in You" on page 212 of the journal and page 222 of this guide.

HAVE LEISURE ACTIVITIES AND SNACKS

Day Three

WORSHIP TOGETHER (1 HOUR)

Prepare a worship table in the center of the room. Cover it with fabric and display an open Bible, a candle, and a small vial of oil to be used in a service of anointing and commissioning. Set up chairs in a circle around the table. Call the group into the circle. Have a volunteer light the candle. Sing or say together the hymn "Gathered Here in the Mystery of the Hour" on page 211 of the journal and page 221 of this guide.

Call to Worship

A leader may say:

We hear your call and are surprised that you invite us to share in your ministry, O God. We are not great or strong, rich or powerful. And yet you call us, leaving us to wonder what you see in us. Who are we? Have you no one else but us?

Scripture Reading

Ask a volunteer to read Luke 4:16–19.

An Anointing

Leader: *Spirit of power, time and again throughout history you have anointed your servants and sent them on mission: to speak your word to the poor, to heal the sick, to free captives—always renewing the face of the earth in such a variety of ways that creation itself sings of your glory and the human family reflects your beauty in a thousand different ways!* (Extends hands over the oil.)

Leader: *Come Spirit of the Living One. Bless this oil of anointing. Make it an oil of gladness and of healing, a lotion of strength and tenderness. We pray that by this anointing our hands and hearts might be strengthened for the work that lies ahead, that we might be compassionate to human need, tender and strong in our care for one another, genuine in our friendship, and faithful to the commitments we have made. Amen.*

The leader now anoints each person. She or he may choose to anoint either the forehead or the back of the hand. In either case, the leader shall moisten his or her thumb with the oil and use the thumb to trace a cross. When anointing each person, the leader may say one of the following phrases, to which the others gathered shall respond: "Blessed are you, (name)."

If there are fewer people to anoint than the number of blessings suggested here, the leader should select those statements most fitting for the individuals in your group—or combine more than one. If there are more people than the number of blessings written here, the leader should feel free to repeat some—or create more.

Leader: *May you spread your gentleness wherever you go.*
All: *Blessed are you, (name). (Repeat after each blessing is spoken by the leader.)*
Leader: *May you speak with those who are voiceless.*
Leader: *May you find companions on your journey.*
Leader: *May you dream dreams and see visions of shalom.*
Leader: *May you be strong to confront injustice.*
Leader: *May you feed the hungry in mind, body, and heart.*
Leader: *May you bring laughter to those you meet.*

Leader: *May you find courage with those in despair.*

Leader: *May you see rainbows, the sign of God's promise.*

Leader: *May you give and receive the joy of song.*

Leader: *May you share your gift of wisdom and perception.*

Prayer

One: *O Anointing Spirit, your touch promises wholeness where once there was an ache. May the song we hear lead us toward your rainbow of promise and peace. Amen.*

Close the worship time by singing or saying together the hymn "We Are Your People" on page 224 of the journal or page 230 of this guide.

PACK, CLEAN UP, AND DEPART (30 MINUTES)

Handout

A TESTIMONIAL BANQUET

What would you like others to say about you when most of your life is over? How would you like others to
remember you? What legacy would you like to leave behind?

Here's an opportunity to write your own testimonial in words you would want another to say about you.

We are here today to honor our friend, _____ (enter your name here),

for all that his/her life has meant and for all that he/she has accomplished.

From early on, our friend always was moved by high hopes and goals. He/she always hoped to

_____

_____

_____

_____

_____

Our friend's accomplishments are so many, we cannot mention them all. But I think you'll all agree, he/she will be
remembered most because of

_____

_____

_____

_____

_____

Indeed, if we were to list his or her three most endearing qualities, they would be:

_____

_____

_____

_____

_____

His/her most important contribution was in the area of

_____

_____

_____

_____

_____

It's hard to summarize an entire life in a single sentence. But our friend's life could be summed up by saying

_____

_____

_____

_____

Handout

MENTOR'S OR LEADER'S GUIDELINES

The purpose of this time with your spiritual companion is to reflect on his or her readiness to participate in the rite of confirmation—the public affirmation of baptism.

Both you and the confirmand with whom you are working will grow in faith in the future. We hope that the rite of confirmation will mark one of many times in which faith grows. We hope that confirmands will consider the Christian journey to be an important part of life and seek to grow further in the knowledge, love, and service of God as life goes on. Simply to have the desire and to make the attempt to grow in this direction is all that can be asked of any of us.

The following are some suggested questions that may be used during your time together. These, are only *suggestions*. Feel free to do what seems right to you.

- If you could position yourself under one of the "traffic signs" displayed on this retreat to describe where you are in your journey with God right now, which one would it be? Why?
- What about the Christian faith gives you the most hope?
- What about it do you have the most difficulty understanding?
- What have been some of the high points on your faith journey during the time you have spent with the group (or with your mentor)?
- What have been the low points?
- What's been of particular value to you during this time?
- What do you do during a typical week that you perceive as being of particular service to God?
- What do you think and feel about making a public affirmation of your baptism or about being baptized? Is it something you want to do now? Why or why not?
- What did you compose as your prayer?
- What are some of the questions you still have?

Gathered Here

Text and Music: Phil Porter, 1990

Gath-ered here in the mys-tery of this hour, gath-ered here in one strong

bod - y, gath-ered here in the strug-gle and the power, Spir - it draw near.

This chant may be sung as a round.

Great Work Has God Begun in You

Carol Birkland, 1995

Tune: VERBUM DEI L.M.
William P. Rowan, 1993
Alternate tune: PUER NOBIS NASCITUR

1 Great work has God begun in you, so let the Spir - it
2 In love, God calls you to this day, and gives you strength, these
3 A - round God's ta - ble cel - e - brate the end of bond - age,
4 Great work has God be - gun in you; take on God's love in

fol - low through; The mark of Christ up - on your brow, bap -
vows to say; Take up the faith that you were shown, and
sin, and hate: A feast of love and vic - to - ry, the
all you do, And may that love in you in - crease—now,

tis - mal touch re - mem - ber now.
grow, as - sured you are God's own.
gift of Christ who sets us free.
with God's bless - ing, go in peace.

Bring Many Names

Brian Wren, 1989

Tune: WESTCHASE 9.10.11.9.
Carlton R. Young, 1989

1 Bring man-y names, beau-ti-ful and good, cel-e-brate, in
2 Strong moth-er God, work-ing night and day, plan-ning all the
3 Warm fa-ther God, hug-ging ev-ery child, feel-ing all the
4 Old, ach-ing God, grey with end-less care, calm-ly pierc-ing

par-a-ble and sto-ry, ho-li-ness in glo-ry, liv-ing, lov-ing God.
won-ders of cre-a-tion, set-ting each e-qua-tion, gen-i-us at play:
strains of hu-man liv-ing, car-ing and for-giv-ing till we're rec-on-ciled:
e-vil's new dis-guis-es, glad of good sur-pris-es, wis-er than de-spair:

1–5
Hail   and Ho-san-na! bring man-y names!
Hail   and Ho-san-na, strong moth-er God!
Hail   and Ho-san-na, warm   fa-ther God!
Hail   and Ho-san-na, old,   ach-ing God!

6
great, liv-ing God!

5 Young, grow-ing God, ea-ger,
       on the move,
   say-ing no to false-hood and
       un-kind-ness,
   cry-ing out for jus-tice,
       giv-ing all you have:
   Hail and Ho-san-na,
       young, grow-ing God!

6 Great, liv-ing God, nev-er ful-ly known,
   joy-ful dark-ness far be-yond our see-ing,
       clo-ser yet than breath-ing,
       ev-er-last-ing home:
   Hail and Ho-san-na,
       great, liv-ing God!

I Thank You, Jesus

Words and music: Kenneth Morris, 1948; alt.

Arr. by Joyce Finch Johnson, 1992

For All the Saints

William W. How, 1864; alt.

Tune: SINE NOMINE 10.10.10.4.
Ralph Vaughan Williams, 1906

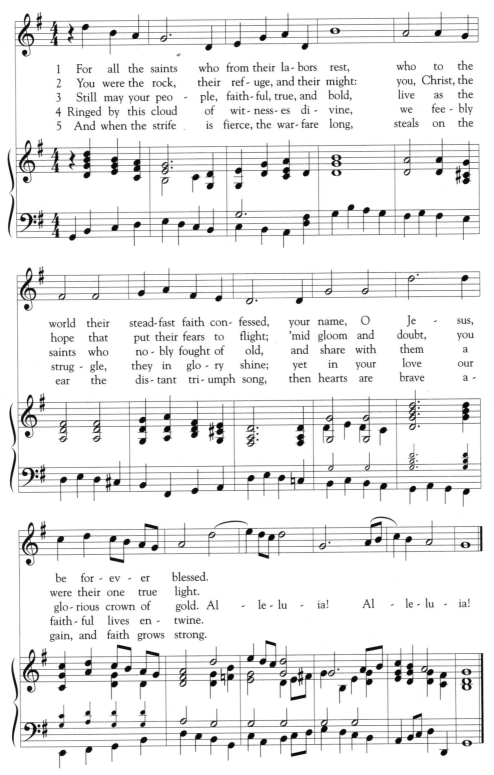

1 For all the saints who from their la-bors rest, who to the world their stead-fast faith con-fessed, your name, O Je - sus, be for-ev - er blessed.

2 You were the rock, their ref - uge, and their might: you, Christ, the hope that put their fears to flight; 'mid gloom and doubt, you were their one true light.

3 Still may your peo - ple, faith-ful, true, and bold, live as the saints who no - bly fought of old, and share with them a glo - rious crown of gold. Al - le-lu - ia! Al - le-lu - ia!

4 Ringed by this cloud of wit-ness-es di - vine, we fee-bly strug - gle, they in glo - ry shine; yet in your love our faith-ful lives en - twine.

5 And when the strife is fierce, the war-fare long, steals on the ear the dis-tant tri - umph song, then hearts are brave a - gain, and faith grows strong.

Let Us Break Bread Together

African American spiritual

Tune: LET US BREAK BREAD
10.10. with refrain
Harm. David Hurd, 1983

1 Let us   break bread to-geth-er   on our   knees;
*2 Let us   drink wine to-geth-er   on our   knees;
3 Let us   praise God to-geth-er   on our   knees;

let us   break bread to-geth-er   on our   knees.
let us   drink wine to-geth-er   on our   knees.
let us   praise God to-geth-er   on our   knees.

Refrain

When I   fall   on my   knees,   with my   face to the ris-ing   sun,

* "Share the cup" *may be substituted for* "drink wine."

My   God, have   mer-cy   on   me.

Spirit of the Living God

Daniel Iverson, 1926

Tune: IVERSON 7.5.7.5.8.7.5.
Daniel Iverson, 1926

Nada te Turbe
(Nothing Can Trouble)

Text: The Taizé Community, 1991   Music: Jacques Berthier, 1991

Na - da te tur - be,   na - da te_es - pan - te.   Quien a Dios tie - ne
Noth-ing can trou-ble,   noth-ing can fright-en.   Those who seek God shall

na - da   le   fal - ta.   So - lo   Dios   bas - ta.
nev - er   go   want - ing. God   a - lone   fills   us.

We Are Your People

Brian Wren, 1973; rev. 1993

Tune: WHITFIELD Irr.
John W. Wilson, 1975

Unison

1 We are your peo - ple: Spir - it of   grace,
2 Joined in com - mu - ni - ty,   trea - sured and   fed,
3 Rich in di - ver - si - ty,   help us to   live
4 Glad of tra - di - tion,   help us to   see

you dare to   make us   Christ to our   neigh - bors
may we dis - cov - er   gifts in each   oth - er,
clos - er than   neigh - bors,   o - pen to   strang - ers,
in all life's   chang - ing,   where Christ is   lead - ing,

1 & 6   *Last time, end*   **2–5**

of   ev - ery   cul - ture   and   place.
will - ing to   lead   and   be   led.
a - ble to   clash   and   for - give.
where our best   ef - forts   should   be.

5   Give, as we ven-ture
      jus-tice and care
            (peace-ful, in-sist-ing,
            risk-ing, re-sist-ing),
      wis-dom to know when and where.

6   Spir-it, u-nite us,
      make us, by grace,
            will-ing and read-y,
            Christ's liv-ing bod-y,
      lov-ing the whole hu-man race.

Be Still

Ps. 46:10

Music: Anon.

Be still and know that I am God. Be still and know that

I am God. Be still and know that I am God.

Tú Has Venido a la Orilla
(You Have Come Down to the Lakeshore)

Cesáreo Gabaraín, 1979; alt.
Transl. Madeleine Forell Marshall, 1989; alt.

Tune: PESCADOR DE HOMBRES
8.10.10. with refrain
Cesáreo Gabaraín, 1979
Harm. Skinner Chávez-Melo, 1987

1 Tú has ve-ni-do a la o-ri-lla, no has bus-
2 Tú sa-bes bien lo que ten-go: en mi

1 You have come down to the lake-shore seek-ing
2 You know full well my pos-ses-sions. Nei-ther

ca-do ni a sa-bios, ni a ri-cos, tan só-lo
bar-ca no hay o-ro ni es-pa-das; tan só-lo

nei-ther the wise nor the weal-thy, But on-ly
trea-sure nor weap-ons for con-quest, Just these my

Estribillo (Refrain)

quie-res que yo te si-ga. Je-
re-des y mi tra-ba-jo.
ask-ing for me to fol-low. O
fish-nets and will for work-ing.

sús, me has mi-ra-do a los o-jos;
Je-sus, you have looked in-to my eyes;

son - ri - en - do,   has di - cho mi nom - bre;
kind - ly smil - ing,   you've called out my name.

en la a - re - na   he de - ja - do mi bar - ca;
On the sand   I   have a - ban - doned my small boat;

jun - to a ti   bus - ca - ré o - tro mar.
now with you   I   will seek o - ther seas.

3 Tú ne-ce-si-tas mis ma-nos,
   mi can-san-cio que a o-tros des-can-se,
a-mor que quie-ra se-guir a-man-do.
   Estribillo

4 Tú, Pes-ca-dor de o-tros ma-res,
   an-sia e-ter-na de al-mas que es-pe-ran.
A-mi-go bue-no, que a-sí me lla-mas.
   Estribillo

3 You need my hands, my ex-haus-tion,
   work-ing love for the rest of the
      wea-ry—
A love that's will-ing to go on lov-ing.
   Refrain

4 You who have fished oth-er wa-ters;
   you, the long-ing of souls that are
      yearn-ing:
As lov-ing Friend, you have come
   to call me.
   Refrain

Amazing Grace, How Sweet the Sound
(Onuniyan tehanl waun)

St. 1–4, John Newton, 1779; alt.
St. 5, *A Collection of Sacred Ballads*, 1790
Lakota trans. Stephen W. Holmes, 1987

Tune: AMAZING GRACE C.M.
(NEW BRITAIN)
Columbia Harmony, Cincinnati, 1829
Arr. Edwin O. Excell, 1900

1 A - maz - ing grace, how sweet the sound, that
2 'Twas grace that taught my heart to fear, and
3 Through man - y dan - gers, toils, and snares, I
4 My God has prom - ised good to me, whose
5 When we've been there ten thou - sand years, bright

saved a wretch like me! I once was lost, but
grace my fears re - lieved; How pre - cious did that
have al - read - y come; 'Tis grace has brought me
word my hope se - cures; God will my shield and
shin - ing as the sun, We've no less days to

now am found, was blind but now I see.
grace ap - pear the hour I first be - lieved!
safe thus far, and grace will lead me home.
por - tion be as long as life en - dures.
sing God's praise than when we'd first be - gun.

1 O-nu-ni-yan te-hanl wa-un,
    Ma-shi-cha tke wa-ni,
    Wo-wash-te kin i-ye-wa-ye,
    wi-cho-ni wan-bla-ke.

2 Wo-wash-te he chan-te ma-hel,
    wash-ag-ma-ya-yin kte,
    Wo-wi cha-ke kin un le-hanl,
    o-a-pe kin wan-na.

3 O-ta kig-le te-ke wan el,
    eg-na i-ma-cha-ge,
    Wo-wash-te kin hel ma-wa-ni,
    Wash-te o-ma-ju-la.

4 O-to-ka-he-ya chi-ya-tan,
    o-hin-ni-yan ya-un,
    Wa-kan-tan-ka wo-wi-tan kin,
    yu-ha ma-wa-ni kte.

5 Wa-kan-tan-ka ya-tan un-we,
    Wa-kan-tan-ka ya-tan,
    Wa-kan-tan-ka ya-tan un-we,
    wa-kan-tan-ka a-men.

Called as Partners in Christ's Service

Jane Parker Huber, 1981

Tune: BEECHER 8.7.8.7.D.
John Zundel, 1855

1 Called as part-ners in Christ's ser-vice, called to min-is-tries of grace,
2 Christ's ex-am-ple, Christ's in-spir-ing, Christ's clear call to work and worth,
3 Thus new pat-terns for Christ's mis-sion, in a small or glob-al sense,
4 So God grant us for to-mor-row ways to or-der hu-man life

We re-spond with deep com-mit-ment fresh new lines of faith to trace.
Let us fol-low, nev-er fal-tering, rec-on-cil-ing folk on earth.
Help us bear each oth-er's bur-dens, break-ing down each wall or fence.
That sur-round each per-son's sor-row with a calm that con-quers strife.

May we learn the art of shar-ing, side by side and friend with friend,
Men and wom-en, rich-er, poor-er, all God's peo-ple, young and old,
Words of com-fort, words of vi-sion, words of chal-lenge, said with care,
Make us part-ners in our liv-ing, our com-pas-sion to in-crease,

E-qual part-ners in our car-ing to ful-fill God's cho-sen end.
Blend-ing hu-man skills to-geth-er gra-cious gifts from God un-fold.
Bring new power and strength for ac-tion, make us col-leagues, free and fair.
Mes-sen-gers of faith, thus giv-ing hope and con-fi-dence and peace.

Wakantanka Taku Nitawa
(Many and Great, O God, Are Your Works)

Dakota hymn, Joseph R. Renville, 1842
Paraphr. by R. Philip Frazier, 1929; alt.

Tune: LACQUIPARLE 9.6.9.9.9.6.
Native American melody (Dakota)
Adapt. Joseph R. Renville, 1842
Harm. James R. Murray, 1877

Creeds and Statements of Faith

APOSTLES' CREED

I believe in God, the Father almighty,

    creator of heaven and earth.

I believe in Jesus Christ, God's only Son, our Lord,

    who was conceived by the Holy Spirit,

    born of the Virgin Mary,

    suffered under Pontius Pilate,

    was crucified, died and was buried;

    he descended to the dead.

On the third day he rose again;

    he ascended into heaven,

    he is seated at the right hand of the Father,

    and he will come to judge the living and the dead.

I believe in the Holy Spirit,

    the holy catholic Church,

    the communion of the saints,

    the forgiveness of sins,

    the resurrection of the body,

    and the life everlasting. Amen.

—English Language Liturgical Consultation[1]

UNITED CHURCH OF CHRIST STATEMENT OF FAITH IN THE FORM OF A DOXOLOGY

We believe in you, O God, Eternal Spirit,

God of our Savior Jesus Christ and our God,

and to your deeds we testify:

> You call the worlds into being,
>
> > create persons in your own image,
> >
> > and set before each one the ways of life and death.
>
> You seek in holy love to save all people from aimlessness and sin.
>
> You judge people and nations by your righteous will declared through prophets and apostles.
>
> In Jesus Christ, the man of Nazareth, our crucified and risen Savior,
>
> > you have come to us
> >
> > and shared our common lot,
> >
> > conquering sin and death
> >
> > and reconciling the world to yourself.
>
> You bestow upon us your Holy Spirit,
>
> > creating and renewing the church of Jesus Christ,
> >
> > binding in covenant faithful people of all ages, tongues, and races.
>
> You call us into your church
>
> > to accept the cost and joy of discipleship,
> >
> > to be your servants in the service of others,
> >
> > to proclaim the gospel to all the world
> >
> > and resist the powers of evil,
> >
> > to share in Christ's baptism and eat at his table,
> >
> > to join him in his passion and victory.
>
> You promise to all who trust you
>
> > forgiveness of sins and fullness of grace,
> >
> > courage in the struggle for justice and peace,
> >
> > your presence in trial and rejoicing,
> >
> > and eternal life in your realm which has no end.

Blessing and honor, glory and power be unto you.

Amen.[2]

A Service of Dedication for Confirmands, Leaders, and Mentors[3]

Here is a service of dedication that can be used at the beginning of a faith formation program before the opening retreat is held. It assumes that the pastor and other leaders will have met beforehand with the confirmands, leaders, parents or guardians, and mentors (if mentoring is a part of the program). It would be most appropriate to have this celebration during a regular service of worship, with the entire congregation present. This portion of the liturgy could follow the Service of the Word. At that time the pastor would invite the confirmands, leaders, and mentors to come forward before the assembled congregation to be introduced. A brief description of the faith formation process could be made. Then the following liturgy could be used.

THE JOURNEY OF FAITH

Pastor (or another leader): All Christians are on a journey. It is a journey to a place where we seek to find meaning in life, to that place where we come to know God. It is a journey away from the place where we think of ourselves first, to the place where we can offer ourselves to others. All of us are on this journey for the duration of our lives. Ours is a journey of learning—in which we seek to learn more about God and how to please God. Ours is a journey of growing—in which we seek to mature in those ways we may serve God more faithfully.

These young people come before us today because they have come to a significant point in their own journeys. They are about to engage in an intentional faith formation process together, with the hope that, at its conclusion, they may join us in publicly affirming the Christian faith into which we have been baptized.

These adults from our congregation have agreed to be present with the youth as guides [and mentors] for the length of this process. As such, they will share with them their own faith, learning along with them.

But faith formation requires the support of the entire community of faith. Therefore, as these people take their next steps in faith, they need our support, encouragement, and prayers. I therefore ask each of you to express your commitment to the next segment of the faith journey these young people are about to make.

Pastor (addressing the confirmands): Do you desire to join with one another and with your leaders [and mentors] to journey together in the Christian faith? Do you wish to learn and grow more fully in the ways of God, Christ, and the Spirit?

Confirmands: I do.

Pastor (addressing the leaders [and mentors]): Do you desire to join with each other and with the confirmands to journey together in the Christian faith? Do you wish to learn and grow more fully in the ways of God, Christ, and the Spirit?

Leaders [and Mentors]: I do.

Pastor (addressing congregation): Will you, the people of [congregation] give your support to these sisters and brothers in Christ, to uphold them and encourage them in faith wherever possible, and keep them in your prayers?

Congregation: We will.

BLESSING

For this blessing, the leaders [and/or mentors] stand behind the confirmands, placing a hand on their shoulders. The pastor, deacon, or other worship leader approaches each confirmand and, in turn, makes a cross on the forehead (using oil to anoint each one, if desired) with the thumb, saying the following:

Pastor: [Name], by this sign of God's love, Christ will be your strength; let the Spirit guide you into the way of truth.

As the leaders [or mentors] continue to lay their hands on the confirmands, the confirmands pray the following:

Confirmands: May my ears be open to hear the voice of God; may my eyes be open to see the light of Christ; may my lips speak words of truth.

Leaders [or Mentors] (with hands still on confirmands' shoulders): May your shoulders bear the yoke of Christ; may your heart be filled with faith; may your feet follow in the way God has prepared for you.

Pastor: May the Spirit fill every part of you, and be with you in all you say and do

Pastor (addressing the congregation): Let us pray.

Congregation (unison): Gracious God, you are the One in whom we live and move and have our being. Draw near to these persons who seek to grow in faith. Steadily increase in them, and in us, the desire to follow you, courage to question you, and willingness to learn from you. We ask this through Christ our Savior. Amen.

Pastor (to confirmands, leaders [and mentors]): The peace of God be with you.

Signs of peace may be exchanged. Confirmands and leaders [and mentors] reassume their places in the congregation.

ACOLYTE. An attendant who assists in worship.

ADOPTIONISM. The teaching that Jesus was by birth only human and adopted by God as God's child at the time of Jesus' baptism. It is the opposite of incarnation.

ADORATION. To give honor, glory, and love to God.

ADULTERY. Unfaithfulness to the marriage vow.

ADVENT. The season of the church year that consists of the four Sundays before Christmas.

AFFIRM, AFFIRMATION. To confirm, ratify, or express agreement with and to be willing to assert this agreement with others.

AGAPE. The Greek word for love used in the New Testament for God's love and the way Christians love one another (1 Corinthians 13); God's love in Jesus Christ. Self-giving love, often distinguished from other Greek words for love: *eros* (longing, desire, erotic love) and *philia* (brotherly and sisterly love). The *agape* or feast of love was a common meal of early Christians (1 Corinthians 11:20).

AGNOSTICISM. From the Greek word *agnostos*: unknown or unknowable. A skepticism about or claim that God simply cannot be discovered or known by humans. Distinguished from atheism, which declares that God does not exist at all.

AIMLESSNESS. Having no aim or purpose.

ALMIGHTY. Having power over all; all-powerful.

ALPHA AND OMEGA. "A", the first letter of the Greek alphabet; omega, the first of a sequence or order (Ω), is the last letter of the Greek alphabet, like the English "z". "I am the Alpha and Omega, the first and the last, the beginning and the end" says the Lamb of God, Christ, who is coming soon (Revelation 22:13).

ALTAR. A raised structure used in the performance of religious rites in the Hebrew Scriptures for animal, grain, or incense offerings to God and in today's Christian church for the celebration of Holy Communion. Also called the communion table, Lord's table, or holy table.

AMEN. "So be it." A word used to express agreement.

ANGEL. A messenger of God.

ANOINT. To apply oil, ointment, or fragrances to the body. This was done in ancient times for a number of reasons: anointing the head as part of body care and cleansing (Matthew 6:17); anointing the head as a religious ceremony of initiation into the office of prophet, priest, or king (the title Messiah or Christ means the anointed one); a way of ministering to the wounded and the sick (Isaiah 1:6, Luke 10:34); a preparation of the dead for burial (Luke 23:56).

ANTHEM. A sacred composition for a choir, often with words from the Bible.

APOSTLE. One who is sent out to preach the gospel; a missionary.

APOSTLE'S CREED. A statement of faith from the early Christian church.

ASCENSION DAY. The fortieth day after Jesus' resurrection; commemorates the ascension into heaven (Acts 1:3–11).

ASH WEDNESDAY. The first day of Lent, so named because of a service in which ashes are placed on the forehead or back of the hand.

ASSOCIATION. A group of United Church of Christ congregations in a given area that organize for ministry and mission.

ATHEISM. A belief that there is no God. *See also* AGNOSTICISM.

ATONEMENT. "At-one-ment"; reconciliation between people and God through Christ.

BAPTISM. The sacrament through which God's grace, love, claim, and covenant are expressed to a person and through which that person is incorporated into Christ and the church. *See also* IMMERSION.

BEATITUDES. Blessings or statements about blessedness or happiness. Jesus's beatitudes are found in Matthew 5:3–12 and Luke 6:20–26.

BEGOTTEN. Brought into being, created.

BENEDICTION. From the Latin words *bene* (well) and *dicero* (to say). To praise, speak well, bless. The words spoken to a congregation at the end of a service of worship by the minister of God, or at other times when God's blessing is asked for.

BIBLE. The book made up of writings accepted by Christians as inspired by God and having divine authority; the Hebrew and early Christian Scriptures (also called the Old and New Testaments).

BIBLICAL CRITICISM. Critical judgment by biblical scholars based on the tools of analysis to find out as much as possible about Scripture. Not negative criticism, but constructive and challenging questions to get a clearer understanding of the meaning of Scripture, such as the following: What is the form and structure of the text? What kind of literature is it (history, story, laws, poetry, sayings, liturgy, legend, etc.)? Where does it fit in the whole book? Who wrote it and why? What was happening around that time? How did the first hearers understand it? What does it say to us in our day?

BLESS, BLESSING, BLESSED. The giving and receiving of God's good will and grace, bringing prosperity and happiness: long life, children, crops, herds, wisdom, righteousness, peace. Jesus spoke the blessings called Beatitudes (Matthew 5:2–12). The sign of blessing was often the laying on of hands (Matthew 19:15).

BODY OF CHRIST. A metaphor for the church found in the writings of the apostle Paul.

BUDGET. A plan of how much money is to be spent and for what purposes.

BULLETIN. A brief statement of the latest news; a regular publication of an organization; a worship bulletin.

CALL. A summons to a specific duty or vocation. In the church ministers are called to ministry in a community.

CATECHISM. Oral instruction—often using question, answer, correction—of those preparing for admission to church membership by learning the essentials of faith, discipline, and morals. These persons were called "catechumens" in the early church. The official manual for such instruction, such as the Heidelberg Catechism or the Evangelical Catechism.

CATHOLIC. Universal, applying to the whole Christian church. Sometimes used to mean Roman Catholic. *See also* ECUMENICAL and UNIVERSAL.

CHALICE. The cup used for wine in Holy Communion.

CHANCEL. The area surrounding the altar or communion table in a church.

CHOIR. An organized group of singers, usually in a church.

CHRIST. The Greek word for Messiah.

CHRISTIAN. A follower of Christ; one who accepts Christ as Savior and follows Jesus' teachings.

CHRISTIAN STORY. The whole faith tradition of the Christian people, however that is expressed or embodied.

CHURCH. The community of all believers in Christ; a body of believers holding the same beliefs and following the same practices, as in a denomination; often used incorrectly to refer to a building.

CHURCH YEAR. *See* LITURGICAL YEAR.

CLERGY. People who have been ordained to the ministry of Word and sacrament.

COMMANDMENT. An order; decisive declarations of God or Jesus, as in the Ten Commandments.

COMMISSION. An authorization to perform certain duties or take on certain powers. To authorize, empower, or give a commission.

COMMUNICANT. One who partakes of the sacrament of Holy Communion.

COMMUNION. A full spiritual relationship between people; participation in the sacrament of Holy Communion; a denomination.

CONCEIVED. Brought into life or existence.

CONFERENCE. A regional or state organization of United Church of Christ congregations.

CONFESSION. An admission of wrongdoing or sin; a statement of belief.

CONFIRMAND. A person preparing for the rite of confirmation.

CONFIRMATION. A rite of the church in which a person affirms his or her baptism. In many local churches, the rite of confirmation is preceded by a time of faith exploration and formation.

CONGREGATION. Christians in a local church when they are gathered for worship, education, mission, work, or deliberation.

CONGREGATIONAL. A form of church government in which the congregation is the basic unit of decision-making.

CONGREGATIONAL CHRISTIAN CHURCHES. One of the two denominations that joined to form the United Church of Christ in 1957. *See also* EVANGELICAL AND REFORMED CHURCH.

CONSCIENCE. The sense or consciousness of right or wrong; an inner voice that impels us to do right in harmony with God's will.

CONSECRATE. To declare sacred or holy; to dedicate or set apart for the service or worship of God.

CONSISTORY. The governing body of a congregation; the church council.

COVENANT. A solemn agreement between two or more people; an agreement between God and people.

CREATION. The universe and everything in it.

CREED. A statement of belief.

CRUCIFIXION. A form of execution used by the Romans in the first century in which a criminal was nailed or bound by the wrists or hands and feet to a cross to die. The manner in which Jesus was put to death.

CUP, THE. The chalice; often used in place of the word *wine* in speaking of the communion elements.

DEACON. From the Greek word *diakonos*, literally a servant or one who waits on tables (Luke 17:8, 22:25–27). Jesus described his ministry as one who came not to be served, but to serve (Mark 10:45). In the early Christian community, the offices were ministries serving God and the brothers and sisters of the fellowship. Today a deacon is a lay minister who serves the church.

DEBTS. Often used in place of *trespasses* in the Prayer of Our Savior to mean sin or wrongdoings.

DEDICATE. To set apart to the service or the worship of God.

DEMON. A person or thing regarded as evil or cruel; an evil spirit.

DENOMINATION. A group of congregations that have the same beliefs and the same type of church government.

DEVIL. The personification of evil; an evil spirit.

DISCERNING, DISCERNMENT. Perceiving or recognizing, as in perceiving or recognizing the will of God.

DISCIPLE. The English form of the Latin *discipulus* (from *discere*, to learn); thus, a disciple is a learner, pupil, apprentice. The Jews were disciples of Moses (John 9:28); both John the Baptist and Jesus had disciples as followers. In the Gospels it refers to the large group of men and women who followed Jesus, including the Twelve.

DISCIPLESHIP. Being a disciple or follower of Christ.

DIVINE. Pertaining to God.

DOCETISM. A belief that Jesus Christ only seemed to be human but really wasn't.

DOXOLOGY. A hymn or chant in praise of God; frequently refers to the hymn beginning "Praise God from whom all blessings flow."

EASTER. The day on which we celebrate the resurrection of Christ.

ECCLESIASTICAL. Having to do with the church.

ECUMENICAL. Worldwide; a consciousness of belonging to the worldwide Christian fellowship. *See also* CATHOLIC and UNIVERSAL.

ELDER. An officer of the church who helps the pastor in caring for the spiritual life of the members. (In some congregations, this is the deacon's role.)

ELEMENTS. The bread and wine (or grape juice) used in Holy Communion.

EPIPHANY. The season of the church year that celebrates the coming of the Magi as the revelation of Christ to the Gentiles. It begins on January 6.

EROS. Greek word for longing, desire, erotic love. *See also* AGAPE and *PHILIA*.

ETERNAL LIFE. Continuing community with God in this life and after death.

EUCHARIST. From *eucharisita*, the giving of thanks. Holy Communion or the Sacrament of the Lord's Supper (1 Corinthians 11:20), which was the common meal, *agape*, commemorating the last supper of Jesus with his disciples.

EVANGELICAL. Contained in the four Gospels; a Protestant denomination holding certain beliefs.

EVANGELICAL AND REFORMED CHURCH. One of the two denominations that joined to form the United Church of Christ in 1957. *See also* CONGREGATIONAL CHRISTIAN CHURCHES.

EVANGELISM. Telling the good news of God's redeeming love in Christ.

EVIL. Morally bad; contrary to divine law.

FAITH. Belief and trust in God.

FAITH FORMATION. An intentional process of growth in faith.

FAMILY. Persons bound together by blood ties or mutual commitments that are sustained by shared memory and common hope.

FELLOWSHIP. Communion; an organization of Christians in the church.

FONT. The basin containing water for baptism.

FORGIVENESS. Forgiveness is God's word and act whereby we sinful humans are put into a true and right relationship to God; it is an act of grace, undeserved by us, a true gift to repentant sinners who trust God's promise in Jesus Christ. In the Bible there are many metaphors for forgiveness, such as: covering a blemish (Psalm 78:38), paying a debt (Luke 7:43), an act of healing (Psalm 103:3), forgetting iniquity (Jeremiah 31:34), a pardon (Isaiah 55:7), carrying away a burden, or being gracious. Repentance (conversion, turning) is required for forgiveness—not as merit, but in recognition that forgiveness is both needed and possible, and thus accepted.

FUNERAL. A service of worship remembering a person who has died.

GENERAL SYNOD. The national decision-making body of the United Church of Christ.

GLORY. Honor and praise given to God in worship.

GOOD FRIDAY. The Friday before Easter Sunday; marks the day when Jesus was crucified. It is called "good" because of the new life won for us in Jesus' death.

GOSPEL. The good news of God's love in Christ; one of the four New Testament books that deal with the life and teachings of Jesus.

GRACE. Divine mercy, love, and forgiveness, granted without any consideration of what one really deserves; a prayer of blessing or thanks offered at mealtime.

HALLOWED. Blessed; holy; to be held in reverence.

HEAVEN. Where God dwells; the fulfillment of life on earth.

HELL. The Anglo-Saxon word for the abode of the dead; the place of punishment for sin committed during life. Hell is a biblical symbol for judgment, condemnation, and punishment—not a geographical location.

HOLY COMMUNION. Another name for the Lord's Supper.

HOLY GHOST OR HOLY SPIRIT. The third Person of the Trinity who is ever-present to guide us in the way of God.

HYMN. A song of praise, adoration, or prayer to God.

IDOL. An image made to represent God and used as an object of worship.

IDOLATRY. Worship of an idol; excessive love or veneration for anything.

IMMANENT, IMMANENCE. Living, remaining, or operating within.

IMMERSION. Baptism by submerging a person in water.

IMPOSITION OF ASHES. Placing ashes on the forehead, often in a worship service on Ash Wednesday.

INCARNATION. The coming of God in the person of Jesus; becoming flesh or human. *See also* ADOPTIONISM.

INTERCESSION. A petition or entreaty on behalf of someone else; mediation; a prayer *to* God *for* another person.

INVOCATION. Calling on God, often at the beginning of a worship service.

JUSTICE. Fairness, righteousness, wholeness.

KINGDOM OF GOD. A way of life in which the rule of God as revealed in Jesus Christ is accepted. *See also* HEAVEN and REALM OF GOD.

KOINONIA. The Greek New Testament word for the communion, community, and communalism that Christians claim is unique because it comes from their common relationship to God in Christ. Paul often used it for the fellowship of grace and gospel; it is *agape* love shared. *See also* AGAPE.

LAITY. Literally means "the people" and usually refers to all church members except the ordained clergy.

LAST SUPPER. The meal Jesus shared with the disciples on the night before his death. Another name for the sacrament of Holy Communion.

LECTERN. A reading desk from which the Scriptures are read.

LECTIONARY. A prescribed schedule of weekly scripture readings.

LENT. The season of the church year leading up to Easter.

LITANY. A prayer in which invocations and supplications are read or sung with alternated responses by the congregation.

LITURGICAL COLORS. Colors associated with each season of the church year that are used in worship.

LITURGICAL YEAR. The seasons of the church year: Advent, Christmas, Epiphany, Lent, Easter, and Pentecost.

LITURGY. Forms or rituals for public worship.

LORD'S SUPPER. The sacrament instituted by Christ through which we remember Christ's life and death on the cross for us and through which we receive the promise of new life. *See also* HOLY COMMUNION.

MARTYR. A witness to Christ; one who voluntarily suffered death for refusing to renounce Christ.

MAUNDY THURSDAY. The Thursday before Good Friday. *Maundy* comes from the Latin *mandatum*, meaning command; it refers to Jesus' word the night of the Last Supper: "A new commandment I give you, that you love one another; even as I have loved you, that you also love one another" (John 13:34).

MENTOR. A wise and loyal advisor.

MERCY. Forgiveness; love that overlooks harm that has been done to one.

METAPHOR. A figure of speech in which one thing is compared to another by saying that one item actually *is* the other.

MINISTER. A Christian who serves, helps, gives, comforts, protects, shepherds. Also, a Christian set apart by ordination to preach the word, administer the sacraments, conduct worship, and do all of the above ministries too. One of the offices in the church—along with teachers, evangelists, elders, overseers—that is a translation of *diakonos* or deacon.

MINISTRY. The act of ministering or serving.

MISSION. The ministry of the church when directed toward others and the world.

MISSIONARY. One who is sent to preach the gospel, to teach, and to heal in the name of Christ.

NARTHEX. The part of the church that leads into the main part; the vestibule.

NAVE. The sanctuary; the part of the church where the people sit. *See also* SANCTUARY.

NEWNESS OF LIFE. A gift of God through Christ; the continual change of mind and action in accordance with God's will.

OMEGA. The first of a sequence or order (Ω) is the last letter of the Greek alphabet, like the English "z". (Alpha is the first letter of the Greek alphabet, "A".) "I am the Alpha and Omega, the first and the last, the beginning and the end" says the Lamb of God, Christ, who is coming soon (Revelation 22:13). *See also* ALPHA.

ORDAINED MINISTER. One authorized to conduct Christian worship, preach and teach the gospel, administer the sacraments, and exercise pastoral care and leadership.

OUR CHURCH'S WIDER MISSION (OCWM). The work the United Church of Christ does in the United States and throughout the world for which people in local churches contribute money.

PALM SUNDAY. The Sunday before Easter; the beginning of Holy Week commemorating the waving of palms and the subsequent betrayal and crucifixion of Christ. Also known as Palm Sunday.

PARABLE. A story that illustrates a moral or religious principle.

PARISH. Originally the geographical area and people belonging to one pastor and church, a portion of a diocese. Today, in Protestant churches, it means simply a local church community and its members.

PAROUSIA. The Greek word meaning the coming or the presence. Used in the New Testament for the coming (again) of Christ. It is part of the Christian confession about the end and purpose of the human story. "He shall come to judge the quick and the dead" (Acts 10:42 KJV; Apostles' Creed).

PASSION SUNDAY. *See* PALM SUNDAY.

PASSOVER. The greatest Hebrew festival. It became a memorial of Yahweh's deliverance of Israel from slavery in Egypt and the founding of the covenant. In the New Testament and the Christian community, it became the background in time and meaning for the Last Supper, the death and resurrection of Christ as the liberator, and a new covenant with God.

PASTOR. The minister in charge of a congregation; from the Latin word meaning shepherd, therefore one who leads and takes care of the flock as a shepherd cares for sheep.

PEACE. In Greek and everyday American thought, peace is negative as "the absence or end of war." In the Bible, peace means what is affirmed by the Hebrew word *shalom*—wholeness, well-being, goodness that is free from misfortune, injustice, and violence. This tradition is reaffirmed by the New Testament where it is said of Christ, "He is our peace" (Ephesians 2:14–17). This peace is part of the meaning of love (Romans 12:28, 2 Corinthians 13:11).

PENTECOST. From the Greek meaning fiftieth day, because it is the fiftieth day, or seventh Sunday, after Easter, commemorating the events recorded in Acts 2 when the Holy Spirit came upon the early apostles. Sometimes called *Whitsunday*, a shortened form of white Sunday, for the white robes of those newly baptized during the festival.

PETITION. A request; that part of a prayer in which we ask God for something.

PHILIA. Greek word for brotherly and sisterly love. *See also* AGAPE and EROS.

PLURALISM. The quality or state of being more than only one of class or ethnic group; diversity and difference within a group; variety.

PRAYER. Speaking, listening, and responding to God either alone or with others.

PROPHET. One inspired by God to speak in God's name.

PROTESTANT. A person who belongs to one of the churches that has grown out of the Reformation begun by Luther, Zwingli, Calvin, and others; a protestor.

PROVIDENCE. Divine guidance or care. Another word for God.

PSALM. A sacred song or poem.

PULPIT. A raised platform, sometimes enclosed, where the minister stands while preaching.

QUICK, THE. The living; a phrase used in Acts 10:42 (KJV) and the Apostles' Creed.

RABBI. A Hebrew word meaning master or teacher.

REALM OF GOD. A way of life in which the rule of God as revealed in Jesus Christ is accepted. *See also* HEAVEN and KINGDOM OF GOD.

RECONCILIATION. Bringing back harmony after a misunderstanding; returning to community with God after sin has brought about separation.

REDEEMER. One who rescues or delivers another by paying the price; Christ, who rescues and delivers people from the slavery of sin.

REFORMATION. Changing into a new and improved form; the religious movement of the sixteenth century that reformed the church and resulted in the formation of various Protestant churches.

REPENTANCE. Feeling sorry for what one has done wrong and resolving to change one's life according to God's will. *See also* FORGIVENESS.

REREDOS. The screen or wall behind the altar of a church, made of wood, stone, or fabric and usually decorated with Christian symbols or images.

RESURRECTION. Being raised from death, as in Jesus' resurrection.

REVELATION. God's sharing of identity, will, and purpose.

REVISED COMMON LECTIONARY. A book containing a prescribed schedule of weekly scripture readings.

REVISION. A revised edition (as of the Bible); a new, improved, or up-to-date version.

RIGHTEOUS, RIGHTEOUSNESS. Doing that which is right; free from wrong or sin.

RIGHT HAND OF GOD. Biblically a position of honor and power in relation to God.

RITE. A ritual, or a prescribed form of conducting a religious ceremony, such as the rite of confirmation or marriage.

SABBATH. The seventh day of the week (Saturday) when the Hebrew people rested and worshiped God; used by Christians for Sunday.

SACRAMENT. A religious act and visible sign of God's grace and presence; baptism and Holy Communion, as instituted by Christ.

SACRED. Consecrated as being holy; set apart for the service and honor of God; dedicated and entitled to reverence and respect because of association with the divine; worthy of religious veneration. Holy in contrast to the profane and secular.

SACRIFICE. An offering to God; giving oneself for another, as in Christ's sacrifice to save all people.

SALVATION. The saving of people, especially our deliverance from sin through Christ's sacrifice; freedom from sin and community with God. The word literally means wholeness.

SANCTUARY. A place set aside and dedicated for the worship of God and therefore holy, such as the church sanctuary where the *sanctus* is said or sung. It also has the meaning of an asylum, a refuge, or a protected place where one is immune from the law in the presence of a higher law or authority.

SATAN. A name sometimes used in the Bible for the Devil, Demon, or the Adversary.

SCHISM. Church splitting; willfully separating oneself from the unity and community of the church to form a rival religious group.

SCRIPTURE(S). Sacred writings; the Bible.

SECULAR, SECULARISM. From the Latin *saeculum*, meaning "this age" or "the world"; worldliness. It is often used as the opposite of *the sacred* to indicate the difference between the church and the world.

SEMINARY. From the Latin *seminarium*. A professional school preparing men and women for ordination and service in the church.

SERMON. Proclamation of the Word of God; a discourse by a minister, based on a passage of scripture, for the purpose of religious instruction and inspiration.

SHALOM. Wholeness, health, justice, and peace. A shalom person is what the Bible means by the new person in Jesus Christ. A shalom society is what is envisioned by the rule of God bringing justice and righteousness.

SIN. Separation, being separated from God, from other people, from what is best in oneself.

SOUL. The essential self; the deep spirit in people.

SPIRIT. The breath of life; the soul; the Holy Spirit.

STATEMENT OF FAITH. The statement adopted by the United Church of Christ in 1959 and revised in 1977 and 1981 for use in worship and other settings as a testimony to the historic faith of the church.

STEWARDSHIP. The management of one's time, talents, and possessions in accordance with the will of God; thinking of all one has as a sacred trust to be used in service for God and humanity.

SYNAGOGUE. An assembly of Jewish persons for worship and religious study.

SYNOD. A church assembly or council, as in the United Church of Christ General Synod.

TEMPTATION. That which entices, especially to do evil; that by which one is tested or tried.

TESTAMENT. A solemn agreement or covenant; one of the two main divisions of the Bible—the one being the result of the covenant made between God and the Israelites on Mount Sinai; the other the result of the covenant made through Christ for all people.

THEOLOGY. Literally, "God talk"; the knowledge of God; the study of religion and religious ideas.

TITHE. A tenth part of something given as a contribution or tax for religious purposes—for example, giving ten percent of your annual income to the church.

TORAH. Law; commandment. Used as a title for the five books of Moses (Genesis, Exodus, Leviticus, Numbers, Deuteronomy), which contain the history of God's law for the children of Israel. An essential part of the covenant.

TRANSCENDENT, TRANSCENDENCE. Existing apart from the material universe.

TRANSLATION. Writings, such as the Bible, changed from one version or language into another.

TRESPASSES. Often used in place of *debts* in the Prayer of Our Savior; sin or wrongdoing.

TRINITY. God in three beings: God, Christ, and Holy Spirit (or Creator, Redeemer, and Sustainer). The Trinity is celebrated on the eighth Sunday after Easter in the liturgical year.

TRIUNE. Three in one; one God in three beings.

UNIVERSAL. Including all people on earth. *See also* CATHOLIC and ECUMENICAL.

VERSION. A particular translation of the Bible.

VISION. In the Bible, a vision is an ecstatic experience or dream in which new knowledge is revealed through something seen—whether experienced internally or externally.

VOCATION. A call to enter a certain career. The term is used more broadly in the church to mean a call to ministry and service in your particular occupation.

VOW. To make a solemn promise; to swear, pledge, consecrate—especially during a religious ceremony where a covenant is being affirmed, for example, marriage vows, confirmation vows, baptismal vows.

WAY, THE. The early Christians were sometimes called "people of the way" (Acts 19:23). They were followers of Jesus, who said, "I am the way, and the truth, and the life" (John 14:6).

WEDDING. The act of becoming married, the marriage ceremony and festivities.

WITNESS. A person who sees and can give a firsthand account of something.

WORD OF GOD. The truth of God revealed in the writings of the Bible, in Jesus Christ, and through the Holy Spirit.

WORSHIP. Honoring God; the act whereby believers enter into communion with God.

A GUIDE FOR YOUTH LEADERS

WORKING WITH YOUTH IN A FAITH FORMATION PROGRAM IS BOTH JOYFUL AND CHALLENGING. IT IS IMPORTANT BOTH FOR LEADERS TO UNDERSTAND THE YOUTH IN YOUR PROGRAM, AND FOR YOUR CONGREGATION TO GIVE SPECIAL CARE TO THE RECRUITMENT AND SUPPORT OF THOSE WHO WILL BE LEADERS IN THE PROGRAM.

Understanding the Youth in Your Group

Younger youth are actively forging identities that are different from the parental identities which they have shared in large measure. In adolescence, the process becomes more pressing as physical maturation inspires a new sense of power and possibility apart from parents. In developing a unique identity, youth test the life boundaries established by their parents and other adults. They seek to discover how far they may go in new and different directions. More and more their peers will be the models to which they compare their own identity, independence, and ability. However, both they and their peers experience great uncertainty as a result of the same changes that give them their sense of power and possibility: "What is happening to me? Why is my body acting this way? Why am I feeling this way inside? Why are 'they' treating me in that way?" No wonder young adolescents seem so mixed up and unpredictable. They are! Their bodies and emotions, peers and parents give them very mixed messages: "You're just a kid. Act like an adult!"

In this confusing and rapidly changing state of affairs, younger youth need understanding and supportive care as well as clear boundaries and expectations. With all of their internal inconsistencies, they need some external consistency from adults. They also need opportunities to be in dialogue with adults who give them unconditional love and witness to vital faith and life.

Older youth may already have weathered some of the more turbulent storms of early adolescence. They probably have developed some thinking skills to help them sort through the changes and challenges of moving from childhood to adulthood. Their capacity for abstraction is far greater. That is, they can generalize principles from the particulars of their experience and apply those principles to later experiences, even somewhat different ones.

Older youth have become more accustomed to the emotional ups and downs of their lives, although they may still be troubled by them. They also are learning new relationship-building skills. As they become more at ease with themselves, they become more at ease with one another. However, there is still a lot of exploration and testing to be done, especially as to the boundaries of human relationships. For many older youth, testing has a decidedly sexual quality. It also has, for some, a vocational quality. In other words, older youth may be searching for their place in relationship to others personally and professionally, asking, "Who will I be and what will I do?"

Policies and Procedures

When young persons are placed in our charge, they deserve the best care and protection we can give. Every congregation readily acknowledges this. Yet how we accomplish this task requires special attention.

State and federal laws, the courts, and even insurance carriers all have something to say about adults working with children and youth. Most states require that adults working with children and youth undergo background checks. Generally no adults working with children and youth are exempted from this scrutiny. Depending on your state, this may involve letters of reference or a combination of practices that can include fingerprinting and FBI checks. Check with your state offices to know about specific requirements for your congregation.

While screening adults does not guarantee there will not be problems, it does send clear messages that your congregation cares about its children and youth and is serious about ensuring their protection. Likewise, this is how your congregation protects itself from liability suits and other legal actions.

These are not comfortable nor familiar practices for many churches. If it has not already done so, your congregation should establish policies concerning sexual exploitation, sexual harassment, and a manual of practices in case exploitation occurs. Specific policies should be drafted for youth programs. These policies and practices should cover: the use of permission forms for trips; information sheets for parents/guardians; how guests are or are not to be included in activities; medical information and treatment permission forms; covenants defining appropriate and inappropriate behavior for adult and youth participants; how misconduct and violations of covenants will be handled; and background screening procedures for adults.

The following materials include sample forms for conducting an adult background screening. These materials are provided to help the Leadership Team become aware of the procedures and questions that are necessary to establish policies and practices for the faith formation program and for the congregation as well. These are samples; the resources should not be used without consulting legal counsel.

Additional information is available from your conference or association office; your state's offices for education or human services; the Minister for Education in Human Identity and Youth and Young Adult Programs, United Church Board for Homeland Ministries (216-736-3789); the Office for Church Life and Leadership of the United Church of Christ (216-736-2130); and Christian Ministry Resources in their publication *Church Law and Tax Report* (1-800-222-1840).

Sample Adult Advisor Form

Name   _____

Address   _____

            _____

            _____

Home Phone _____

Work Phone _____

If you need more space to answer the following questions, use additional sheets of paper and attach them to this form. Be sure your name and home phone number are on each.

Have you ever been found guilty, or plead guilty or no contest, to a criminal charge alleging actual or attempted sexual harassment, exploitation, misconduct, physical abuse, or child abuse by you?

Yes _____ No _____   If yes, give a short explanation of the charge.

Has a civil or ecclesiastical complaint ever been made against you alleging actual or attempted sexual harassment, exploitation, misconduct, physical abuse, or child abuse by you?

Yes _____ No _____   If yes, give a short explanation of the charge.

Is there any fact or circumstance involving you or your background that would call into question you being entrusted with responsibilities involving youth in our programs?

Yes _____ No _____   If yes, please provide a brief explanation.

(continued on next page)

RELEASE AND AUTHORIZATION

I acknowledge that the information provided in the application is true and complete. I authorize _____ (name of the congregation) and/or their agents to investigate all statements contained in this application. I also authorize all persons and entities to respond to inquiries concerning me, to supply verification of the information provided in this application, and to comment on and state opinions regarding my background and character. I hereby release all such individuals and entities from all liability and responsibility arising from doing so.

Signature   _____

Date   _____

Sample Reference Form

(Make copies for as many references as your state requires.)

Name _____

Address _____

_____

_____

Home Phone _____

Work Phone _____

Relationship to you _____

Name _____

Address _____

_____

_____

Home Phone _____

Work Phone _____

Relationship to you _____

Sample Letter to References

Dear _____,

_____ gave us your name as a reference and authorized us to seek this information as indicated by the signature below. He/she is under consideration as a youth advisor in the youth programs at _____ (name of your congregation). As part of our responsibility, we are required to ensure the safety of youth in our programs and care.

There are legal requirements that churches and others must fulfill in order to protect youth and to shield against potential lawsuits. One of those requirements is to take reasonable actions to ensure that people with a history of sexual abuse and misconduct are prevented from involvement in youth programs. A standard and accepted way to do this is through a background check.

Enclosed is an "Adult Advisor Reference Response Form," which we would like you to complete and return to us in the enclosed envelope.

We want to emphasize that we are required to seek this information about all persons who work with youth at _____. There is *absolutely no implication* that this reference request suggests any of these statements are true about _____ (name).

It is responsible and right to protect the youth in our care. We are sure that you understand and appreciate the need to do this.

Thank you for your cooperation and assistance. We look forward to your prompt reply.

Sincerely,

_____

(name)

_____

(title)

Reference authorized by

_____

Enclosure

Sample Adult Advisor Reference Response Form

This is a reference for _____. To the best of your knowledge, has the person named above ever been found guilty, or pleaded guilty or no contest, to a criminal charge alleging actual or attempted sexual harassment, exploitation, misconduct, physical abuse, or child abuse?

Yes _____   No _____   If yes, give a short explanation on a separate piece of paper and attach to this form. Please include your name and the name of the person seeking a reference on that sheet.

To the best of your knowledge, has the person named above ever had a civil or ecclesiastical complaint made against him or her alleging actual or attempted sexual discrimination, harassment, exploitation, misconduct, physical abuse, or child abuse?

Yes _____   No _____   If yes, give a short explanation on a separate piece of paper and attach to this form. Please include your name and the name of the person seeking a reference on that sheet.

To the best of your knowledge, is there any fact or circumstance involving the person named above that would call into question her or him being entrusted with responsibilities in youth programs and activities?

Yes _____   No _____   If yes, give a short explanation on a separate piece of paper and attach to this form. Please include your name and the name of the person seeking a reference on that sheet.

Signature   _____

Date   _____

Name   _____

Address   _____

_____

Home Phone   _____

Work Phone   _____

Life is a challenge. To attempt to follow in the footsteps of Jesus of Nazareth is difficult without help from one's faith community. Throughout the history of the church, those with experience have shared their encouragement and wisdom with the less experienced. A mentor program offers an organized way to do this.

During the rite of confirmation, the pastor asks the candidates:

Do you promise, by the Grace of God, to be Christ's disciple . . . to resist oppression and evil . . . to show love and justice . . . to witness to the work . . . of Jesus . . . to grow in . . . faith . . . to be a faithful member . . . furthering Christ's mission in the world?[1]

Accordingly, the candidates for confirmation say:

I promise, with the help of God.

How can a young person know what these promises entail? How can one prepare for and practice resisting evil? showing love and justice? witnessing to the work of Jesus? growing in faith? being a faithful member? being Christ's disciple?

One of the goals of faith formation is discipleship, to follow in the footsteps and service of Jesus of Nazareth, the Christ. Discipleship is a way of life, not a body of doctrine or dogma. Education for this way of life needs to be personal and positive, experienced and practiced, rooted in the shared faith of church members, in theology, and in biblical knowledge. One way to further discipleship is to create and foster partnerships in faith between mentors and confirmands in the congregation.

What is a mentor? Literally, a mentor is an advisor. The name is taken from the person of that name in Homer's *The Odyssey*. Mentor was a friend of Odysseus and teacher of his son, Telemachos. In the broadest sense, a mentor is a person of wisdom who cares enough about someone younger or less experienced to invest time, patience, and energy in a relationship that helps the younger or less experienced person grow in ability and confidence. In sum, a mentor is a wise, loyal advisor and teacher.

Even though some congregations have only recently discovered mentoring as a way to encourage faith growth, it has been practiced in the church for hundreds of years. Kenneth Smith describes one such mentoring relationship:

One of the earliest descriptions of the relationship between a mentor and a young person in the Christian tradition was given by a young person around 250 A.D. He was Gregory of Thaumaturgus and his mentor was Origen, the great teacher and Greek theologian at the famous catechetical school in Alexandria. The school had been started by Origen's mentor, Clement of Alexandria. In his writings, Gregory recalls with affection the way he was treated by Origen. From his recollections we can discover some characteristics of the ancient Christian mentor Clement of Alexandria.[2]

Some important characteristics of a mentor are:

- A mentor is usually older or more experienced in the area to be studied than the learner.
- A mentor offers a scope of knowledge and understanding that is wider than the learner's.
- A mentor is dedicated to the subject to be studied.
- A mentor values the learning process and is invested in the progress of the learner.
- A mentor genuinely cares for the learner.
- A mentor is able to encourage and support the learner and, at the same time, maintain healthy, positive boundaries.

In religious mentoring, the partnership may involve sharing one's faith convictions, praying together, searching the Scriptures for wisdom and guidance, struggling with issues of justice and ethics, investigating the inner workings of one's church, and serving people as Christ's disciples.

In a formal church program, a mentor is an active adult member of the congregation who agrees to enter a supportive relationship with a confirmand for a specific length of time to explore faith and discipleship. In religious mentoring, both partners in the relationship bring unique gifts of faith to each other. Mentoring in the church includes:

- **The gift of *experience*.** The mentors have experienced the struggle with good and evil, faith and doubt, hope and discouragement. They have "been there" and may not be as likely to be overwhelmed by life's contrasts and contradictions. Therefore, they can sympathetically listen to and support confirmands in their journey of faith.

@ **The element of** *practice*. Mentors are committed Christians and active church members. They have already chosen to be disciples of Christ and to serve God's people in concrete ways. They are willing to work side by side with someone growing in Christian discipleship.

@ **The ingredient of** *caring*. A mentor in the church genuinely cares for the confirmand and the confirmand's family, friends, problems, opinions, and interests. A mentor tries to practice unconditional love.

Guidelines for Your Church's Mentor Program

GOAL STATEMENT

However you organize a mentor program, you will need to answer the question, "Why?" Why is your congregation interested in a mentor program? What does the rite of confirmation mean? What do you believe is to happen in the faith formation process? What is the goal and purpose of a mentor program? Each congregation has a wide range of religious backgrounds, traditions, expectations, and disappointments. There are suggestions in the section called "Confirmation in the Local Church" (pages xiii–xviii) that will help you incorporate mentoring into the larger context of faith formation in your congregation.

Your congregation may find it helpful to organize meetings open to anyone interested in the mentor program. These gatherings of interested church people are an opportunity to hear faith stories and what has helped or hindered members' struggles to be disciples of Jesus Christ. Questions need to be asked about what is necessary and helpful in learning how to live a life of discipleship.

One church came to the conclusion that their faith formation program leading to the rite of confirmation had discipleship as its goal. They wanted to confirm people who more closely resembled the lifestyle, beliefs, and values of the disciples of Jesus Christ.[3] Your congregation needs a clear goal statement to help focus on the content, time line, and leadership of a mentor program.

CONTENT

Affirming Faith has many suggestions for the specific content of a mentor program using this resource. If your faith formation group is using the resource in sessions or in retreats, there are questions or activities in the *Confirmand's Journal* that can help initiate conversations between a youth and his or her mentor. Another option for some congregations, especially those with only one or two confirmands, is to use the resources of *Affirming Faith* entirely in a mentoring program. In that case, mentors will have all the session suggestions with which to work.

Your congregation may want to add or adapt these resources to fit your own circumstances. For example, in one congregation the deacons prepared a list of questions for discussion with the confirmands at a meeting with the church council prior to the day of confirmation. The confirmands were also invited to write a short statement of faith. During the six months prior to confirmation Sunday, the mentor and confirmand met monthly to discuss the questions and formulate responses. In this example, the mentor is a supportive reference person as the confirmand articulates a statement of faith. Just prior to confirmation Sunday, the deacons met with each confirmand (mentors and parents present) to discuss his or her reflections on the questions, statement of faith, experience with God and the church, and commitment to discipleship. The meeting ended with a celebration.

The relationship between mentor and confirmand may be recognized and "blessed" in a worship service, both at the beginning and end of the relationship. There is a dedication service on pages 240–41 (pages 236–38 in the journal) that may be used at the beginning of a faith formation program. Mentors may choose to participate in the rite of confirmation with confirmands, affirming their own baptisms and symbolizing for confirmands the repeatable nature of the rite. Often mentors and confirmands make and share vows of commitment to be active in the church in specific ways and these vows may be dedicated on the day the rite of confirmation is celebrated. In one mentor program, the mentor and confirmand commit to meeting once monthly for a year after the rite of confirmation for the purpose of mutual support and encouragement in faith and discipleship.

The content of your congregation's mentor program can bear the distinct imprint of your community of faith and what is important to your members in their journey of faith.

TIME LINE

How long does the mentor program last? What length of time will mentors and confirmands work in partnership? It depends on the traditions of your congregation, the design of the faith formation process, and the content of the program. Those who have organized mentor programs usually find that the longer mentors and confirmands are together, the better. Good relationships take time to develop and become richer through time. Some congregations are able to begin the process to select mentors two years before the rite of confirmation and extend the mentor relationship a full year beyond the day the rite of confirmation is celebrated.

The mentor program is an investment in relationships among people who are mutually supportive in a life of discipleship. The more time given to these unique relationships, the more effective they become.

HUMAN RESOURCES

Who organizes, manages, and inspires a mentor program? Everyone in the congregation can witness the working of this program in the life of the church. The support of church members gives energy to the mentor program and, in turn, the program strengthens faith and commitment within the congregation.

One person in the congregation should take overall responsibility for coordinating the mentoring program. This person can be available to consult with mentors, to clarify expectations, and to help the experience flow smoothly. It is important that mentors, as well as parents or guardians, youth, educators, and church officers be represented on the planning team for the congregation's Faith Formation Committee (see "Confirmation in the Local Church," page xiii).

The church council, board, consistory, elders, diaconate, Christian education committee, and other appropriate groups in the church can be important sources of supervision and support. They can help interpret and integrate the mentoring program into the life of the church. They can support and be included in the group gatherings of mentors and confirmands to encourage, and be encouraged, in a life of Christian discipleship.

MENTORS

At the heart of the mentor program are the mentors themselves. They are faithful members of the congregation who are a rich and sometimes hidden source of wisdom, support, and understanding for confirmands.

A mentor may be any active church member willing to participate in the joys and obligations of the mentor program. Some programs stipulate that a confirmand cannot have a close relative for a mentor. This stipulation helps the confirmand to develop relationships with committed Christians outside of their family circle. Generally it is best if mentors are *at least* a few years older than the confirmand (post–high school) in order for the confirmand to reap the benefits of experience and maturity.

MENTOR SELECTION

Congregations have different criteria for selecting mentors. Expectations will vary depending on the length and content of the program. Mentors should meet all the criteria for adult leaders of youth in your congregation. The section "A Guide for Youth Leaders" (pages 255–62) provides specific information on developing these criteria.

In some congregations confirmands choose and contact their own mentors. In other congregations the pastor or faith formation leader takes this responsibility. Another alternative is for the confirmands or the congregation to suggest potential mentors who may then be matched with confirmands by the pastor or another leader. For a variety of reasons, it often works best when final discernment is left to the pastor or another leader. Look for the best and most fruitful mentor for each *individual* confirmand, considering his or her preferences and suggestions.

However you choose to select mentors, those who are being asked need to know the privilege and responsibility of the position. Be clear about the time commitment involved in mentoring and give them time to think about their decision. Also give them the freedom to say no. Interpret the possibility of a "No" to confirmands as a realistic appraisal of a member's limits and abilities and not a rejection of the confirmands themselves.

Some congregations suggest that confirmands choose mentors of the same gender. More often congregations find it better to be flexible, choosing the best person to fill the needs and challenges of this unique partnership. In one congregation, a 15-year-old boy never had the opportunity to form relationships with his grandmothers. His first choice for a mentor was a woman in her late seventies who was, indeed, a grandmother. She had served the congregation in every conceivable way in sixty years of membership. This mentor later told, with great delight, the experience of her outings with the confirmand into the world of pizza parlors and hamburger hangouts and the excitement of entering the world of teenagers. It was a very fulfilling match for both partners.

The goal of the mentor selection process is to match people who can be a blessing to each other as they learn to grow in the discipleship of Jesus Christ. To review the key factors in a mentor selection, look for:

@ a committed Christian and active member of the congregation

@ someone who has the maturity and life-experience to be an effective advisor and teacher

@ someone who can be effective with a particular confirmand

MEETINGS WITH CONFIRMANDS

Mentors need to find appropriate times and places to meet with confirmands. It is increasingly important to organize mentoring in a way that deals with concerns about the safety of each youth. Many congregations have made it a policy that a mentor *not* meet with a confirmand in complete privacy. Meetings are to take place in an environment where there are other people present. For example, a mentor and a confirmand are never alone in a separate room with the door closed. This does not mean, however, that conversations must all take place publicly. Confirmands and mentors may meet at a separate table or space where conversation may happen, but in view of others. Mentors can be encouraged to take advantage of times when there are other activities happening at your church building. Mentors and confirmands might meet on Sunday when others are present, or before (or after) a church supper, or at the church office when others will be there. Two or more mentors might schedule a time to meet with confirmands at the church or mentors can be in contact with the confirmand's parents about other appropriate times and places to meet. A mentor and confirmand could meet at the confirmand's home when parents are home or it might be possible to meet in conjunction with some other activity in which the confirmand or mentor participates, or to meet at a public place such as a library or restaurant.

MENTOR TRAINING

It is important to offer help and support to mentors in their important work. Mentor training may consist of an evening with all or some of these components:

- **Shared faith journeys.** The worship service from the beginning of the opening retreat, "On a Faith Journey" (pages 3–16), is an excellent way to begin an event for mentors, inviting them to worship and to share stories of those who have helped them grow in faith.

- **Provide a historical grounding.** See page 263 of this guide for the historical background of mentoring. You might tell how your congregation came to choose a mentoring approach. If there are mentors who have worked with youth in the past, invite them to share stories about their relationships.

- **Provide an overview of the congregation's faith formation program.** Spend time as a group reviewing the sessions in *Affirming Faith*. Give each mentor a copy of *Affirming Faith: A Confirmand's Journal*. Discuss the schedule for your program, giving dates when sessions and/or retreats will be held, so that mentors may focus on sessions at appropriate times. The contents of the journal, especially the "Questions to Consider," can be used to spark discussions when the confirmand and mentor meet. Indicate if you want them to be a part of the opening and closing retreats, field trips, witness and service projects, and so on. Hear concerns and answer questions mentors may have.

Each congregation will need to develop a training model to fit its context. The more people involved in all areas of the mentor program, the more intentional the sharing of faith will be among generations of Christians. This increases our love and knowledge of God, our appreciation of one another, and our commitment as followers of Jesus Christ.

A GUIDE FOR WITNESS

AND SERVICE

JESUS . . . GOT UP FROM THE TABLE, TOOK OFF HIS OUTER ROBE, AND TIED A TOWEL AROUND HIMSELF. . . . YOU ALSO OUGHT TO WASH ONE ANOTHER'S FEET.   —JOHN 13:4, 14B

TRULY I TELL YOU, JUST AS YOU DID IT TO ONE OF THE LEAST OF THESE WHO ARE MEMBERS OF MY FAMILY, YOU DID IT TO ME.   —MATTHEW 25:20

Many Christians have stories to tell about how involvement in a ministry of the church has changed their faith. Participating in rebuilding a home for Habitat for Humanity, traveling with a work camp to Puerto Rico, volunteering to deliver Meals on Wheels, responding to the needs of those whose homes or communities were destroyed in a flood or earthquake—any of these experiences can be faith forming for those who participate. Serving on a church committee, planning a special worship service, visiting with those who are homebound, teaching in the church, helping to cook a meal, working in the church's food pantry—any of these experiences can be faith forming for those who participate. Whether close to home or far away, being involved in witness and service can change one's faith.

The church has responded over many centuries to Jesus' challenge to engage in ministries of witness and service. Today the United Church of Christ through the work of local churches, associations, conferences, and national instrumentalities offers many opportunities for church members to be involved in significant ministries that serve others and give witness to God's love for the world.

You may wish to include opportunities for witness and service as part of your local church's faith formation program. This guide is designed to help your planning committee or leadership team organize ways for young people to engage in these activities. In a local church where there is a mission committee, that group might help plan this part of the faith formation program. In other congregations the leadership team, including both youth and adults, will do this planning. In yet other places, the congregation's Christian education committee may be the appropriate group.

Many congregations find that making witness and service an integral part of the faith formation program greatly enhances the experience for youth. We suggest that you plan this involvement early in the program, so that there will be time to discuss and reflect upon the experiences. Below is a process that may be used at an opening retreat, or one of the first meetings of your faith formation group, to plan these activities. There are two *Affirming Faith* sessions—session 17, "Followers of Christ," and session 18, "Witness and Service"—for which it will be helpful for confirmands to bring reflections on ministries in which they have engaged. The *Confirmand's Journal* also provides opportunities for reflection on these witness and service activities.

Planning Witness and Service Activities

On a sheet of newsprint write "witness" and "service." Then brainstorm about the words. Have members of the group say what comes to mind when they hear each of these words. These might be one-word responses or phrases. Ask for a volunteer or volunteers to record the suggestions. List the responses on the newsprint.

Explain that *witness* is the translation of the Greek word *martyr*. Originally martyrs referred to those who were witnesses of Christ's life and resurrection. Later it came to mean those who had undergone hardship or suffering, including death, for their faith. Explain that *service* is related to the terms *servant* and *slave* and refers to one who does work for another. One may serve God though work or prayer. *Service* also brings to mind a service of worship.

Read aloud two passages of scripture: John 13:3–7 and Matthew 26:31–46. Ask the group to discuss how the terms witness and service are connected. Which activities in the scripture passages are witness? Which are service? Next ask members of the group for suggestions they have regarding service-oriented activities that they themselves are involved in or have been involved in sometime in the past. List these on newsprint as "Ways That I Am Serving." Then invite them to consider ways in which they might take on new forms of service-oriented activities. As a group they might wish to choose one of these activities to put their faith into action.

At this meeting invite members of the group to reflect with you on the following questions:

- How do you now understand the biblical call to service?
- Why is it important to engage in servanthood? How does the practice of servanthood reveal what you believe?
- In our culture servanthood is not something that is seen as being a cool thing to do. How might your commitment to becoming a servant be a costly one?
- In what ways does your congregation witness to, as the Statement of Faith says, "being servants in the service of others, to proclaiming the gospel to all the world and resisting the powers of evil"?
- What insights about service and witness have you been offered by the church in the past?
- What benefits are there from serving?

@ Who serves you? How does it feel to be served?

@ What form of service will you now pursue?

There are several possible ways you might help youth in your faith formation program participate in a service activity. You will need to discuss which of these best fits the needs of the young people in your program and the needs of your church community.

PLAN A GROUP PROJECT

Your faith formation group could undertake a project together. Make a list of the service projects in which your congregation is or might be engaged. Discuss how youth are or might be involved in these projects. Ask them to help decide which project they would be interested in undertaking. As a group, chose one service project to undertake and lead for the congregation. Some examples of projects which have been done by youth are:

@ Clean up at the community center.

@ Assist in the delivery of food to the soup kitchen.

@ Help a newly arrived immigrant family, making them feel welcome.

@ Assist a neighboring congregation that needs volunteer help for their vacation church school program.

PLAN INDIVIDUAL APPRENTICESHIP PROJECTS

Another way to involve youth in witness and service is to pair them with members of the congregation who are doing specific ministries. You might begin by making a list on newsprint of the names of those with whom youth might work. Who is preparing Holy Communion? Who visits the sick? Who volunteers often to help care for the congregation's building and grounds? Who does the church's newsletters? After making this list, have each confirmand choose a type of service they would want to help with. Make plans to call the contact people to volunteer to help with these ministries. This activity, done as part of the congregation's faith formation program, can emphasize that discipleship is a continuous, growing part of a Christian's life, one that involves learning by doing. If this option is chosen, there will need to be careful coordination with those in the church who organize volunteer ministries.

VISIT MISSION SITES OF THE CHURCH

"A Guide for Field Trips" (pages 289–91) has many suggestions for ways to visit mission sites of the church. Any of these visits could also include a time when your group could do a volunteer project for the place you visit. Being involved in doing something will be a positive addition to the visit for youth.

PLAN A WORK CAMP EXPERIENCE

For many youth, a work camp may be a highlight of faith growth. Perhaps your conference's outdoor ministry program has already organized a work camp experience for youth that your congregation could join. Or your congregation could form a committee to organize a work camp for your group.

The Voluntary Service Program of the United Church of Christ can provide a list of possible work camp sites. Contact the Minister for Volunteer Services, United Church Board for Homeland Ministries, 700 Prospect Avenue, Cleveland OH 44115 (216-736-3266).

Your conference's resource center may have a copy of the video *With Hammers, Paint, and Love*, which tells the story of how one congregation organized a work camp experience for youth.

"A Guide for Retreats" (page 275) has helpful, practical information about planning short-term retreat experiences. Most of that information will apply to planning a work camp.

From the list of activities the group has compiled, you may wish to arrange for each member or the entire group to become involved in one or more of the service-oriented activities. One of the benefits of doing a group-oriented activity is the fun and community-building that often take place while serving.

Each group participant may want to sign a pledge to engage in at least twenty hours of service as part of this process.

Once confirmands have chosen witness and service activities in which they wish to be involved, the leadership team should help connect their desires to the life of the congregation. Some youth will need assistance in contacting others in the life of the congregation who are already engaged in service ministries. It is helpful for the congregation to recognize and celebrate these commitments. Consider printing the names of those who serve in the church bulletin or newsletter. Recognize them in worship and bless the ministries in which they are involved. This conversation in the faith formation group will probably identify some ministries in which young people are *already* involved. Include and honor these prior commitments as well as those newly made through this process.

A GUIDE FOR RETREATS

THIS GUIDE IS DESIGNED TO PRESENT AN OVERVIEW OF RETREATS IN GENERAL AND SPECIFICALLY TO HELP YOU ORGANIZE RETREATS EITHER IN PLACE OF, OR IN ADDITION TO, WEEKLY SESSIONS. IF YOU DECIDE TO USE RETREATS IN YOUR FAITH FORMATION PROGRAM, A "RETREAT PLANNING CHECKLIST" IS PROVIDED ON PAGE 282 TO HELP YOU ORGANIZE.

Foundational Understandings

What is a retreat? They come in a variety of sizes, shapes, and styles. Generally:

- A retreat is a gathering, sometimes convened either at your church building or a place "away," such as a camp or retreat center.
- A retreat can be conducted over the course of a morning, a day, or several days.
- A retreat can provide opportunities within large and small groups to deliver information, reflect upon and share responses, participate in activities, and experience communally (if the retreat is long enough) the common events of life such as eating, sleeping, exercise, play, and work (service).

Why should you consider a retreat format for your congregation's faith formation program? What are the advantages of a retreat format? A retreat format can vividly combine many important elements of our Christian life: study, worship, play, service, and fellowship. Compared to a series of weekly sessions, participants can explore the same amount of content or even more. With longer blocks of time available, there is more opportunity in a retreat to develop and reinforce a theme and to do activities that take longer than one hour.

Integrating and assimilating learning experiences is easier. Rather than referring to things experienced in a session several weeks (or months) ago, the leader can refer to information shared and discussed only hours (or one day) before.

A retreat format is ideal for including confirmands from other congregations. Retreats may be especially attractive to congregations who have only a few confirmands. Several congregations can combine to create a faith formation program with many participants. In this arrangement, the congregations share in planning and leading, thus reducing the workload on individual adult and youth leaders while increasing support and camaraderie among the leaders.

A retreat often requires lay involvement and participation, thus the faith formation program becomes a congregational effort and the laity who attend may learn and have as much fun as the confirmands. A group of adult confirmands may also participate in the faith formation retreat.

A program of retreats requires fewer scheduled events but demands commitment from confirmands. Rather than asking your confirmands and advisors to fit many sessions into their personal schedules, with a retreat format there are fewer events to schedule.

In schedule conflicts (e.g., with band practice, sports, social events, and other activities) the confirmands must decide and commit themselves to attend this one-time faith experience.

Retreats do require extra planning and the use of additional space beyond a single meeting room. They require leadership participation and concentrated attention over more than just one hour. There may be additional transportation, lodging, and meal expenses involved.

For most people retreats are special, popular, and fun. They are eagerly anticipated and long remembered. And retreats can be very powerful. Due to the possible intensity of experiences, persons who attend may find their lives are changed. The message and ministry of Christ may come alive as they never have before.

Practical Considerations

Refer to "Confirmation in the Local Church" (pages xiii–xviii) for suggestions about planning your congregation's faith formation program and forming a leadership team. Be sure to include confirmands in both planning and event leadership.

Although some spaces of time within the retreat may be left open for the confirmands to plan for themselves, the leadership planning team must begin long before the event by developing the overall framework of the retreat. Your team must make decisions about the following.

FOCUS

What is the focus of this faith formation event? Does it replace one or more of the sessions? Will retreats be in addition to sessions, offering further opportunities to reflect, integrate, and respond to faith-forming experiences?

If you choose to have one or more retreats in place of individual sessions, the retreats can focus on the whole unit, using the session designs to encompass ninety-minute time blocks within the retreat schedule.

A day may be divided into three major blocks of productive time: morning, afternoon, and evening. These
time blocks may then be divided into segments, each of which may contain one of the following: session
designs (including worship), organized play, and free time.

It is best to provide a variety of activities as the day progresses and, over the course of the retreat, to
include all of the above elements. On a sheet of paper, lay out your progression of events within each
time block, and ascribe beginning and ending times to each event to insure they may be accomplished
in the time you have. Be realistic about your time estimates and be sure to include extra time for tran-
sitions, introductions, movement or travel from one area or site to another, set-up, break-down, and
clean-up.

SITE

The number of confirmands determines site selection. Obviously it must be of sufficient size to comfortably
house your group and permit the activities that you envision. At the least there should be one room free
from outside distraction and large enough to comfortably contain your entire group and sufficient rooms
or spaces to allow for small group gatherings, activity centers, planning team meetings, sleeping arrangements (as needed), and other activities you envision.

Sites might include your church facility, a conference camp or retreat center, or a commercial site. The final
decision will depend on your budget, the size of your group, and the time of year.

All sites have limitations that may potentially reduce the effectiveness of your retreat. A site with many
recreational opportunities may be great for exercise and fun, but it may also be distracting. A site with
no recreational opportunities may enhance a study atmosphere, but might also lead to a one-sided (all
work and no play), boring retreat. If you use your church site, remember to coordinate your use of worship, meeting, and kitchen space with other groups who might be present.

Some overnight retreats have one room for both men and women. In other retreats, they have separate
rooms. Your planning team needs to decide upon a policy and how to handle this. The key is to have
proper adult supervision. Confirmands generally behave better when in mixed company. For some, it is
a completely new experience and may be a healthy way to experience the other gender in a safe and
family-like atmosphere.

TRANSPORTATION

If your site requires travel to reach, you will need to arrange for vehicles and drivers. Does the congregation's
insurance provide coverage for travel to and from a retreat site? Be sure your drivers know the places and
times for departing and returning. Be sure to give confirmands specific instructions about what to bring.

MEALS

If the retreat will cover meal times, you will need to make plans for meal preparation, serving, and eating. If meals or cooking facilities are not available at the site, perhaps outside eating establishments can supply your meals. Alternatively, you can structure your retreat to begin and end between meals and only offer snacks. The sharing of food is always a welcome addition to any retreat and a concluding meal can provide an intimate closure.

LEADERS AND ADVISORS

It is good to have a ratio of one adult advisor for every six to eight confirmands. There should be at least one man and one woman at the event. If your group of confirmands is younger, more boisterous, and active, you may want more adults. If your group is more mature, you may need fewer adults present. Also consider the number of sleeping rooms your group will use and how adults will supervise multiple rooms.

These advisors should be asked not only to undertake specific tasks and responsibilities but also to participate and interact in all group activities. Throughout the retreat, advisors are to adhere to the same rules given to the confirmands (e.g., regarding smoking, drinking, leaving the site, etc.). Adults should sign community covenants as the youth do. Sample community covenants for youth and adults are offered on pages 284 and 285.

Advisors should be committed Christians who are able to talk about their faith, who enjoy relating to youth, and (if on an overnight retreat) who won't need ten hours of uninterrupted sleep. The choice of persons to be present at a retreat needs to be prudent to ensure the safety and well-being of the youth in your charge. Some conferences, associations, and local churches now require a screening process of potential adult leaders to ensure that they have not been involved in situations that could be injurious to youth. See "A Guide for Youth Leaders" (pages 255–62) for more information.

Who are the lay leaders in your congregation who could help plan your retreat? Who can help coordinate, provide transportation or other logistical support, or lead portions of a retreat? Who might give a short talk on their faith journey or offer what the United Church of Christ means to them? What persons might be available who are associated with the United Church of Christ at the conference or national level? What leaders of other faiths might be available to attend and speak of their traditions and faith heritage? Ideally the retreat leaders, adult and youth, should be part of your planning team. They will feel more ownership of the retreat if they have had a say in the areas they will lead.

Once recruited, leaders need to be informed of what is expected of them in terms of time commitment and skills. They need to be apprised of decisions already in place concerning the retreat, as well as any preestablished goals, limitations, or requests. The convener of your planning and training meetings should provide a clear agenda of the items to discuss and the decisions to be made. If the site is unfamiliar, it should be described and made as familiar as possible either by showing photos, slides, maps, or arranging a pre-retreat visit.

OTHER CONCERNS

In your planning process, after you decide upon your overall theme, develop activities and programs in support of that. Then you are ready to make a list of your logistical needs. For each activity, list the props, equipment, media, supplies, and people you are going to need to make the activity happen.

Beyond specific activities, look at the retreat as a whole, and list other personnel and physical things you will need such as: first aid kit, notebook paper, pencils, notebooks, Bibles, presentation board and markers, video player and monitor, audio tape or CD player and music tapes or CDs to play as confirmands arrive, between activities, or at a dance.

Be sure to arrange and prepare the space as much as possible to enhance and reinforce the purpose of your retreat. Have a colorful banner welcoming the confirmands and stating your theme. This is a fellowship event, so as confirmands arrive have music playing and something such as a game going on. In study areas, have chairs arranged to focus and maximize attention. Have any required props set up and ready to go. In general, make your site as functional and attractive as possible. Make it obvious to the confirmands that you are ready and eager to welcome them at this retreat.

If you are preparing and/or serving meals or snacks, make a list of what is needed. If meals are being prepared elsewhere, have arrangements been made? Are there any special dietary needs? If participants need extra cash to pay for food, have they been told beforehand?

Be safety conscious. Always have a list of emergency phone numbers, medical treatment forms, and first aid supplies available. Prior to the retreat, have a parent or guardian sign a form for each confirmand authorizing medical intervention in the event of an accident or illness. Your conference office or camp will have copies of the forms they require minors to complete for their programs. Check with the laws of your state regarding the requirements of this form. Call the hospital closest to your retreat site to determine what they will require to treat one of your group. Some hospitals may require the photocopy of both sides of the person's medical insurance card. Your group may be able to purchase retreat-specific insurance coverage from your congregation's insurance carrier.

Two information sheets should be prepared, one for participants and one for parents or guardians. These sheets should include information about the place and time of departure and return; phone numbers for the site and emergency phone numbers; and actual and extra cash needs. The participant sheets should also include information about the event schedule and what to bring or what to leave at home.

Confirmands must be made aware that their behavior is a reflection upon themselves, their family, and their congregation, and that they are expected to behave accordingly. Have each confirmand and leader sign a community covenant prior to the retreat agreeing to certain standards of behavior regarding drugs, alcohol, smoking, sexual activity, violence, the property and privacy of others, and respecting God's creation. Sample covenants may be found on pages 284 and 285. As stated in the covenants, any confirmand whose behavior becomes unacceptable will be removed from the group, his or her parents or guardians will be called, and the confirmand will be sent home. The planning committee should have a process for handling such a situation.

During a retreat, some activities may be very personal and powerful. There may be some emotional outpouring and crying. Youth are in a wonderfully expressive and passionate time of life. But some emotional expressions may go beyond the expected. Remember, this is a confirmation retreat and is not designed to confront, heal, or solve deep emotional or mental stress or illness. If you face such a situation, be comforting and caring, but don't try to "fix" her or him. Allow the confirmand the space and freedom to express himself or herself and then to return to the group when ready. In a crisis you may need to seek, or recommend, professional help.

Retreats are an integral component of this resource. They may provide great opportunities to explore one's relationship to God, explore one's faith, and build fellowship. When conducted well, retreats can be settings for experimental and experiential learning and for building memories that will last a lifetime.

Retreat Planning Summary

THEME

How will the retreat help the larger design of your program? Be clear about the topic to be considered and leadership for teaching/learning activities. If you are planning a unit retreat, be sure all sessions are adequately reflected in the retreat content.

LEADERSHIP

Both youth and adults need to be recruited for planning and event leadership. These should be persons who have skills and abilities that are clearly identified for everyone and that will be utilized in planning as well as during the event.

ATTITUDE

As you prepare for this retreat, keep in mind the youth who have expressed an interest in your congregation's faith formation program. Prayerfully consider the individuals and details of the retreat. Allow room for the Spirit to guide you and the leadership team in all you do.

SETTING

A setting with adequate facilities will enhance the retreat. A room with carpets and movable chairs will provide for a relaxed atmosphere. Accessibility to the outdoors and nature can enhance reflection time. A setting with a park or hiking trails would be helpful. Be sensitive to the particular needs of your group, keeping in mind the physical abilities of each member.

FOOD

Be conscious of what youth like to eat. Bring plenty of snacks for the evening and think about the special lunch program being planned. Plan the menu, taking into consideration any special dietary needs.

RECRUITMENT

After you have decided on a time and a place for the retreat, notify the confirmands and their parents or guardians. Announcements during worship and in a newsletter are helpful, but there is nothing better than sending out a flyer with the details about the retreat followed up by a personal invitation on the phone or in person.

REGISTRATION

Be sure all required permission forms are obtained from the parents or guardians. Decide on a registration closing date and the least number of participants needed to make the retreat work.

Retreat Planning Checklist

Dates   _____

Themes   _____

_____

_____

PLANNERS AND LEADERS

Adults   Youth

_____   _____

_____   _____

_____   _____

_____   _____

TRANSPORTATION

Who   Telephone Numbers

_____   _____

_____   _____

_____   _____

_____   _____

FOOD

[Use a separate sheet for menu planning. Have one sheet for each meal and snack time.]

Meals _____   Snacks _____

PROGRAM

Schedule _____   Bibles _____

Resource Books _____   Songbooks _____

MULTIMEDIA

VCR_____   Audiotapes or CDs _____

Monitor _____   Tape or CD Player_____

Videotapes _____   Extension Cords _____

Projector _____

ART AND OFFICE SUPPLIES

Pencils _____   Paper _____

Crayons/Markers _____   Masking Tape_____

Newsprint _____   Paints _____

Others   _____

PARTICIPANTS

Permission Slips_____   Health/Medical Treatment Forms_____

Community Covenants

_____(youth)

_____(adults)

Parent/Guardian

Information Sheet_____

Participant Information

Sheet _____

Youth Covenant

Because God calls us to be a community of faith and leaders in Christ's church, I covenant with God and with one another to conduct our life together at the retreat in a manner that promotes a community of faith.

1. I will participate in all activities, working together to learn and grow from my retreat experience.

2. I will treat all people with dignity and respect.

3. I will respect the property of all people.

4. I will use the facilities made available to us with care. If I hurt or accidentally damage property, I will take responsibility for the damage done and inform an adult leader.

5. I will not smoke if I am not allowed and if it is prohibited by state law. If my parent(s)/guardian(s) and the law allow, I will only smoke in outside areas, except at outdoor group activities.

6. I will not bring or use alcohol and/or illicit drugs, realizing that such behavior is destructive to Christian community and would require my dismissal. Prescribed drugs must be left with an adult leader.

7. I will not engage in sexual activity.

8. I will observe the following guidelines for visiting the rooms of members of the opposite sex: doors must stay open at all times and visitation hours are during lunch, dinner, and optional time.

9. I will be mindful of my roommates' rights to privacy.

10. I will be in my room for "Lights out" and honor the curfew time.

11. I will not travel alone or leave the facility after dark. If I wish to leave the facility during the day (optional time), I will obtain permission.

Remember, while you are attending the retreat you are a representative of your local church and of the entire United Church of Christ. Please keep this in mind and behave accordingly. Violation of this covenant could mean returning home at your own expense before the event's conclusion.

Participant's Signature _____

Date   _____

Parent's/Guardian's Signature _____

Date   _____

Adult Leader's Covenant

Because God calls us to be a community of faith and leaders in Christ's church, I covenant with God and with one another to conduct our life together at the retreat in a manner that promotes a community of faith.

1. I will participate in all activities, working together to learn and grow from my retreat experience.
2. I will treat all people with dignity and respect.
3. I will respect the property of all people.
4. I will use the facilities made available to us with care. If I hurt or accidentally damage property, I will take responsibility for the damage done.
5. I will smoke only in outside areas, except at outdoor group functions.
6. I will not bring or use alcohol and/or illicit drugs, realizing that such behavior is destructive to Christian community and would require my dismissal.
7. I will not engage in sexual activity.
8. I will observe the following guidelines for visiting the rooms of members of the opposite sex: doors must stay open at all times and visitation hours are during lunch, dinner, and optional time.
9. I will be mindful of my roommates' rights to privacy.
10. I will honor the lights out curfew.
11. I will not travel alone at night or leave the group after dark.
12. I realize that as an adult advisor, I am responsible for my group twenty-four hours a day. I am conscious of my role as model for my group.

Leader's Signature _____

Date   _____

Sample Field Trip Permission Form

(This is not a legal form. Always consult your legal counsel.)

Youth's Name   _____

Trip to   _____

Dates of the trip _____

Method of transportation_____

Departing on   _____ at _____

From   _____

Returning on   _____ at _____

To   _____

Name of person to contact in an emergency _____

Phone   _____

Relationship to youth _____

Alternate name of person to contact in an emergency _____

Phone   _____

Relationship to youth _____

Parent's/Guardian's Signature _____

Date   _____

(Some states require the addition of the following information on the form:

"Consent must be given by a parent or legal guardian; stepparents, grandparents, and foster parents cannot authorize travel.")

Sample Medical History and
Medical Emergency Consent Form

(This is not a legal form. Always consult your legal counsel.)

Youth's Name _____

Home Phone _____

Parent/Guardian Phone _____

Additional Phone_____

In case you cannot be reached, is there someone else who could be notified?

Name _____

Phone _____

Relationship to youth _____

Name _____

Phone _____

Relationship to youth _____

Insurance Carrier _____

Membership number _____

Please attach photocopies of the front and back of your insurance card.

Name of Youth's Physician _____

Phone _____

Name of Youth's Dentist _____

Phone _____

Are there any medical problems we should be aware of?

_____

_____

_____

_____

_____

_____

Are there any allergies we should be aware of?

_____

_____

_____

Are there any dietary needs we should be aware of?

_____

_____

_____

Is any medication taken regularly?_____

If yes, what is the medication?_____

What is it taken for? _____

When is it taken?_____

What are the medical procedures?_____

Date of last Tetanus Booster?_____

I give authority to the advisor in charge of this activity to grant permission to a medical doctor to examine and provide treatment if necessary.

Parent's/Guardian's Signature _____

Date   _____

I do not give authority to the advisor of this activity to grant permission for medical treatment. I, or the persons named above as alternate contacts, must be contacted and will assume responsibility for the youth if emergency medical treatment is necessary.

Parent's/Guardian's Signature _____

Date   _____

(Some states require the addition of the following information on the form:
"Consent must be given by a parent or legal guardian; stepparents, grandparents, and foster parents cannot authorize travel.")

A GUIDE FOR FIELD TRIPS

FIELD TRIPS ARE OPPORTUNITIES TO MOVE BEYOND THE FAMILIAR SETTING OF YOUR LOCAL CHURCH OR COMMUNITY AND SHOULD BE AN IMPORTANT FACET OF YOUR CONGREGATION'S FAITH FORMATION PROGRAM. FAITH IS EXPANDED WHEN WE EXPERIENCE HOW OTHER PEOPLE WORSHIP GOD, SEE HOW THEY LIVE OUT THEIR FAITH, AND LEARN HOW THEY HAVE BEEN INFORMED AND SHAPED BY THEIR HERITAGE. THE LEARNINGS FROM FIELD TRIPS OFTEN SURPRISE EVEN THE LEADERS. WE ENCOURAGE YOU TO INCLUDE FIELD TRIPS AS AN INTEGRAL ELEMENT IN YOUR FAITH FORMATION PROGRAM RATHER THAN AS AN OPTIONAL ACTIVITY.

Planning Ahead

To take your group to any off-site location, you will need to make arrangements with the place to be visited, secure signed field trip permission forms from parents or guardians (see page 286), and provide for transportation. Contact the site well in advance to make an appointment for your group. Ask when the best time to visit is. At some sites a tour of the facility may be helpful. At other places you might offer to do a service project for the organization as part of your visit. If you are attending a public function such as worship or a special activity of a congregation, inquire about how your group will participate. For some new worship experiences, your group members may be able to participate more fully if you "walk through" the liturgy with them before you go. At other times you may discover that the surprising element of a new experience leads to new faith.

If your congregation or a group within it has an ongoing relationship with another congregation or you have supported a local UCC or ecumenical ministry, consider arranging a visit to that site.

Field Trip Possibilities

WORSHIP WITH OTHERS FROM THE CHRISTIAN TRADITION

Seek out worship experiences that are different from those typical in your congregation. The pastor and other leaders may know of congregations in your community or nearby where worship includes liturgy that would be new to members of your congregation. For example, if you do not use the liturgy of the

"Great Easter Vigil" on the Saturday before Easter, you might find a neighboring congregation that does. Even within the United Church of Christ there is a great diversity of worship styles. You might want to travel within your association or conference to worship with another UCC congregation or visit a congregation with a different racial or ethnic make-up than your own. You might consider a worship experience with an intentional Christian community such as a monastery or abbey. Consider setting up a "worship tour" to visit several congregations over a period of time.

After each experience arrange a time for the group to reflect upon their experience. What did the service have in common with your congregation's worship? How was it different? What was familiar to you? What was new? List elements in this service and in your congregation's worship that could have derived from the same source. What characteristics and images of God were included in the worship you experienced? Did the congregation greet you or offer you refreshments? What did you learn from this experience?

VISIT SERVICES OF OTHER FAITHS SUCH AS BUDDHIST, BAHA'I, MUSLIM, OR JEWISH

Visit and talk with a representative about their faith, their religious customs and practices, their holy days and celebrations, and how their faith tradition informs and shapes their daily lives.

Following your visit discuss what you observed and experienced. In this visit you will have learned about how another tradition informs the lives of its members. What did you learn about your faith and life? Consider extending an invitation to those you meet to visit your congregation. What would they learn about your life?

If it is too far for your group to travel to visit one of these groups, consider inviting a speaker, renting an informational video, or ordering materials from the group of your choice.

ARRANGE TO VISIT A MISSION PROGRAM IN YOUR COMMUNITY OR A NEARBY CITY

There are many possibilities to visit a mission program, including a food pantry, Habitat for Humanity project, Meals on Wheels program, a shelter or group home, a hospital chaplaincy, a jail chaplaincy or ministry, an advocacy organization, or a truck-stop ministry. Often there are ecumenical agencies in larger cities that can help set up visits with ministries they help fund. Your conference office can help you locate ministries supported in your area by gifts from the United Church of Christ.

One challenge in arranging this type of field trip is to visit at a time when the program or ministry of the group is in action. For many of these groups you will have a better experience if you can go on a weekday rather than a weekend. Consider organizing the trip on a weekday when the youth in your group have a day off from school or a holiday. Many public school districts schedule two or three in-service days each year on a Monday or Friday when the youth in your faith formation program could make such a visit. Some school districts are willing to provide time out of school for such activities.

You may want to consider how your group could establish a longer term relationship with one or more of these ministries. Find out how you can help. Have group members make a report to your congregation about the ministry. Perhaps your faith formation group will lead your whole congregation into involvement in the mission of a group you have visited. "A Guide for Witness and Service" (pages 271–74) has more information about how your group may organize ways for individuals and the group to participate in witness and service ministries.

Following your visit discuss the experience. How is faith strengthened for those who participate in serving others? How is faith strengthened for those who are served by the ministry?

VISIT ORGANIZATIONS OR SITES RELATED TO THE UNITED CHURCH OF CHRIST

Your conference or association office would welcome a visit from your faith formation group.

The UCC national offices in Cleveland, Ohio, New York City, or Washington, D.C., can arrange for groups to tour the facility and to meet with the various national ministries of the church.

There are health and welfare agencies closely related to the United Church of Christ. There is a list of these agencies in the *UCC Yearbook*. They welcome visits from groups.

Schools, colleges, and seminaries affiliated with the United Church of Christ are also listed in the *UCC Year-book*. If your group knows a student attending a UCC institution, you might want to visit there. UCC landmarks such as Plymouth Rock, in Massachusetts; the Amistad Research Center, in New Orleans; or Deaconess Hospital in the Saint Louis area are examples of such field trip experiences.

If possible, arrange for a representative to talk with your group about the relationship to the United Church of Christ and learn some of their history. Afterward, review and discuss the role of this setting in the life of the United Church of Christ. Name some of the people who make this place important to your faith. How does your congregation benefit from and relate to this setting? How could your congregation make more use of this setting in learning and celebrating your faith?

Coordinating Field Trips with Sessions

There are two sessions when field trips are especially appropriate. Session 2, "Worship" (pages 25–32), is an excellent time to organize one or more worship visits during the program. Session 18, "Witness and Service" (pages 161–67), is the other time when field trips will especially enhance learning for your group.

INTRODUCTION

1. "The Constitution and Bylaws, United Church of Christ" (Cleveland, Ohio: Executive Council for the United Church of Christ, 1992).

CONFIRMATION IN THE LOCAL CHURCH

1. Urban T. Holmes III, *Confirmation: The Celebration of Maturity in Christ* (New York: Seabury Press, 1975), 27.
2. *United Church of Christ Book of Worship* (New York: United Church of Christ Office for Church Life and Leadership, 1986), 10.

CONFIRMATION: THEN AND NOW

1. *Book of Worship*, 143. Used by permission.
2. Ibid., 145. Used by permission.
3. William R. Myers, ed., *Becoming and Belonging: A Practical Design for Confirmation* (Cleveland: United Church Press, 1993), 190.
4. For a fuller treatment of this issue, see Peter R. Monkres and R. Kenneth Ostermiller, *The Rite of Confirmation: Moments When Faith Is Strengthened* (Cleveland: United Church Press, 1995).

OPENING RETREAT: ON A FAITH JOURNEY

1. Wayne Rice, *Up Close and Personal* (El Cajon, Calif.: Youth Specialties, 1989).
2. Mike Yaconelli and Wayne Rice, *Super Ideas for Youth Groups* (Grand Rapids, Mich.: Zondervan, 1979).
3. Henri J. M. Nouwen, *Reaching Out: The Three Movements of the Spiritual Life* (New York: Image Books, 1986), 156.
4. "Prayer of Our Savior," in *The New Century Hymnal* (Cleveland, Ohio: The Pilgrim Press, 1995), 56–57. Used by permission.
5. Adapted from *Book of Worship*, 529. Used by permission.
6. Adapted from Ron DelBene with Mary and Herb Montgomery, *The Breath of Life: A Simple Way to Pray* (Nashville: Upper Room Books, 1996).
7. Adapted from *Book of Worship*, 165.

SESSION 1: SHARING OUR STORIES

1. Thomas H. Groome, *Christian Religious Education: Sharing Our Story and Vision* (San Francisco: Harper and Row, 1980), 192.

SESSION 2: WORSHIP

1. *Book of Worship,* 19.
2. *Webster's Ninth New Collegiate Dictionary* (Springfield, Mass.: Merriam-Webster, 1983).
3. Ibid.
4. "God, Speak to Me, That I May Speak," words by Frances Ridley Havergal, 1872, alt., in *The New Century Hymnal* (Cleveland, Ohio: The Pilgrim Press, 1995), 531. Used by permission.

SESSION 3: GOD'S MISSION AND THE HISTORY OF OUR CONGREGATION

1. Burton H. Throckmorton Jr., *The Gospels and the Letters of Paul: An Inclusive-Language Edition* (Cleveland, Ohio: The Pilgrim Press, 1992). Used by permission.
2. Mission Statement of the United Church of Christ, report of General Synod XVI (1987). Used by permission.

SESSION 6: THE HISTORY OF THE UNITED CHURCH OF CHRIST

1. *In Mission: A Calendar of Prayer for the United Church of Christ, 1996–97* (Cleveland, Ohio: United Church Board for World Ministries and United Church Board for Homeland Ministries, 1995), July 7–13. Used by permission.

SESSION 7: THE STATEMENT OF FAITH

1. Allen O. Miller, *The United Church of Christ Statement of Faith: A Historical, Biblical and Theological Perspective* (New York: United Church Press, 1990), 9.
2. *Basis of Union of the Congregational Christian Churches and the Evangelical and Reformed Church with the Interpretations 4,* quoted in Roger L. Shinn, *Confessing Our Faith: An Interpretation of the Statement of Faith of the United Church of Christ* (New York: The Pilgrim Press, 1990).
3. Shinn, *Confessing Our Faith,* 25.
4. These summaries come from Shinn, *Confessing Our Faith.* They appear in the table of contents and as subheadings in the second part of the book.

SESSION 8: GOD CREATES

1. "Creation," *The Interpreter's Dictionary of the Bible,* ed. George A. Buttrick, vol. 1 (Nashville: Abingdon Press, 1962), 728.

2. Walter Brueggemann, *Genesis: A Bible Commentary for Teaching and Preaching* (Louisville: Westminster/John Knox, 1982), 40.

3. Miller, *The United Church of Christ Statement of Faith,* 18–19.

SESSION 9: GOD SEEKS AND SAVES

1. See Paul Tillich, *The Shaking of the Foundations* (New York: Charles Scribner's Sons, 1948).

2. LindaJo H. McKim, *The Presbyterian Hymnal Companion* (Louisville, Ky.: Westminster John Knox, 1993), 200.

SESSION 11: JESUS CHRIST, HUMAN AND DIVINE

1. Shinn, *Confessing Our Faith,* 67–68. Used by permission.

2. Ibid., 68–69.

3. Louis Cassells, "The Parable of the Birds," in *Advent: A Calendar of Devotions* (Nashville: Abingdon, 1976). Used by permission.

SESSION 12: JESUS CHRIST, CRUCIFIED AND RESURRECTED

1. Martin B. Copenhaver, *To Begin at the Beginning: An Introduction to the Christian Faith* (Cleveland, Ohio: United Church Press, 1994), 41. Used by permission.

2. *Book of Worship,* 495. Used by permission.

SESSION 13: JESUS CHRIST, RISEN SAVIOR

1. Alan Boesak, *Black and Reformed* (Maryknoll, N.Y.: Orbis Books, 1984), 29.

2. Adapted from *Book of Worship,* 149. Used by permission.

SESSION 14: GUIDED BY THE SPIRIT

1. Elizabeth Roberts and Elias Amidon, eds., *Earth Prayers from around the World* (San Francisco: Harper, 1991), 188. Used by permission of Elizabeth Roberts.

2. Jacqueline McMakin with Rhoda Nary, *Doorways to Christian Growth* (San Francisco: Harper, 1984), 211–12.

SESSION 15: BOUND BY THE SPIRIT

1. *Webster's New World Dictionary of the American Language, Second College Edition* (New York: Simon & Schuster, 1984), 326.

2. Shinn, *Confessing Our Faith,* 83.

3. Ibid.

SESSION 19: THE SACRAMENTS

1. Preamble, *The Constitution of the United Church of Christ* (Cleveland: Executive Council of the United Church of Christ, 1992).

2. Douglas Horton, *The United Church of Christ* (New York: Thomas Nelson & Sons, 1962), 89.

3. Ruth C. Duck, *Gender and the Name of God: The Trinitarian Baptismal Formula* (New York: The Pilgrim Press, 1991), 163. This book has a complete discussion of the reasons for seeking alternatives for the baptismal formula and the theological problems which need to be addressed.

4. Horton, *The United Church of Christ,* 89.

5. Ibid., 91.

SESSION 21: JUSTICE AND PEACE

1. Adapted from *Make a World of Difference: Creative Activities for Global Learning* (New York: Church World Service, The Office of Global Education, National Council of Churches, USA, 1989), 63. Used by permission.

2. As reproduced in Maren C. Tirabassi and Kathy Wonson Eddy, *Gifts of Many Cultures: Worship Resources for the Global Community* (Cleveland, Ohio: United Church Press, 1995), 64.

SESSION 22

1. Copenhaver, *To Begin at the Beginning,* 225.

CLOSING RETREAT

1. *Book of Worship,* 149. Used by permission.

2. Adapted from Mark Link, *Breakway: Twenty-eight Steps to a More Prayerful Life* (Allen, Tex.: Argus Communications, 1980), 51.

3. Adapted from George Appleton, ed., *The Oxford Book of Prayer* (London: Oxford University Press, 1985), 91.

4. Ibid., 90.

5. Juanita J. Helphrey, comp., *Worship Resources* (Minneapolis: United Church of Christ Council for American Indian Ministries, 1991), 28. Copyright 1991, United Church of Christ Council for American Indian Ministries. Used by permission.

MUSIC AND WORSHIP RESOURCES

1. *Book of Worship,* 881. The English translation of The Apostles' Creed was prepared by the English Language Liturgical Consultation (ELLC), 1988. Used by permission.

2. Ibid., 885. Approved by the Executive Council in 1981. Used by permission.

3. Maynard Beemer et al., *Responsible Faith: A Course for Confirmation Education and the Rite of Confirmation* (Madison: Wisconsin Press, 1981), 29–30.

A GUIDE FOR MENTORING

1. *Book of Worship,* 149.

2. Kenneth Smith, "The Teacher as Mentor" in *Parish Teacher* (June 1980).

3. Ibid.

RELATED READING

Anderson, Yohann. *Songs*. San Anselmo, Calif.: Songs and Creations, 1978.

Bailey, Betty Jane, and J. Martin Bailey. *Youth Plan Worship*. New York: The Pilgrim Press, 1987.

Borg, Marcus. *Jesus: A New Vision*. San Francisco: HarperSan Francisco, 1993.

Browning, Robert L., and Roy A. Reed. *Models of Confirmation and Baptismal Affirmation*. Birmingham, Ala.: Religious Education Press, 1995.

Caldwell, Elizabeth Francis. *Come Unto Me: Rethinking the Sacraments for Children*. Cleveland, Ohio: United Church Press, 1996.

Coleman, Lyman. *Serendipity Youth Ministry Encyclopedia*. Littleton, Colo.: Serendipity House, 1985.

Confirming Our Faith: A Confirmation Resource for the United Church of Christ. New York: United Church Press, 1980.

Copenhaver, Martin B. *To Begin at the Beginning: An Introduction to the Christian Faith*. Cleveland, Ohio: The Pilgrim Press, 1994.

Davies, J. G., ed. *The Westminster Dictionary of Worship*. Philadelphia: Westminster Press, 1979.

Driver, Tom. *The Magic of Ritual: Our Need for Liberating Rites That Transform Our Lives and Our Communities*. San Francisco: HarperSan Francisco, 1991.

Dunn, David, et al. *A History of the Evangelical and Reformed Church*. Cleveland, Ohio: The Pilgrim Press, 1990.

Groome, Thomas H. *Christian Religious Education: Sharing Our Story and Vision*. San Francisco: Harper and Row, 1980.

————. *Sharing Faith: A Comprehensive Approach to Religious Education*. New York: HarperCollins, 1991.

Gunnemann, Louis H. *The Shaping of the UCC: An Essay in the History of American Christianity*. New York: The Pilgrim Press, 1977.

————. *United and Uniting: The Meaning of an Ecclesial Journey*. New York: The Pilgrim Press, 1987.

Hambrick-Stowe, Charles E., and Daniel L. Johnson, eds. *Theology and Identity: Traditions, Movements, and Polity in the United Church of Christ*. Cleveland, Ohio: The Pilgrim Press, 1990.

Hamilton, Virginia. *In the Beginning: Creation Stories from Around the World*. Orlando: Harcourt Brace Jovanovich, 1988.

Harris, Maria. *Fashion Me a People: Curriculum in the Church*. San Francisco: Harper and Row, 1988.

Hohenstein, Mary. *Games, Games, Games*. Minneapolis: Bethany House Publishers, 1980.

Holmes, Urban T., III. *Confirmation: The Celebration of Maturity in Christ*. New York: Seabury Press, 1975.

Imaging the Word: An Arts and Lectionary Resource. 3 vols. Cleveland, Ohio: United Church Press, 1994, 1995, 1996.

International Commission on English in the Liturgy. *Rite of Christian Initiation of Adults*. Collegeville, Minn.: The Liturgical Press, 1988.

Jones, Cheslyn, Geoffrey Wainwright, and Edward Yarnold, eds. *The Study of Liturgy*. New York: Oxford University Press, 1978.

Justice, Peace, and the Integrity of Creation. Geneva, Switzerland: World Council of Churches, 1990.

Kavanaugh, Aidan. *Confirmation: Origins and Reform*. New York: Pueblo Publishing Co., 1988.

Kispaugh, Charles, and Barbara Bruce. *Friends in Faith: Mentoring Youth in the Church*. Nashville: Discipleship Resources, 1993.

Make a World of Difference: Creative Activities for Global Learning. New York: Church World Service, The Office of Global Education, National Council of Churches (USA), 1989.

McCarthy, Scott. *Celebrating the Earth: An Earth-centered Theology of Worship with Blessings, Prayers, and Rituals*. San Jose: Resource Publications, 1987.

Miller, Allen O. *The United Church of Christ Statement of Faith: A Historical, Biblical, and Theological Perspective*. New York: United Church Press, 1990.

Monkres, Peter R., and R. Kenneth Ostermiller. *The Rite of Confirmation: Moments When Faith Is Strengthened*. Cleveland, Ohio: United Church Press, 1995.

More New Games! New York: Dolphin Books/Doubleday, 1981.

My Confirmation: A Guide for Confirmation Instruction. Rev. ed. Cleveland, Ohio: United Church Press, 1994.

Myers, William. *Becoming and Belonging: A Practical Design for Confirmation*. Cleveland, Ohio: United Church Press, 1994.

The New Century Hymnal. Cleveland, Ohio: The Pilgrim Press, 1995.

New Games Book. New York: Dolphin Books/Doubleday, 1976.

One Hundred and One Ways to Help Save the Earth. Washington: The Greenhouse Crisis Foundation (GCF) and the National Council of the Church of Christ (USA), 1990.

Reimer, Sandy, and Larry Reimer. *The Retreat Handbook*. Ridgefield, Conn.: Morehouse Publishing, 1987.

The Revised Common Lectionary. Nashville: Abingdon, 1992.

Roberts, William O., Jr. *Initiation to Adulthood: An Ancient Rite of Passage in Contemporary Form*. New York: The Pilgrim Press, 1982.

Schmemann, Alexander. *Liturgy and Life: Christian Development through Liturgical Experience*. New York: Department of Religious Education, Orthodox Church in America, 1974.

Shinn, Roger L. *Confessing Our Faith: An Interpretation of the Statement of Faith of the United Church of Christ.* Cleveland, Ohio: The Pilgrim Press, 1990.

Tirabassi, Maren C., and Kathy Wonson Eddy. *Gifts of Many Cultures: Worship Resources for the Global Community.* Cleveland, Ohio: United Church Press, 1995.

Trimmer, Edward A. *Youth Ministries Handbook.* Nashville: Abingdon, 1994.

United Church of Christ Book of Worship. New York: United Church of Christ Office for Church Life and Leadership, 1986.

von Rohr, John. *The Shaping of American Congregationalism, 1620–1957.* Cleveland, Ohio: The Pilgrim Press, 1992.

Walker, Williston. *The Creeds and Platforms of Congregationalism.* Cleveland, Ohio: The Pilgrim Press, 1990.

Weinstein, Matt, and Joel Goodman. *Playfair.* San Luis Obispo: Impact Publishers, 1988.

Westerhoff, John. *Will Our Children Have Faith: Bringing Up Children in the Christian Faith.* Minneapolis: Winston Press, 1980.

Wezeman, Phyllis Vos. *Peacemaking Creatively through the Arts: A Handbook of Educational Activities and Experiences for Children.* Brea, Calif.: Educational Ministries, 1990.

White, James F. *Introduction to Christian Worship.* Nashville: Abingdon, 1990.

———. *Sacraments as God's Self-Giving.* Nashville: Abingdon, 1983.

Yarnold, E. *The Awe-Inspiring Rites of Initiation: Baptismal Homilies of the Fourth Century.* St. Paul, Minn.: Slough, 1972.

Zikmund, Barbara Brown. *Hidden Histories in the United Church of Christ.* 2 vols. New York: The Pilgrim Press, 1984, 1987.

Affirming Faith Response Form

Name of Church _____

Contact _____

Address_____

_____

_____

Telephone Number _____

(If additional paper is needed, please include your name and reference to the question being answered.)

How many young people were in your group? _____

Who led the program? _____

What were the ages of the young people?_____

1. In general, what is your impression of *Affirming Faith*?

2. How did you use the materials—in group sessions, with mentors, or on retreats?

3. If you used sessions, which ones did you use?

4. If you used any additional resources, which ones did you use?

5. Does the material in the sessions adequately reflect the Statement of Faith, focus scriptures, and themes?

_____yes   _____no

If no, which sessions do you think need strengthening?

6. Are the session activities relevant and age appropriate for young people?

_____ yes _____ no

Do you have any additional comments about activities?

7. If you used the *Confirmand's Journal*, was it helpful?

8. What was most helpful about this resource?

9. What was least helpful about this resource?

10. "If I were changing this resource, I would . . . " (Please be as specific as possible, including page number when referring to *Affirming Faith*.)

Additional Comments

Thank you for your response.

Please return the completed form to:
Editor, Curriculum Office
United Church Press
700 Prospect Avenue
Cleveland, Ohio 44115